1906–73
The Maggie Murphs
A History of Margaret Morrison Carnegie College

CarnegieMellon

1906–73
The Maggie Murphs
A History of Margaret Morrison Carnegie College

By Edwin Fenton

❧

To the Maggie Murphs:
Pioneers in Women's Education
at Carnegie Mellon University

❧

Library of Congress Control Number 2003112524
ISBN 0–88748–412–3

Printed and bound in the United States of America
10 9 8 7 6 5 4 3 2 1

Contents

Preface

Ninety men earned master's degrees from Margaret Morrison, but since MMCC was a women's college, we opted, for the sake of simplicity, to use alumnae (the feminine plural) when referring to the graduates. We hope that the male graduates understand this editorial decision.

Margaret Morrison Carnegie College began as one of the four divisions in the Carnegie Technical Schools, an institution that became the Carnegie Institute of Technology in 1912 and Carnegie Mellon University in 1967. Originally a trade and technical school designed to serve working women from the Pittsburgh area, it became a technical college offering both professional degrees and education in the liberal arts and sciences. Its programs in the humanities, social sciences and science were absorbed into departments in the newly-formed Carnegie Mellon University in 1968, after which the last remaining programs in its two professional schools were phased out. Its last students graduated in 1973. This volume, written primarily for Margaret Morrison alumnae, documents the history of this intriguing school in both words and pictures.

This book has been a community effort. The idea for a volume to commemorate Margaret Morrison Carnegie College and its alumnae originated with Mary Phillips, the Director of the Margaret Morrison Carnegie College Program. She persuaded more than 200 Margaret Morrison alumnae to submit reminiscences to be included in the volume, and identified additional alums who contributed telephoned interviews. I drafted each interview and sent it to the interviewee who edited the draft—in some cases rewrote it completely—and returned it, often with visuals to be added. The information from all these individuals shaped the volume in many ways. So did conversations with members of the Advisory Committee and with Maggie Murphs I have met on a variety of occasions. In addition, I remember many Margaret Morrison students from the classes I taught at Carnegie Tech from 1954–1973.

The book is based on voluminous files in Carnegie Mellon's archives. Two talented and remarkably patient archivists, Jennie Benford and Kathleen Behrman, not only found what I requested, but unearthed many files and individual documents that had escaped my attention. These sources gave life to the material in the institutional histories published by the Carnegie Tech/Mellon Press: Arthur W. Tarbell covered the first two administrations (1900–1935); Glen U. Cleeton wrote about Robert Doherty's years (1935–1950); Austin Wright discussed John C. Warner's administration (1950–1965); and Ludwig F. Schaefer's volume covered the Stever and Cyert administrations (1965–1990). My own centennial history attempted to interpret the entire 100 year period, 1900–2000. In addition to the archivists and the members of the Advisory Committee—Agnes (Cancelliere) Campbell '35, Norene (DiBucci) Christiano '64, '71, Lois (Shoop) Fowler '47, Evelyn (Alessio) Murrin '57, Angela Pollis '50, Helen Pollis '45, Louisa (Saul) Rosenthal '44, Virginia (Page) Sheedy '31, and Hilary Zubritzky '70, '72—I owe particular votes of thanks to several individuals. Mary Phillips had her fine hand in every aspect of this project, and Erwin Steinberg read the entire manuscript. I owe particular thanks to three talented colleagues. Tracey DePellegrin Connelly prepared an excellent index. Carolyn Grundy, a meticulous editor and proofreader, saved me from a host of transgressions. Libby Boyarski, owner of Boyarski Design, and her two children, Luisa and Colin, designed the entire volume. Going far beyond a designer's customary contributions, Libby spent many hours in the archives seeking visuals that made exactly the correct point. Among other contributions, Luisa labored valiently in the Carnegie Mellon Archives and Colin skillfully scanned the line drawings that enliven the book. Tim Kaulen from Photography and Graphic Services at Mellon Institute and Brian Herman from Broudy Printing Inc. took great care in reproducing archival photos that varied greatly in quality. I, of course, am responsible for any shortcomings that remain.

Edwin Fenton

Edwin Fenton

Office of the President

On behalf of the entire Carnegie Mellon community, it is my great pleasure to present you with this copy of *The Maggie Murphs: A History of Margaret Morrison Carnegie College*. More than 6,200 "Maggie Murphs"—as well as approximately 90 male master's students—graduated from Margaret Morrison Carnegie College (MMCC) between 1906 and 1973. During this period, the college was recognized as a vital force for top-quality education and vocational training for young women. As the college grew, students and alumnae challenged gender barriers and paved the way for today's coeducational university, one that is fundamentally committed to equal opportunity for all women.

The history of Carnegie Mellon's first women is one of hard work, life-changing experiences, and lots of fun. Thanks to the generosity of over 200 alumnae and alumni, who added their reminiscences to the university's archival records, *The Maggie Murphs: A History of Margaret Morrison Carnegie College* opens windows directly into the college experience during these critical decades. Through this project— the brainchild of Mary Phillips, director of the MMCC Program, and Ted Fenton, emeritus professor of history—the entire Carnegie Mellon community has become more deeply aware and appreciative of the crucial role women have played throughout the university's distinguished history.

As president of Carnegie Mellon, it has been a special pleasure to meet many Margaret Morrison alumnae in Pittsburgh and across the country. I know first-hand what talented and committed individuals you are. Your contributions to your communities and institutions are truly remarkable. And your interest in today's Carnegie Mellon women—exemplified by your creation of an endowed MMCC scholarship program for women undergraduates—is a fitting tribute to the Margaret Morrison spirit and an inspiration to us all.

With heartfelt appreciation, deep respect, and loving regard, Carnegie Mellon honors and celebrates you, its Margaret Morrison Carnegie College alumnae and alumni. Enjoy *The Maggie Murphs*!

Jared L. Cohon

Jared L. Cohon
President
Carnegie Mellon
July 16, 2003

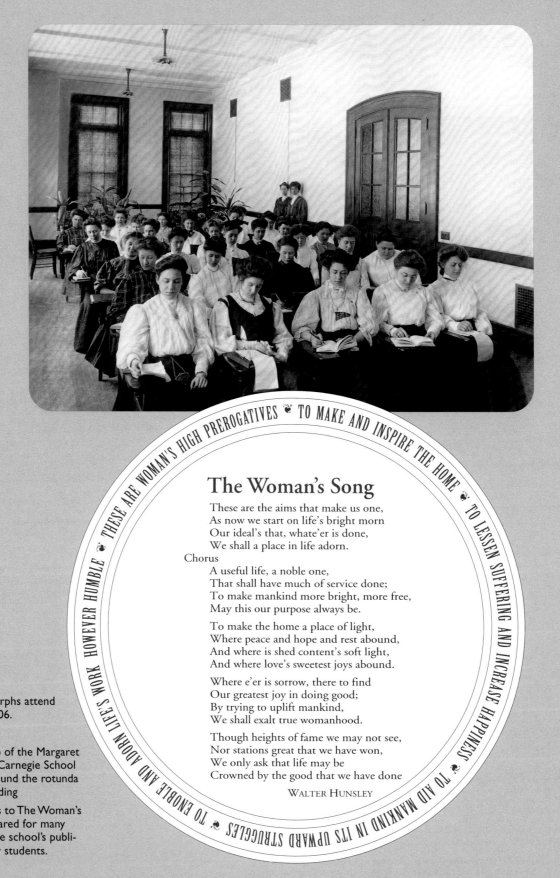

The Woman's Song

These are the aims that make us one,
As now we start on life's bright morn
Our ideal's that, whate'er is done,
We shall a place in life adorn.
Chorus
A useful life, a noble one,
That shall have much of service done;
To make mankind more bright, more free,
May this our purpose always be.

To make the home a place of light,
Where peace and hope and rest abound,
And where is shed content's soft light,
And where love's sweetest joys abound.

Where e'er is sorrow, there to find
Our greatest joy in doing good;
By trying to uplift mankind,
We shall exalt true womanhood.

Though heights of fame we may not see,
Nor stations great that we have won,
We only ask that life may be
Crowned by the good that we have done

WALTER HUNSLEY

Top:
Maggie Murphs attend
class in 1906.

Bottom:
The motto of the Margaret
Morrison Carnegie School
carved around the rotunda
of the building

The words to The Woman's
Song appeared for many
years in the school's publications for students.

Chapter 1

1906–12
The Margaret Morrison Carnegie School for Women

The dinner at Hotel Schenley during which Andrew Carnegie read a letter offering to found a technical school

November 15, 1900 marked the beginning of an adventure in women's education. On that day Andrew Carnegie read a letter to the trustees of the Carnegie Institute—the library, museum, and music hall he had founded in the Oakland area of Pittsburgh in the 1890s. In the letter he offered to found a technical and trade school to serve working men and women from the Pittsburgh area. One of the branches of that school, the Margaret Morrison Carnegie School for Women (MMCS), opened officially in 1906. By the time that the Carnegie Technical Schools (CTS) became Carnegie Institute of Technology in 1912, Margaret Morrison had grown into a thriving institution although its focus had begun to change significantly from the one its founder had envisioned.

"To die rich is to die disgraced."
Andrew Carnegie Founds the Carnegie Technical Schools

Andrew Carnegie had emigrated from Scotland at the age of 13 in 1848. Steam looms had replaced the handlooms on which his father, a weaver, made a living. With the family's welfare declining, Carnegie's mother, Margaret Morrison Carnegie, decided to move with her husband and her two sons to Pittsburgh to join her sister, who lived in Allegheny on what is now Pittsburgh's north side. Andrew had a meteoric career, starting as a bobbin boy in a textile mill, and becoming successively a telegrapher, a railroad executive, an entrepreneur in a dozen businesses, and finally a steel baron and the richest man in the world. "To die rich is to die disgraced," he wrote even before he began to give away his huge fortune.

9

Top left:
Window bearing Andrew Carnegie's motto, "My Heart is in the Work"

Top right:
Mrs. Hamerschlag digs the first shovelful of earth for Margaret Morrison Hall.

Bottom:
The original campus looking across the deep valley in what is now the middle of the campus towards Forbes Street, now Forbes Avenue

At the age of 14, Carnegie had begun his own self education, studying bookkeeping at night after a 12-hour work day and borrowing books from the library of a local citizen to read in his spare time. Once he became successful, he began to study his roots in Scotland and to examine technical schools in both the United States and Great Britain. In his letter of gift to the Carnegie Institute, he pointed out that more than half of the men and women who studied at two British technical schools worked during the day and studied to improve themselves at night. Clearly, he intended his new school to offer similar opportunities to young men and women from the Pittsburgh area.

In 1903 the City of Pittsburgh provided a site for the new school, 32 acres of land bordering Schenley Park in Pittsburgh's Oakland section. The trustees appointed an advisory committee to make plans for the new school. Its three members, all men, included Arthur Arton Hamerschlag, superintendent of St. George's Trade School in New York City. Hamerschlag had attended neither high school nor college. Like his schooling, his teaching and administrative careers had taken place entirely in trade schools, an unusual background for a future college president.

In its 1903 report, the advisory committee recommended a broad plan of secondary technical and trade education. Their plan revealed the quandary in which they found themselves as they tried to define the new school:

These courses should not encroach upon the field or purposes of your Universities....Your Committee has, therefore, tried to eliminate anything which would lead to duplication....The Carnegie Technical Schools, embodying a scheme of Secondary Technical Education should be pitched between the Elementary Courses of Grammar Schools and the Engineering Courses of the Universities, without encroaching on the General Courses of your High Schools. There exists in Pittsburgh and vicinity absolutely no school of any kind that will enable a young man to acquire the rudiments of a trade. There exists no school which offers similar opportunities to young women.... The instructors in these branches must be chosen from those who have proven in commercial work their ability and their mastery of the subject.

The committee divided the new educational enterprise into four schools, each with its own faculty, building, laboratories, and shops. They were originally named the School of Science and Technology, the School of Fine and Applied Arts, the School for Apprentices and Journeymen, and the Margaret Morrison Carnegie School for Women. The School for Apprentices and Journeymen, offering only trade courses, could grant only two-year certificates, but the remaining three schools could also offer three-year diplomas. The trustees chose committee member Arthur Arton Hamerschlag to be the schools' first director, a title later changed to president.

Margaret Morrison:
The School and Building

The 1903 plan suggested that, like the other three schools, Margaret Morrison should focus on trade and vocational training and offer diploma programs in secretarial studies, household economics, costume design, and general science.

This school should be strictly practical in character, and should have for its principal aim the training of young women to earn their livelihood. It should offer courses of two different and separate grades: First, short courses of a trade character for those of comparatively little natural ability and intellectual training,… to train them for more responsible positions. [Second,] the courses of instruction for the technical branches of the school designed to be of about three years in length. The courses of instruction in the day and evening classes in the trade section of the school should be as short as is consistent with the proper instruction in the various subjects taught.…

We have grouped in a purely tentative manner subject to revision in a later report, the following courses of instruction: Technical Courses for Dressmakers, Costume Designers, Professional Housekeepers, Librarians, Secretaries, etc. Trade courses for Milliners, Seamstresses, Stenographers and Typewriters, Bookkeepers, Office Assistants, Cooks, Waitresses, Housekeepers' Assistants, and perhaps additional courses such as: Compositors, Upholsterers, Bookbinders, Box Makers, Leather Workers, etc., etc.

Note what is missing: among others, options in any of the liberal arts or sciences, courses in management, and majors in homemaking. The original plan for Margaret Morrison provided training (not education) in a number of traditional technical and trade fields long dominated by women. Yet, by the time Carnegie Mellon's Board of Trustees voted to phase out Margaret Morrison as a separate college, the overwhelming majority of its students were being educated for careers in the liberal arts, the sciences, and management. The transition occupied 70 years and began soon after the doors of the new school opened.

Victorian ideals that prescribed domesticity for women and public life for men dominated nineteenth century women's education. Victorian women's culture upheld religion, morality, homemaking, and the family. These ideals led to rigid rules about women's behavior in colleges and universities, rules that did not apply to men. Late in the century, new forces began to make their way. The most notable women's colleges of the day—the so-called Seven Sisters: Vassar, Wellesley, Byrn Mawr, Radcliffe, Barnard, Mount Holyoke and Smith—focused their curricula on the classical tradition, in imitation of eastern men's colleges. Their students studied Latin, Greek, the social and natural sciences, history, and literature. They were heavily involved in off-campus political and social reform movements, such as settlement associations. By emphasizing trade and technical education for women, Margaret Morrison's planners rejected both of these contemporary trends. The curriculum they proposed in 1903 resembled Pittsburgh's high schools of a decade later more than they paralleled education in the Seven Sisters.

Knowing how deeply Andrew Carnegie admired his mother, the trustees decided to name the women's school after her. Carnegie was delighted. He so idolized his mother that he had delayed his marriage until after she died. In 1906, when work was underway on the new building for the women's school, Carnegie wrote the following reply to a letter from the secretary of the Board of Trustees about the name they had selected.

Dear Mr. Church:

The tribute to my mother is exquisitely fine, and one she would have rejoiced in receiving. The interest she took in women everywhere was extraordinary. She became the sage of the neighborhood, and was constantly in demand in time of trouble, by the neighbors.

I am delighted with the action of the Trustees. Please say to one and all that I am deeply touched by this remembrance of one to whom I owe everything that a wise mother ever gave to a son who adored her.…

Always yours, Andrew Carnegie

Andrew Carnegie's mother, Margaret Morrison Carnegie

The Brave Women of Margaret Morrison

The surroundings were absolutely devoid of any home-like appearance: bare brick walls, cement floors, and every now and then an iron-bound pillar to vary the monotony. Here it was that these brave young women battled with such new and strange objects as Terrestrial Evolution, Industrial Economics, and Food Values.... A few red letter dates stand out boldly in our memories. Hallowe'en and Valentine Day, for instance, when dances broke the gloom. But it was on Founder's Day (November 15) that we permanently emerged from our chrysalis and shone forth in all our glory.... Arrayed in robes of white and carrying yellow flowers, we took our places as C.T.S students.
—*The Thistle*, 1908, p. 196.
The Thistle was, and still is, the school's yearbook.

Top:
Margaret Morrison's Charter Class

Bottom:
The newly constructed Margaret Morrison Hall

Margaret Morrison's first day students, its Charter Class, entered the doors of Industries (now Porter) Hall, the first building on the campus, on September 17, 1906. This day-school class included 65 students. Forty-two were Pittsburgh residents, 22 lived in nearby suburbs, such as Wilkinsburg and Allegheny, and one came from Massilon, Ohio. The Charter Class of the night school opened on October 8, 1906 with 111 students enrolled, more than half again as many as the day school. Ninety-four of these students listed Pittsburgh as their residence; the remaining 17 came from nearby suburbs.

Members of the charter classes must have spent much of their spare time on campus watching their future home rise a few hundred muddy yards away. The 1907 *Thistle* described the new building in words that appear in the right hand margin of page 13.

The 1903 plans for Margaret Morrison had not mentioned the homemaking arts. Instead they proposed curricula to prepare students to become housekeepers or housekeeper's assistants. The model apartment in

the Margaret Morrison building included a butler's pantry and a maid's room, important for these trades but not for the homes of typical housewives. The emphasis on home-making, so vital to the home economics programs that developed in Margaret Morrison, seems to have had three origins. One was the interests of the students, as their comments in the last sentence (right hand margin, page 13) in *The Thistle* indicate. The second may have been the Board of Trustees. Lucian Scaife, a bachelor and board member, wrote the words that were carved inside the portico at the entrance to the Margaret Morrison building. Scaife penned these words on the stationery of the Duquesne Club, an institution that neither admitted women as members nor permitted them to use its facilities.

Duquesne Club
Pittsburgh

To make and inspire the home;

To lessen suffering and increase happiness;

To aid mankind in its upward struggles;

To ennoble and adorn life's work, however humble;

These are woman's high prerogatives.

The third was Margaret Morrison's first dean, Anna B. Smith, who was a product of women's education in eastern schools. She described the ideal she sought for the school in the following words:

To so train and equip each student so as to give her the highest possible efficiency as a home maker, with an understanding of the problems and responsibilities of wifehood and motherhood in affecting the mental, moral and physical well-being of the home, and through the home of society and state. This sound basis being given each student, to further safeguard her future by equipping her with such specific training as to make her an efficient and self-respecting wage-earner in case of need.

No matter what the origins of the change, within a few years the curriculum of the freshman year had shifted in part from women's occupations to the roles of women as wives and mothers. The curriculum focused on home economics and included required courses in cooking and needlework.

MARGARET MORRISON CARNEGIE
SCHOOL FOR WOMEN

The New Building

1 The basement is devoted almost exclusively to the laundry department. All machinery is of the most modern kind, for both steam and hand methods.

2 On the second floor are the large study hall, the reference library, and the classrooms.

3 The kitchen is equipped with twelve of the latest type of French ranges, arranged in two rows through the center of the room, side by side and back to back.

4 In the east wing the arts of sewing, dressmaking, and millinery are taught. Power sewing machines, as well as foot-treadle sewing machines are installed.

5 The east wing of the fourth floor contains a large gymnasium, having a stage at one end. Great things are expected from this department, not only a tremendous lot of muscular development, but also the histrionic arts.

6 Last but not least in our estimation is the unique and beautiful model apartment, containing a living room, dining room, two bedrooms, bathroom, a kitchen, a butler's pantry and maid's room. Here...we will be taught the proper furnishings and organization of the home; and when all is said and done, this is the thing that appeals to most of us.
—*The Thistle*, 1907, pp. 108–109

The Students

Low tuition and few entrance requirements quickly attracted students to the new school. Tuition in the day school was $20 a year for Pittsburgh residents and $30 for others. The night school was an even greater bargain: five dollars for Pittsburghers and seven dollars for others. Applicants for the technical courses had to be at least 16 years old. If they had not graduated from an approved high or preparatory school, they could still gain admittance by passing examinations in three of four subjects: English, mathematics, science, and general history or geography. Entrance requirements for the certificate courses were even less rigorous. Night school applicants, for example, only had to be at least 16 years old and present themselves for a personal interview.

Spurred by an avalanche of applicants, the new school for women grew steadily as the registrar's figures indicate:

ENROLLMENT MMCS, 1906–1912

Year	Day	Night	Total	Day Grads	Night Grads
1906-07	104	120	224		
1907-08	219	175	394		
1908-09	281	240	521	43	30
1909-10	234	240	474	31	29
1910-11	264	212	476	48	43
1911-12	239	246	485	50	60

Andrew Carnegie should have been delighted with these enrollment figures. He wanted his new school to serve boys and girls (as the early documents usually referred to students) from the Pittsburgh area. During the entire six-year history of the Carnegie Technical Schools, 95 percent of registered students came from Pittsburgh and its immediate suburbs. Most out-of-town students roomed with families chosen from a list approved by the school. In 1908, Margaret Morrison rented a home on nearby Northumberland Street to be used as a dormitory called Morrison Hall. Ten girls lived and ate there, carefully supervised by a matron. Everyone else commuted.

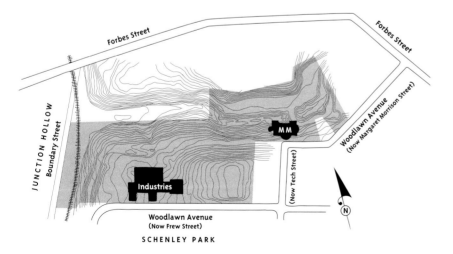

Those who lived too far from the campus to walk usually took streetcars. Trolley lines connected nearby towns to the city. Students from outlying areas took one trolley

downtown and joined other CTS students at transfer points for the ride up Forbes Street to the campus. They got off the car at a stop in front of the Carnegie Institute, walked across the bridge over Junction Hollow to Woodlawn Avenue (now Frew Street) next to Schenley Park, and then up Woodlawn and across the campus to the Margaret Morrison building.

The trip from outlying suburbs, door to door, often took an hour-and-a-half. Many commuters spent three hours a day, fifteen hours a week, 600 hours a year and 1800 hours in the three years it took to earn a diploma, on streetcars. Fare in 1906 was a nickel. Most commuters carried their lunches or purchased lunches made by the senior household girls, who served 200 people each day in the Margaret Morrison lunchroom. The Carnegie Technical Schools had no student union and only a primitive lunchroom for men in Industries Hall.

Commuting helps to account for two characteristics of these Margaret Morrison students: they were frequently ill, and many of them dropped out of school. Every dean's report from 1906 through 1912 commented on the poor health of Margaret Morrison students and attributed it in part to the strain of commuting. In her 1911 Annual Report, Dean Clara Linforth West wrote:

(Our students') specific ailments are due in the majority of instances to poor hygenic conditions, lack of proper nutrition, and a generally unintelligent mode of life. These disadvantages are further aggravated by the difficulties of transportation that I have already alluded to and which sap the too slight strength of the girl still more.

Such a state of affairs calls for preventive measures much more than for ordinary medical treatment of individual cases…. [H]ere again the need for better housing for students near the School is so evident that it scarcely needs comment. We ought for the sake of health to have dormitory accommodation for at least one hundred young women within easy walking distance of the School building.

The high drop out rate—over two-thirds of the typical plebe (freshman) class who entered the day school failed to graduate with their class—also testifies to the conditions Dean West indicated. A heavy classroom schedule and the lure of wedding bells contributed to both academic difficulties and the high drop out rate.

The staff of Margaret Morrison included a registered physician who examined students twice each year. Both physical training and athletics were designed to contribute to better health. A gym occupied much of the east wing of the fourth floor of the building. Students took gym classes there and participated in intramural volleyball and basketball leagues. Each class in both the day school and the night school had teams. Margaret Morrison's deans frowned on interscholastic sports, arguing that sports should provide recreation and physical fitness rather than athletic competition.

In 1909, *The Thistle* presented a picture of the social life of Margaret Morrison girls. In retrospect, it seems unexciting. The school sponsored a few informal dances to the delight of its students, and a number of teas given mainly for the seniors. At one of these teas, the girls learned that Dean Anna Smith had become engaged and would resign from her post.

The school also sponsored the Junior Promenade, the Junior Phantom Dance to welcome the incoming plebes, and a vaudeville show featuring talent among the plebes. The Dramatic Club performed "Alice in Wonderland" and a Christmas pageant in the Margaret Morrison gym. A newly formed Glee Club gave its first concert in May, and a number of girls formed the Guild, an organization that raised money for charities. Finally, two local sororities, Delta Kappa Epsilon with 12 members and Phi Sigma with 14 began to function. *The Thistle* failed to mention two more intriguing aspects of social life: strolling through Schenley Park with boys from the rest of Tech, and hours of conversation and good fellowship on streetcars going to and from campus.

Margaret Morrison seems somewhat removed from the rest of the Carnegie Technical Schools. Like the rest of the schools, it had its own building, where only women studied. By late in 1907, MMCS had its own column in *The Tartan*, the CTS weekly newspaper, with an editor and business manager in charge. The column described receptions, speakers, and events in the college and carried a gossip column that paralleled a similar column for men. *The Tartan's* stories emphasized men's sports and included long articles on technical subjects, such as the use of the slide rule, of little interest to typical MMCS students. No parallel stories devoted to women's interests appeared.

A Communication

I am not a suffragette, yet I speak of woman's rights and woman's wrongs. Woman was created in the image of God just as much as man, and it is a crime to deface that image. To hinder her growth in any way is to deface it. Her mind may be just as active and able as man's but it is not like man's. Therefore, to educate her as a boy is educated is to hinder her development into a symmetrical woman.

Primarily, then, she must be educated as a woman. First of all she must learn to know her own possibilities and limitations, and when she has aquired self-control and balance of power, she may learn the use of a paddle. Then she may safely paddle her own canoe down the stream of time with no more serious mishaps than an occasional ducking and sprinkling of freckles.
—*The Thistle,* 1909, p. 183

Left:
MMCC junior class basketball team in 1909

Dean Smith Graduates

"It seems quite fitting to us that when we graduate, Miss Smith will "graduate" with us, and take her place in what a true woman considers the happiest place on earth—a home of her own."
—The Thistle, 1909, p. 190

Top:
The first dean of Margaret Morrison Carnegie School, Dean Anna Smith

Bottom:
The faculty of Margaret Morrison pictured in the 1909 *Thistle*

The Faculty

Two deans, Anna Beckwith Smith (1906–09) and Clara Linforth West (1909–12) led the Margaret Morrison Carnegie School for Women. Both were the products of eastern schools, and each had teaching and administrative experience in technical schools. They struggled with a host of problems as they tried to get the new institution established and running smoothly. Their serious problems included a new and inexperienced faculty.

In 1908–09 the faculty consisted of 32 members, one dean, one professor, two assistant professors, 22 instructors, four assistant instructors, one lecturer and an assistant Secretary-Registrar. Two faculty members held M.D. degrees, one had a B.S. and Pd.B. and five had B.A.s. The remaining 24 had no college degrees although some of them taught academic subjects, such as history or English, and one was a department head. Most faculty members taught trade and technical courses in such fields as millinery, typewriting, practical dressmaking, or cookery. Given their backgrounds and schedules, it comes as no surprise that none of them conducted research or published.

This faculty had little in common with the women and men who led the major women's colleges of the time. The latter were largely members of the middle and upper classes, and had graduated and held advanced degrees from eastern universities. Many of them were caught up in attempts to reform American society and change the roles of women in that society. By emphasizing technical education, Margaret Morrison was blazing a new path.

The faculty always included from four to seven men. Most of them belonged to the faculty of the School of Applied Science and taught the science and mathematics courses in separate sections for MMCS girls. All of them held collegiate degrees, but existing records reveal nothing about their opinions of their students.

Faculty turnover alarmed school officials. Although we have no precise data, comments in student publications indicate that most of the teachers were young, not much older than some of their students. Each year several faculty members found marriage more attractive than the classroom. Breaking in new faculty, many of whom had never experienced a collegiate setting, presented numerous problems, particularly in a school that did not yet have department heads to assist and supervise inexperienced teachers. After coping with these problems for three years, Dean Smith became Mrs. Harry Hart, leaving Pittsburgh to go to a ranch in the west. Her successor, Clara Linford West, had been Professor of Social Ethics in charge of the Household Arts Department.

As the school changed, the quality of the faculty improved steadily. Four of the five new hires in 1911, for example, had bachelor's degrees. These women taught the new academic courses that provided the cultural element missing in the original MMCS curriculum as well as the scientific basis for courses in home economics. The transition from a vocational school to a college faculty was well under way.

The Curriculum and Alumnae Careers

The 1906 General Catalogue of the Carnegie Technical Schools described the curriculum for the regular technical courses as follows:

These courses offer an opportunity for specialization leading to productive skill in occupations for which women are best adapted.... The first year's work is general in character and must be assumed by every student unless she can give satisfactory evidence of having covered similar ground in another school of approved rank. The elements of the curriculum are English, Mathematics, Drawing, Use of the Needle,

Preparation of Food, Personal Hygiene, Social Ethics, Principles of Science, and Economics.

Second and third year students could then specialize in one of five curricula designed for matrons and managers, house-keepers, stewards and dieticians, record and filing experts, secretaries, or dressmakers and designers.

Margaret Morrison also offered special short courses—just a few sessions—in drawing and millinery for a limited number of students, particularly housewives, not enrolled in the regular day school. The night school offered two-year trade courses leading to a certificate in one of five fields: stenography, cooking, sewing, millinery, and bookkeeping and office work.

The curriculum evolved steadily between 1906 and 1912. In a detailed report for the 1911–12 academic year, Dean White described a host of changes in courses for the day school. They included new courses in inorganic and physiological chemistry, new literature and history courses in which students read the *Iliad* and the *Odyssey,* a new emphasis on the biological and cultural development of the family, new courses in psychology and French, and the development of an option in teacher preparation. MMCS graduates rapidly moved into teaching positions in local high schools that were developing trade courses much like those originally designed for the Carnegie Technical Schools. As a result, Margaret Morrison opened an option for a fourth year of study that included the education courses required by the State Department of Education. A new option in institutional management was on the drawing boards. Margaret Morrison Carnegie School was well

on its way to becoming Margaret Morrison Carnegie College, whose students studied for a bachelor of science degree.

The night school continued to flourish. Several departments offered additional classes and extended their programs to three years with plans for a fourth year well under-way. The two-year trade school emphasis of the 1906 program was steadily falling away as public high schools began to offer similar courses.

The annual reports of the deans began to list the names of Margaret Morrison graduates who held excellent positions in Pittsburgh stores, offices, and industries. Secretaries and dieticians were in short sup-ply, and so were teachers for the new tech-nical courses opening in area high schools. The goal of the original planners—to pro-vide excellent training for jobs in industry and business in the Pittsburgh area—was clearly succeeding. Graduates did not forget their alma mater. A few grateful alumnae formed an alumnae association that held periodic meetings on campus.

In Retrospect

Margaret Morrison Carnegie School for Women began life as a vocational and trade school. In 1903 its preliminary plan-ners envisioned a school in which girls, as Margaret Morrison documents usually called women students, from the Pittsburgh area could increase their knowledge and skills in their chosen vocation or trade. The original faculty consisted largely of skilled workers such as milliners, cooks, secretaries, or housekeepers. Even before the school opened, its leaders introduced a different element—an emphasis on women's roles as housewives and mothers. During the follow-ing six years, the school drifted even further away from its original set of goals. By 1912, a better-educated faculty had introduced a wide array of courses in the sciences and hu-manities both for general education and as the basis of education for professional life. Alumnae were succeeding in jobs through-out the Pittsburgh area. The curriculum had expanded slowly until by 1912 the school was prepared to offer bachelor's degrees in the new Carnegie Institute of Technology.

Left:
Margaret Morrison students draw original ideas for walls and floors.

The Sobriquet Maggie Murphy

The originator of the nick-name by which the students of the women's college have long been known had, curiously enough, no association with Carnegie. In the summer of 1907 Ralph K. Merril, '08, and a friend, Albert W. Schenck, chanced to pass a building that was under course of erection on the campus. On being asked to what use the new hall was to be devoted, Merrill replied that it was the Margaret Morrison Carnegie School for Women. Schenck then remarked, quite casually, "Why not call it Maggie Murphy for short?" Merrill, who was on the staff of the *Tartan* at the time, referred in the next issue to the girls' school as "Maggie Murphy." "The thing caught on," Merrill wrote recently, "and I believe has stuck until the present day."
—From Dean Arthur Wilson Tarbell's *The Story of Carnegie Tech: Being a History of Carnegie Institute of Technology from 1900–1935.* Pittsburgh: (Carnegie Institute of Tech-nology, 1937), p. 250

17

The Way We Were:
My Family and I Span a Century at Carnegie Mellon

Clara Herron
*Pittsburgh,
Pennsylvania*

- *General Studies '47*
- *Pi Delta Epsilon
  President*
- *Phi Kappa Phi*
- *Mortar Board*
- *Tartan Editor*
- *Tri Publications*
- *I. R. C. President*

Catherine C. Ihmsen
*(Clara's mother)
Pittsburgh,
Pennsylvania*

- *Household Arts '09*
- *President, first MMCC
  graduating class*

Fourth Annual Night
School of Applied Science
Banquet Program, 1909

18

*I*f my mother, Catherine Clare Ihmsen, MM'09, hadn't caught rheumatic fever, she might never have been president of Margaret Morrison's first graduating class. After missing months of classes in high school, she skipped her senior year and enrolled in the Carnegie Technical Schools. In those days, admission did not require a high school degree. A commuter, she rode the trolley from her south side home on Carson Street and walked over the bridge past Flagstaff Hill to classes. They were held in Industries Hall, the first building on campus. The Margaret Morrison building opened the next year. Like many of her classmates, she majored in Household Arts and delighted in the modern labs and classrooms in the shining new building, not yet besmirched by smoke from Andrew Carnegie's mills.

If Mother hadn't had dark hair, she might never have met James W. Herron, president of the 1910 Civil Engineering Night Class, and I might never have been born. A young acquaintance wanted brides-maids with blonde, red, brown, and black hair. Mother's tresses qualified as nearly black. Jim Herron had been recruited as an usher for the wedding, and Dad and Mom sat next to each other at dinner. When she got home, she told her mother, "I made a hit tonight." Six weeks later she engineered a "porch party" and invited Jim as escort to a girl who was moving out of town. Smart girl, my mother. With the competition out of the way, Dad and Mom were married on October 4, 1911.

My father was hired a year later as superintendent of construction for Rockview Penitentiary. Later the family moved to Huntingdon, Pennsylvania, where Dad became superintendent of the reformatory. By then he was already an expert on penal care. When they arrived, Mother, alarmed at the quality of prison food, used her Margaret Morrison expertise to fashion new menus. Inmates cleaned their plates. An assistant at the prison wrote Governor Pinchot's office, complaining that there weren't enough scraps left to slop the hogs. According to family lore, Pinchot responded, "The prisoners are more important than the hogs."

My parents had five children, two of whom graduated from Carnegie Tech: J. W. Herron, Jr., Civil Engineering, 1935, and me, Clara Herron, Margaret Morrison, 1947. At first, although he had graduated second in his class, Jim was unable to get a job; it was the middle of the Depression. A golf enthusiast, he decided to caddy at a tournament at the Oakmont Country Club to make a little money. He caddied for an executive from H. H. Robertson Steel, who promptly hired him as a salesman. Years later he retired as the firm's national sales manager.

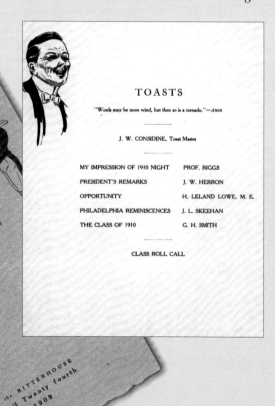

My dad died in 1931. My mother and I lived on Beeler Street just a few houses away from campus, so I walked back and forth to school. On scholarship, I enrolled in Home Economics like my mother, but after one of the faculty, a nice old lady as I saw her, spent a whole semester talking about split pea soup, I changed to social work.

That curriculum also failed to fascinate me; the faculty saved all the good hands-on stuff for graduate school. I had been spending all my Friday nights and Sunday afternoons in *The Tartan* office anyway, so when MMCC added a journalism major to its General Studies program, I took three summer school courses at Pitt and changed direction again.

My first year at *The Tartan* was something else. The office was in a run-down wing of Industries Hall. Several panes of glass were missing from the upper windows, and a large family of pigeons had set up housekeeping in the office. The next year *The Tartan* moved to the top floor of the Carnegie Union, a grand old mansion at the corner of Beeler and Forbes Streets. In my junior year (1945–46), I became editor.

A rumor among students claimed that Tech had a quota on Jewish students. With the late Ben Schwartz, a math major, and Director of Student Personnel and Welfare, Dr. Beryl Warden, we pored over years of records from the admission office, but we found no evidence of a quota, so I lost my chance to become a muckraker. The last sentence I wrote as editor seems to be the only one that impressed my friends. As I ate a cold one at my desk, I wrote, "May all your cheese sandwiches be hot."

After graduation, I started a career in journalism, working at the *Clairton Progress* and then the *Penn Progress* as a reporter and advertising saleswoman. In the early 1950s, I got a job with the *Pittsburgh Post-Gazette,* writing both features and a column called "Shopping with Polly." I worked there for 40 years.

The 1946 journalism honorary Pi Delta Epsilon

First row:
Randall, Sunseri, Bigelman, Dunn, Herron

Second row:
Sweeney, Herlick, Clark, Horridge, Kane

Among my features were stories on pregnant teenagers, hunger in the community, Alzheimer's disease, mental health and for 15 years a series for teenagers covering topics that ran from drug addiction to elephant jokes (for which we interviewed elephants at the zoo). Among many prizes, the best I won was a national award for a story about a man who became a successful business man before he learned to read.

After I retired, I connected to the campus again. I regularly attended plays in the Little Theater, joined the Academy for Lifelong Learning in 1994, and reviewed world events during our years on campus in a talk at my class's fiftieth homecoming in 1997. Looking back, I realize that it's almost a century since my parents enrolled at the Carnegie Technical Schools. What would they think if they could visit now?

Clara Herron
General Studies '47

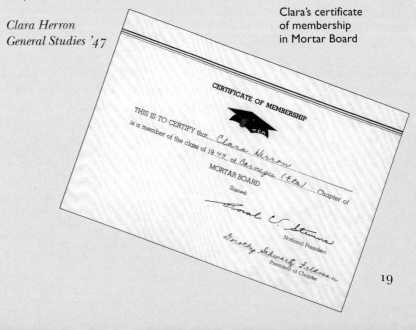

Clara's certificate of membership in Mortar Board

Characteristics of the Technical College for Women

The modern technical college for women differs in three main respects from the academic institutions which give degrees to women.

(1) Preparatory Courses. The technical college does not insist on Latin for entrance. It is more liberal in its entrance requirements than the academic institutions.

(2) Courses of Study for Graduation. The technical college may require for graduation such subjects as English composition and literature, history, natural science, or modern languages. But the greater part of the course consists of specialized or technical courses, most of which are not offered in the academic colleges.

(3) Preparation for a Profession. The technical college resembles a professional school in that each of its graduates is trained with a definite occupation in prospect, so that she is equipped not only with a college degree but with a professional attitude, knowledge, and skill, and can, if she wishes, take a salaried position. The training is expected to raise the occupation in some cases to the level of a profession, as, for example, in the case of homemaking.

Bulletin of the Carnegie Institute of Technology: General Catalogue, 1920–21, pp. 93–94.

Chapter 2

1913–29
Developing a Technical College for Women

For 16 years after 1913, a complex, talented, determined dean, Dr. Mary Bidwell Breed, led Margaret Morrison Carnegie College for Women. Her predecessor, Clara L. West, had resigned after suffering a nervous breakdown. Miss Breed assumed the deanship after a year's interval during which Arthur Arton Hamerschlag, the Director of Carnegie Tech, led the college while the search for a new dean took place. Dean Breed struggled with four major problems: a divided student body, inadequate facilities, an evolving curriculum that included several new majors, and a struggle between an emerging student culture and the values of an older generation. She resigned in 1929, leaving behind a distinguished technical college in which only a few remnants of the trade courses designed mainly for working women remained.

Who Were the Students?

Let's begin at the end of the academic pipeline, at commencement. The number of full-time day school graduates about doubled during Dean Breed's tenure. Although the number of graduates stayed about the same, 81 in 1913 and 84 in 1929, about half of the 1913 graduates were night students who received certificates instead of bachelor's degrees. By 1929, Margaret Morrison had phased out all of its night certificate programs. In all of these 16 years, fewer than half of the girls who entered Margaret Morrison as freshmen stayed to earn their diplomas. Most of the dropouts took place between the freshman and sophomore years.

Opposite page:
Costume design
circa 1920

21

MMCS GRADUATES BY YEARS, 1913-1929

Year	Day	Night
1913	42	39
1914	37	3
1915	40	3
1916	30	3
1917	35	6
1918	38	0
1919	43	0
1920	54	0
1921	47	0
1922	60	0
1923	77	0
1924	64	0
1925	77	0
1926	92	0
1927	94	0
1928	102	0
1929	84	0

Five hundred and seven students enrolled in Margaret Morrison in 1928-29. According to the registrar's figures, 90 percent of these students were Pennsylvanians. Only 13 of them came from outside the tri-state area, that is, Pennsylvania, Ohio, and West Virginia. The figures for the Pittsburgh region highlight the local nature of the student population. Forty-one percent of Margaret Morrison's students resided in Pittsburgh, and an additional 26 percent came from the rest of Allegheny County. Two-thirds of the college's students lived within a streetcar commute of the campus, and well over half of them commuted as late as 1929.

For many years, Tech kept records of its students' religious preferences. In 1929, 78 percent of Tech's women students, including women from both Margaret Morrison and Fine Arts, were Protestant, 12 percent were Roman Catholic, and 10 percent were Jewish. Only two students were Eastern Orthodox. Both these figures and students' names indicate that relatively few of the southern and eastern European immigrants who had emigrated to labor in Andrew Carnegie's mills sent their offspring to Margaret Morrison.

The new college attracted girls who were interested in technical rather than liberal arts education. During Dean Breed's tenure, Margaret Morrison added preparation for three new professions: science, library work, and social work. Home Economics, a discipline that included Costume Economics, Household Economics, and Home Arts and Crafts, attracted most of the students throughout Dean Breed's administration. In 1913–14 home economists were 42 percent of the total enrollment. In 1921–22 they were 45 percent and in 1928–29, 46 percent. Secretarial Studies always occupied second place ahead of Social Work and Library Work. A few students always majored in science, and after 1916, an increasing number of secretarial students enrolled in an English minor, the first step in the direction of a liberal arts degree.

DEGREES AWARDED AT COMMENCEMENT 1913, 1921, 1929

	1913	1921	1929
Costume Economics	5	8	15
Household Economics	19	21	6
Home Economics	0	0	20
Home Arts & Crafts	0	2	0
Secretarial Studies	3	14	27
General Science	0	1	3
Library Work	0	0	6
Social Work	0	0	7

Academic standards for admission rose steadily. In 1913 Margaret Morrison automatically admitted all applicants with a secondary school diploma. If not a high school graduate, applicants could still gain admission by passing entrance examinations given at Margaret Morrison. In addition, the school required candidates to present themselves for a personal interview. By 1929, however, all candidates were required to have earned a secondary school diploma, and the personal interviews became more demanding. Despite these increased standards, Dean Breed complained constantly about the quality of work that her students were doing.

In her annual reports, she argued that admission standards were too low, students were often sick and needed better diets and more sleep, dormitories were inadequate, and most of all, students spent too much time in frivolous activities such as dancing. More about that later. Like academic standards, tuition rose from $30 a year ($40 for non-Pittsburghers) in 1913 to $300 for all students in 1929.

Margaret Morrison's small enrollment presented severe financial problems to Carnegie Tech's officials. The Margaret Morrison building had been designed to educate between 750 and 900 students. Yet, during the 1920s, enrollment ranged between a low of 325 in 1920–21 and a high of 538 in 1926–27. Moreover, the large freshman dropout rate that sometimes approached 50 percent meant that class size for upper division courses for majors were so small that they became uneconomical.

A letter from President Baker to Dean Breed in 1925 noted that 40 Margaret Morrison classes contained fewer than ten students and asked her to see if she could combine some of them. These small classes, however, were upper-division courses for majors that could not be blended together. Seniors in social work and home economics, for example, required specialized courses in their disciplines.

Margaret Morrison students praised the personal attention that the faculty gave to them, but the financial burden imposed by that attention was excessive. The college's financial troubles that contributed to its dissolution in 1973 had their origins much earlier in the school's inability to attract enough students to fill its classes, particularly in the upper three years.

During the years between 1913 and 1929, then, most Margaret Morrison students came from Pittsburgh and its immediate suburbs. Most of them lived at home and either walked to school or commuted by streetcar. About 45 percent of them majored in home economics and another 25 percent in secretarial studies, the two traditional Margaret Morrison professional options. Over the years, their academic quality increased substantially, but still less than half the girls who entered Margaret Morrison as freshmen stayed to earn a degree.

"Those dormitories are a disgrace."

Four changes in the school's physical plant took place during Dean Breed's administration. The entire school rejoiced in 1914 when Carnegie Tech finished a major addition to Margaret Morrison. The new wing included a large, well-lighted library and a room where students could rest between classes. Insufficient funds, however, prevented Tech from including all the additions contemplated in the architect's original plans. According to Dean Breed's 1915 Annual Report, the school still lacked an assembly room large enough to hold the entire student body and needed new facilities for physical training, particularly a better gymnasium and a swimming pool.

The new wing became more accessible to commuters in 1917 when Tech purchased the McGinley property on Forbes Avenue and filled in the ravine that separated this land from the original campus. The traction company opened a streetcar stop at the new campus entrance on Forbes

Top:
Maggie Murphs dine in the Home Management House

Center:
Forbes and Mellon Halls

❧

The Passing of the Original "Little House"

The "Little House" which has always been one of the unique characteristics of M.M.C.S. passed out of existence last fall. It was a laboratory where every member of the Household Economics Department was given an opportunity to put into practice all the theories and principles which modern art and science have conceived for the housekeeper's use.
—*The C.I.T. Alumnus,* March 1919, p. 14

❧

Street. Instead of walking across the Junction Hollow bridge and making their way up Woodlawn Avenue (now Frew, Tech and Margaret Morrison Streets) to the Margaret Morrison building, students could cut across the campus to their classrooms. Hence the name—the Cut—for what is now the lawn between Forbes Avenue and Hunt Library.

The second improvement was the acquisition of the Home Management House on Margaret Morrison Street. Dean Breed's 1920 Annual Report announced this acquisition in quiet tones:

The Department of Household Economics has opened its new Practice House on Woodlawn Avenue, with equipment that puts it in the lead among American institutions of our type, and we hope to see many indirect as well as direct instructional advantages from the use of this beautiful and efficient house.

Carnegie Tech renovated the building completely. In addition to its use in the home management department, it soon became a meeting place for faculty and alumnae, just as Dean Breed had hoped. It replaced the apartment—the "Little House"—that had been a part of the original Margaret Morrison building. Since most Margaret Morrison girls expected to live in

houses and not apartments, the original facility was less than ideal.

The third improvement involved finding adequate dormitories, a more thorny facilities problem. In 1913 Margaret Morrison rented three houses on Woodlawn Avenue that the school used as dormitories for out-of-town students. During the next 16 years, the school either rented or bought an additional seven houses, as the map on the following page shows.

Two of these houses—Forbes Hall and Mellon Hall—were well-built mansions, the latter a gift of the family residence from Andrew W. Mellon. The Mellon Annex was originally the stables for the mansion, but Tech renovated them thoroughly. The remaining houses, typical late nineteenth century residences, left much to be desired. They were expensive to operate, with poor heating systems and inadequate bathrooms, kitchens, laundries, and dining facilities. The school clearly needed better—and more—dormitories. Despite annual complaints by Dean Breed and, after 1920, the newly appointed dean of women,

GIRLS' DORMS

Carnegie Tech failed to build or acquire a modern dormitory for women until after World War II when Tech bought and renovated Morewood Gardens.

Although students complained stridently about the dorms, they seemed to have enjoyed dorm life. Small dormitories—most housed fewer than 20 girls and a matron—promoted close friendships and fostered the development of in-group identities that commuting students could not share. The 1924 *Thistle* included photos of the girls living in each group of dorms, each with a short poem.

Woodlawn Dormitories

One hundred little Plebe girls,
All living in a row
While six Junior presidents
The way to wisdom show.

They work so hard all day,
And sleep from dark 'til dawn,
One scarcely ever sees them,
These little Plebes from Woodlawn.

The girls from one of the best of the houses, Mellon Hall, delighted in the antics of dormitory life.

Mellon Hall

A jolly group of Sophomores, Juniors and Seniors make up the Mellon Hall unit. Many gay times have we had—the Hallowe'en Dance with Jack O'Lanterns, cider, and pumpkin pies, which has become a tradition; the Christmas party—the lighted tree, presents, Santa Claus and everything; a Spring Dance to get us in tune for Campus Week; and the Senior Farewell Dinner. Neither can we forget the little informal parties given us by our chaperone.

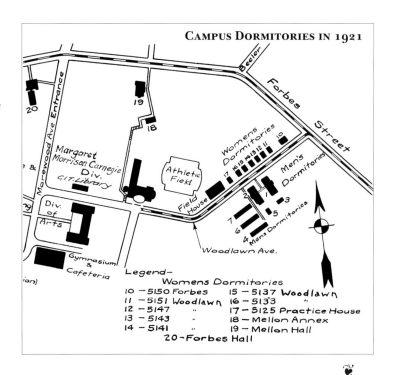

The fourth facilities improvement took place when Tech built a gymnasium on Tech Street in 1924. The administration then renovated the old field house that had stood at the bend of Margaret Morrison Street near the Margaret Morrison building. Renamed the Carnegie Inn, it housed a large dining hall for women students, a faculty dining room, and a student grill. Margaret Morrison then renovated the old dining space in the original Margaret Morrison building and eliminated all of the makeshift dining facilities in the dormitories along Margaret Morrison Street.

An Evolving Curriculum

Dean Breed was born into a distinguished Pittsburgh family. Her mother, Cynthia Bidwell Breed, was a descendant of Jonathan Edwards, a theologian who became president of Princeton. The future dean graduated from the Pennsylvania College for Women, now Chatham College, in 1889 and then attended Bryn Mawr where she earned a Bachelor of Arts degree in chemistry in 1894 and a Master of Arts in 1895. Then she received the Bryn Mawr European Fellowship to study science at Heidelburg University in Germany, the first woman to

Dean Breed Comments on Women's Dormitories

During the past year we have housed two hundred and twenty-two women. The ten houses have been filled practically the entire year. We have lost a number of girls who withdrew their applications for admission when they found that they could not gain entrance to our dormitories. However, there are a number of out-of-town students who live in boarding houses that cannot be supervised by the Institute's officers.
—*Margaret Morrison Carnegie College Annual Report,* 1922, p. 7

Left:
Mellon Hall residents, 1924

Dean Mary
Bidwell Breed

Dean Breed's Comments on Attitudes Toward Margaret Morrison

It is evident that the students from out-of-town represent a somewhat different economic stratum from those living in the Pittsburgh district. The tradition that prevails in Pittsburgh that the Carnegie Institute of Technology is intended solely for students of small means, is not universal in other sections of the country....While we have always had a small number of students from the better element in Pittsburgh, yet even these students reveal by their slightly condescending attitude a certain taint of this misconception. Our problem of enrollment, therefore, is not only of getting numbers, but of getting students from all classes of society especially in the Pittsburgh district.
—*Margaret Morrison Carnegie College, Annual Report,* June 1923, p.1

matriculate at that distinguished institution. Returning to Bryn Mawr, she earned a Ph.D. in 1901 and then served as a faculty member or administrator at several colleges before coming to Carnegie Tech as Dean of Margaret Morrison in 1913. While in Pittsburgh, she lived with her mother in the family home. She was an active member of the Shadyside Presbyterian Church, the Twentieth Century Club, the Bryn Mawr Club, the Women's City Club, and the College Club of Pittsburgh. Dean Breed's policies and her ambitions for Margaret Morrison reflected this background.

Slowly, Dean Breed phased out the night school program. In the past it had attracted students who performed well on an interview and were more than 16 years old. Girls who were not high school graduates and were already employed could cover in four years at night school what candidates for the two-year certificate covered in two years in the full-time day program. They chose one of six fields: bookkeeping, stenography, sewing and dressmaking, millinery, cooking, or handicrafts. Practical courses in these fields took place in hands-on laboratory sessions. By the mid-teens, however, most high schools in the area offered courses in these fields, and when demand decreased, Dean Breed and her colleagues closed the last night school program in 1923.

Special afternoon courses in cooking, sewing, and dressmaking, however, lasted much longer. Each course consisted of 12 three-hour sessions open to students at least 23 years of age who had enough education

to pass any test the department might assign and who wanted to develop skills for use in the home. Women who finished these courses did not earn certificates. The courses continued for many years.

Dean Breed focused most of her energy on the curriculum for the Bachelor of Science degree. Pittsburgh businesses offered many opportunities for the employment of skilled women, and as a result, many proposals for new courses of study surfaced. Although most of them were rejected, Margaret Morrison established new programs in four fields: science in 1913, social work in 1916, a pre-library option in cooperation with the Carnegie Library in 1919, and nursing in 1930.

Curriculum reform focused on the two most popular options, Home Economics and Secretarial Studies. In 1913, classes emphasizing skills—needlework, cooking, or typewriting, for example—dominated the curriculum. Gradually Dean Breed reduced the emphasis on the development of skills in favor of courses in science and the humanities that gave greater professional standing to the degree. All freshmen took the required science courses in chemistry, physics, and biology. Taught by the lecture method, most classes usually included more than 100 students. Classes in English composition were limited to 25 students, however. By the end of her tenure, Dean Breed had reduced the freshman schedule from eight courses per semester to five.

The American Association of University Women recognized these curricular changes in 1925. Before that year, AAUW did not admit graduates of technical colleges, but at its 1925 conference, the organization welcomed alumnae from both Simmons College and Margaret Morrison. Margaret Morrison's alumnae could now rub elbows with graduates of the most distinguished women's colleges in the nation. The trade and technical school that Dean Breed inherited in 1913 had received national recognition of its status as a distinguished technical college.

Two Cultures in Conflict: The Jazz Age

Until 1920, Tech gave Dean Breed responsibility for both the academic and social life of Margaret Morrison students. After 1920, three deans of women: Laura W. Scales (1920–24), Mary Louise R. Brown (1925), and Mary Watson Green (1926–40), assumed responsibility for both the women's dormitories and the social life of Tech's students. Dean Breed and her new colleagues shared viewpoints that were not always those of the students.

Dean Breed promoted positive aspects of the school's social and co-curricular life. As soon as she became dean, she organized the Student Government Association and

THE THISTLE

The Margaret Morrison Social Work Club

GLEN SHUFF	.	.	.	.	*President*
ANNE DOUGHERTY	.	.	.	.	*Vice-President*
VIRGINIA PENTZ	.	.	.	*Recording Secretary*
JOSEPHINE WHITNEY	.	.	*Corresponding Secretary*
ELIZABETH GITT	.	.	.	.	*Treasurer*

Late in the Spring of 1919, the Margaret Morrison Social Work Club burst into being. Belonging by common consent and inclinations to the Sisterhood of Flatheels, stiff hats, tortoise shell glasses, broad intellects and free speech, we plunged into the new project for inspiration and cheer with our customary enthusiasm. Our expectations have not been shattered—we flourish. We even publish annually a club paper—*The Record!*

In the uncertain future, dear classmate, if you feel you morals tottering, if the world has used you ill, if old age or insanity creeps on, if you are lost in a big city—hungry, cold or athirst—look one of us up, and we will fly to you gladly, with a brief-case and a smile—don't forget.

The Thistle, 1921

the Senate. The 11-member Senate was composed of the president, vice president, secretary, and treasurer of the Association, one member from each of the five classes, and the presidents of the dormitories. The Senate held trials of students who violated the honor code and had widespread powers to punish, suspend or, with the consent of the dean, expel students from the school. Carnegie Mellon's archives hold the minutes of the Senate from 1918 through 1944 that describe in detail the trials of hundreds of students who had violated the school's rules.

The honor system taught honesty and good citizenship in an active and dramatic fashion. Each student handbook included a description of the way in which the system functioned.

In addition to the honor system, Dean Breed promoted other attempts to improve the academic and moral climate of the school. She founded The Guild, a philanthropic organization that raised funds

Powers of the Senate

The control of conduct as far as it is connected with the school, whether this be in assembly, lunch room, halls, reading room, park, streets or trolley cars; the control of all forms of dishonesty; the maintenance of high standards of honor in all class work and related matters.
—*Students' Handbook* Margaret Morrison Carnegie School [sic], 1917–1918, p.13

The Honor System.

The foundation stone of the Student Government Association is HONOR. Every student by her matriculation in M. M. C. S. pledges herself to obey the rules of this organization. The Association represents, in the highest degree the united interests of all the students, and as such should be of the utmost importance to each and every one of us.

The Dean and Faculty of the Margaret Morrison Carnegie School hereby grant to the Student Senate the following powers:

The Senate shall have jurisdiction over the conduct of the students so far as it is connected with the school and have power to enforce penalties which the Senate shall determine, with the exception of expulsion, which to be enforced, may be recommended by the Senate and ratified by the Dean.

A. All work, written or oral, for which credit is given done at home or at school, is included in the honor system.

Method of reporting:—

1. A girl who observes another cheating, reports to her class representative to the Senate, within three days after the offense is committed. The Senate then inflicts the penalties which are on first offense:—

  (1) Report to the instructor concerned.

  (2) Announce the whole case in assembly, giving the class and division but not the girl's name.

  (3) Suspension—length of time depending on each individual case.

On second offense:—

  (1) Expulsion.

2. Three days after a girl has told another to report herself to the Senate, she asks the cheater if she has reported; if not, the observer will herself report the case immediately.

B. Quiet regulations of corridors, assembly, class rooms and locker rooms is included in the honor system. Penalties vary, but may be:

1. Losing library privileges.

2. If upper classmen, their upper classmen privileges are taken away for a certain length of time at lunch room, etc.

Students' Handbook Margaret Morrison Carnegie School, 1917–1918

I loved her mouth,
her nose, her eyes.
For this I know
you'd say I'm wise.
You'd call me foolish
without a thought,
If I should say,
I loved her Knot.

The Milk Bar in Margaret Morrison

When we were freshman in 1927, Margaret Morrison maintained a milk bar in the basement. The names of all the underweight (skinny, slender?) freshman girls were put on the Milk List; we were required to drink a glass of milk each morning at a designated time. So we paid for the milk and we drank it. What a laugh for students of today!
—Gertrude (Novak) Kemper
Business Studies '32

for local charities. She promoted a branch of the Young Women's Christian Association that held meetings on campus and invited local clergy to lead them. She introduced Cwens and Mortar Board, national honor societies for women, to the campus, and persuaded each department to organize a club bringing all its majors together to explore their common professional interests. Finally, she helped to promote interscholastic sports teams, primarily to improve student health.

Throughout her tenure, Dean Breed struggled to impose her moral and cultural standards on a somewhat resistant student body. After 1920, newly appointed deans of women joined her in these efforts. The struggle resulted in some caustic denunciations of Margaret Morrison students and their ways in the dean's annual reports. These denunciations increased in fervor during the 1920s, the age of the flapper, jazz, the Charleston, and bathtub gin. A few quotations from Dean Breed's Annual Reports follow:

1920: Our students, unfortunately, are not only infected with the physical ills of the time…but are also subject to the contagion of the current extravagance, waste, pleasure seeking, and irresponsibility.

1923: It is, in my opinion, fallacious and dangerous to assume that social dancing until early morning hours would quicken a true college spirit, or that exploding toy balloons and blowing whistles is anything more than a mask to cover a vacuum not only of ideas, but of interest.

1928: To adapt an educational system so as to develop an all-around personality out of the material so one-sided as we now obtain from our homes and our school systems, will require the patient educational statesmanship of many years. Looking back over a period of years, I note a dying away of active interest in religion and in charitable and philanthropic effort, which is not compensated, at least among the student body of this college, by any increase of interest in the various forms of art and science.

The Dean of Women, Mrs. Laura C. Scales, who was appointed in 1920, echoed Dean Breed's sentiments in her 1924 Annual Report.

The main criticism of the dances is of the choice of orchestras. The dancing is objectionable in proportion to the amount of jazz. This was particularly noticeable at the Junior Men's Promenade where there were examples of the worst dancing of the year.

The Dormitory Council is anxious to provide more simple pleasures for women only. They feel the inadvisability of confining all their life to engagements with men students.

The Dean of Women met all freshman girls on four consecutive Fridays in April and May….In the first two talks, the Dean of Women outlined the history of the world and society anthropologically and ethnologically. In the third lecture, she discussed the biological and psychical traits common to all people, attempting to make plain the necessity for control and training. In the fourth she discussed certain manners and customs of modern life which are different from those of earlier generations. The students expressed the conviction that these talks were what they need and want.

The Plebe Regulations Committee (should) be discouraged to use the "slap-stick" methods that have been used in the past to subdue Freshmen. They rather should use the lecture method— warning freshmen of their shortcomings, giving them an opportunity to mend their ways and finally resorting to a report to the Senate who will recommend probation, counts, suspension or expulsion as the nature of the offense warrants.

In loco parentis could easily have been the motto of both Dean Breed and the three deans of women. They appointed matrons to supervise behavior in the dormitories. They established curfew hours for students in the dorms and in some cases required quiet hours for study. They established regulations

MMC'S GLEE CLUB

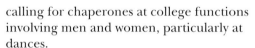

M.M.C.S. May Festival
Group Dances
Seniors — Milkmaids
Juniors — Shepherdess
Sophomores — Fiddler's Dance
Plebes — Maypole Dance
Miss Rachel Beatty of the Senior Class will be
Tucket (Herald)
Miss Florence Bechtel was elected
May Queen

The Thistle, 1918

calling for chaperones at college functions involving men and women, particularly at dances.

During World War I when as many as 8,000 soldiers trained on campus, Dean Breed made vigorous attempts to limit contact between her students and the soldiers. In a letter to President Hamerschlag dated September 12, 1918, she recommended that Tech build "a board walk around the extreme edge of the fill to connect the west side door of Forbes Hall with the path across the cut, so that the path should be as far away from the barracks as possible." In conferences with the military commanders on campus, she later proposed the creation of a zone within which it would be a military misdemeanor for the men in uniform to be seen talking to a woman. The war ended before Tech acted on either of these recommendations.

In addition to a student culture fostered by the administration, Margaret Morrison students developed a parallel, and somewhat rival, culture of their own. They wanted to enjoy life. A major circumstance conditioned the development of that culture: men outnumbered women at Tech by a factor of three to one. Margaret Morrison women had the opportunity for a delightful social life with a bevy of young men competing for their companionship. In 1924, for example, fraternities sponsored sixty dances in one semester. The school also sponsored seventeen dances on Friday and Saturday nights and fifteen tea dances from 4:30 to

6:00 during the same semester. No wonder that the deans complained constantly about the effect of "excessive dancing" on the girls in their charge.

During the teens, Margaret Morrison girls organized May Day celebrations, the lineal ancestor of Campus Week, on a Saturday in May. Only members of the Athletic Association took part. May Day featured several special dances and a group dance by each class.

May Day was phased out after 1920 when Campus Week began. Canegie Tech's Alumni Secretary conceived the idea of a three-day homecoming celebration in May to attract alumni to visit the campus. He asked students to help, and they immediately took over, turning Campus Week into an event that got so far out-of-hand that it was abolished in 1929 to be reinstituted a year later as Spring Carnival. Campus Week featured a migratory dance during which fraternity members and their dates migrated from one frat house to another during a long night of revels, men's and women's athletic events, men's and women's sweepstakes, a queen's coronation ceremony, and a variety of lunches, banquets, and dances. Margaret Morrison students delighted in these revels while their books lay unopened on their desks. Their deans and much of the faculty were dismayed.

During Campus Week, the freshmen buried their Plebe Regulations in an elaborate ceremony called Qualification Day. Tech required all plebes to abide by a set of

The Maypole Dance in 1918

Celebrating May Day

Surprising what the Maggie Murphs of 1918 would do. For May Day we needed forty barrel hoops that we located on Carson Street on the South Side. Two of us set out to get them. It had to be a streetcar job—what else? We chose off hours in the morning to go, but had to take three different trolleys to Tech. The conductors were amazing: they just laughed and gave us the rear platforms and a bit of assistance. When we arrived at Margaret Morrison Street there was plenty of help— hoop rolling, too. How times have changed!
—Florence (Bechtel) Whitwell Costume Economics '18

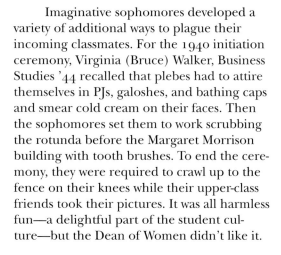

Imaginative sophomores developed a variety of additional ways to plague their incoming classmates. For the 1940 initiation ceremony, Virginia (Bruce) Walker, Business Studies '44 recalled that plebes had to attire themselves in PJs, galoshes, and bathing caps and smear cold cream on their faces. Then the sophomores set them to work scrubbing the rotunda before the Margaret Morrison building with tooth brushes. To end the ceremony, they were required to crawl up to the fence on their knees while their upper-class friends took their pictures. It was all harmless fun—a delightful part of the student culture—but the Dean of Women didn't like it.

Clockwise from top:

1928 Campus Week program

Attendants of the Campus Week Queen, circa 1924

Geisha Girls, 1923 Campus Week

Girls sit astride kiddie cars for the women's sweepstakes, 1924 Campus Week

Dance card, circa 1920

regulations specified in *The Students' Handbook*. The *1917–18 Handbook*, for example, included these regulations among others:

All Plebe women shall wear the Regulation Arm Band; they are permitted to wear only the following pieces of jewelry—one necessary pin, a watch, a fraternity pin; they shall not walk or converse with men while on campus.

All Plebes must use the right-hand stairway and bulletin board.

The following courtesies are required of all Plebes: Holding doors open for faculty and upper classmen. Giving precedence to faculty and upper classmen in the building, on the campus and in the streetcars.

Plebes are not allowed on fourth floor for lunch, between 1:00 and 1:30. This means students who bring lunch also.

Penalties for breaking these rules to be decided upon by the General Student Council.

Alumnae Affairs and Careers

The Margaret Morrison Alumnae Association had been founded in 1909, when members of the charter class received their diplomas. The Association grew steadily throughout Dean Breed's tenure. In order to receive *The C.I.T. Alumnus* and belong to the alumni federation, graduates had to pay an annual fee of two dollars. In 1921, Margaret Morrison's membership led all the schools; 64 percent of its graduates had joined, contrasted to 55 percent of students in Engineering and Science, 31 percent in Industries, and 22 percent in Fine Arts.

Margaret Morrison alumnae met annually for tea in the Home Management House and sponsored numerous dances, teas, theater parties, and bridge parties, proceeds from which usually went to support scholarship funds. During World War I, Association members met to knit garments and roll bandages for the armed forces, a number of alumnae volunteered to serve in YMCA canteens in France, and a few became army nurses.

Fragmentary data from the "Personals" columns in the *Carnegie Alumnus* and the University Advancement Alumni Database contain what we know about the positions held by Margaret Morrison alumnae between 1913 and 1929. There are 110 reports, each one contributed voluntarily in response to general appeals. Of 110 reports, 26 indicated positions as high school teachers, 24 in "business", probably as secretaries, seven in college teaching, seven working in non-profit organizations, six who were self-employed, and five each in libraries and hospitals. Most of the jobs listed seemed to have been at or near entry level, except two supervisory positions in lunchrooms.

In Retrospect

Between 1913 and 1929, Margaret Morrison abandoned its trade school origins and its ambitions to serve Pittsburgh's working women. Led by a distinguished dean, it discontinued its night school courses and its special, short non-degree programs for housewives. An addition to the original building provided 50 percent more space. The school acquired seven additional houses to use as dormitories, a Home Management House, and a new dining facility. New courses in science replaced some of the emphasis on skill development that dominated the school's early curriculum. Four new fields of study—science, social work, library work, and nursing—took their places beside the two traditional Margaret Morrison fields, home economics and secretarial studies. An honor program run by the Senate gave students responsibility for controlling academic honesty. New organizations, such as professional clubs and honorary societies, developed. Although the advent of the Great Depression challenged all of Carnegie Tech, Margaret Morrison was ready to embark on its golden age.

Beneath the surface, however, trouble was brewing. Margaret Morrison's small enrollment presented economic problems and resulted in high overhead charges per student, particularly in several disciplines featuring small classes in upper division courses. The economic problems that contributed so much to the decision to phase out Margaret Morrison in 1973 had their antecedents in Dean Breed's administration. Perhaps these problems entered into her decision to resign as dean in 1929.

Plebes bury their Plebe Regulations during Campus Week, circa 1920

Tea in the "Little House"

The tea in the "Little House" is growing in popularity. About 125 guests attended the last one on January 14th. The house lends itself most delightfully to such affairs, and many come to this tea who are not seen at any other event on the calendar.
—*The C.I.T. Alumnus,* February,1922, p.17

Sema D. Moskovitz
*Pittsburgh,
Pennsylvania*

- *General Studies '49*
- *Alpha Epsilon Phi
President*
- *Cwens*
- *Mortar Board*
- *Phi Kappa Phi*
- *Student Council*
- *Women's Guild*
- *Scotch 'n' Soda*
- *WCIT*
- *Tartan*
- *Cano*
- *Sophomore President*

David Moskovitz
*(Sema's father)
Pittsburgh,
Pennsylvania*

- *Civil Engineering '25, '27*

I was a faculty brat, which worked to my advantage. I always felt at home on the campus, and I knew many faculty members long before I became a student. Interestingly, I have been acquainted with all but one of the presidents of Carnegie Tech/ Mellon. Dr. Baker, the second president, gave a party each Christmas for the children of the faculty. There was a beautifully decorated tree and presents for all the children. We were called up by name to receive our gift from Dr. Baker.

My father, David Moskovitz, had earned his undergraduate degree in civil engineering from Tech in 1925. He graduated first in his class, and went on to earn his doctorate from Brown University. After he joined the Tech faculty, we lived in Squirrel Hill and I attended Taylor Allderdice High School. My future husband, Ivan Faigen, also attended Allderdice.

When it came time to enroll at college, this professor's child had no money to go to college anywhere but Tech. Tuition for faculty children was 10 percent of what others paid. Although Margaret Morrison offered many excellent courses of study, none of them appealed to me. So my father introduced me to Professor Vincent Parisi of the Language Department, who had some plans to make that department broader and more inclusive in its offerings. Intrigued, I enrolled in the General Studies Department in Margaret Morrison.

My courses included four years of German, three of French, two of Spanish, and one each of Italian and Russian. Tech hired professors from Pitt to teach the latter two courses. The classes were small, intimate, and demanding. By taking courses in the Psychology Department and doing supervised practice teaching, I earned a teaching certificate and learned with great delight that I had a flair not only for languages but also for teaching.

My parents had always encouraged me to get involved, and I did so with gusto. I was elected to three honorary societies: Cwens, Mortar Board and Phi Kappa Phi, the all-college scholastic honorary. I worked as proofreader for *The Tartan*; wrote one or two typically undergraduate-type pieces for *Cano*, the literary magazine; and served as secretary for WCIT, the campus radio station. Was it coincidence that Ivan Faigen was station manager during part of that time? In all these and other activities, I formed friendships and enjoyed the opportunities for service that the various organizations provided. Indeed, I have continued to work in a number of service organizations. I call myself a Professional Volunteer.

By far the most memorable activity during those years was being a member of the cast of Scotch 'n' Soda in 1947 and again in 1948 in the production of "The Lady's At Work." I was a tap dancer in the chorus line! And I loved it: the hard work of rehearsals, the late hours, the excitement of being on stage.

Late Afternoon

There was a warm day last summer
Made sleepy-still by insects singing in the grass.
But I, busy with introspective thoughts,
Saw only clouds gathering in the sky,
Did not see the clear green of leaves
Stirred by a breeze I did not feel,
Saw not the beauty of the day
Nor caught the lift to life that it gave,
Till the path led over the height of the hill
Pulling me into the pink and mauve of a sunset
And I saw that the clouds were embroidered with gold.

Ivan returned to campus from the Navy in 1946. We shared a locker in what was then Administration [now Baker] Hall, and did many of the things that other young couples did, such as walking in Schenley Park, visiting the Phipps Conservatory, hanging about in Skibo, and this and that. Ivan graduated in the summer of 1948 and I on June 16, 1949. Following my father's lead, I was first in my class.

Ivan and I were married on June 19, 1949, and we went to live in Waltham, Massachusetts. Because married women couldn't hold permanent positions in schools at that time, I did substitute teaching until our two children, Martha and Ronn, were born. When they were school age, I attended Brandeis University and earned a master's degree in English and American Literature. Then, ten years after Ronn, our third child, Michael, was born. That was the end of my plans to return to teaching, but not the end of my continuing interest in education and service activities.

I ran for School Committee in Wayland, Massachusetts, where we still live, and served for six years, taking my turn as chair. I have been active in both the League of Women Voters and the American Association of University Women for more than fifty years, holding a number of leadership positions on the local, state and national levels. Most recently, I have served as president of the Virginia Gildersleeve International Fund, which provides seed money for women's projects in developing nations.

For the past twelve years, I have been training tutors to teach English to speakers of other languages.

Ivan became CEO of Chu Associates, an antenna research and development company, and founded two other companies, Stainless Steel Coatings and Dispensing Technology, Inc. We maintain close ties to Carnegie Mellon by visiting the campus when we can and by supporting the Andrew Carnegie Society. We have been able to endow several scholarships: the Dr. David and Marion Moskovitz Scholarship for mathematics students, the Faigen Margaret Morrison Scholarship for Women in Modern Languages and the Faigen Margaret Morrison Scholarship for Women in Science.

Both the Faigen and the Moskovitz families have had numerous relatives attending Carnegie over the years, and we now look forward to the possibility of having a grandchild or two do the same. Our roots are planted deeply in Carnegie Tech/Mellon. We are proud to have been among its graduates, and delighted to know that this university will continue to grow and to flourish.

Sema D. (Moskovitz) Faigen,
General Studies '49

Top:
Sema's poem, "Late Afternoon," from the June 1948 *Cano*

Bottom:
The dancing chorus of Scotch 'n' Soda's "The Lady's at Work" from the 1949 *Thistle*

Opposite page:
The WCIT Radio Station staff in the 1947 *Thistle*

Elizabeth Pearsall
Crafton,
Pennsylvania

- *General Science '31*
- *Tartan*
- *Science Club*
- *YWCA*
- *Guild*
- *Volleyball*

Elizabeth's registration
card, 1930

My days at Margaret Morrison began each morning in 1927 on the back seats of streetcars running from downtown to the streetcar stop at the end of Morewood Avenue. Like most Margaret Morrison students, I was a commuter and boarded a streetcar near my parents' home in Crafton. When I changed cars downtown, I always joined a dozen or so Tech students. We huddled together in the back of the streetcar and talked our heads off. Friends made commuting palatable. I rode with them on the trolley and ate lunch with them in Skibo or the Carnegie Inn.

My father, an engineer for Jones and Laughlin, decided that I should attend Margaret Morrison. He thought that Margaret Morrison must be all right since it was a part of Carnegie Institute of Technology. Besides, I had won a Pittsburgh Honors Scholarship that paid my tuition. I had attended Langley High School, an excellent school that prepared students well for college. So I enrolled in Secretarial Studies with an English minor. Writing was my big love.

When I arrived on campus, I was told that all Plebes, as freshmen were called in those days, had to wear black stockings. In addition, we were restricted to specific hallways. We were required to use the stairway to the right as you face the front entrance to the Margaret Morrison building. I loved Margaret Morrison anyway.

Although I was an excellent student, I could never learn to type well, an embarrassing handicap for a future secretary. One of my favorite teachers was Edith Winchester

Alexander, the department head in secretarial studies. She encouraged me to go on, but I liked science and I really wanted to become a doctor. So I switched to a pre-med course in general science. I had to take a lot of extra courses to make up for the ones I had missed. Perhaps I gravitated toward chemistry because I had an excellent chemistry teacher in high school.

I was a complete failure at swimming, but you had to know how to swim in order to graduate. I couldn't swim the length of the pool and back, so I swam back and forth across the width of the pool, holding my breath the whole way as I faked an Australian crawl, and the teacher passed me. So I graduated with a Bachelor of Science degree from Margaret Morrison in 1931 in the depth of the Depression.

When I graduated, I didn't have the money to go to the women's medical college in Philadelphia, so I took a job as a laboratory assistant and secretary in Tech's Metallurgy Department in the College of Engineering and Science. They chose me instead of other candidates because I had excellent grades in science courses and, in addition, I could write well and I could type. How's that for irony—the typing, I mean? Fortunately I began to work with the electron microscope, one of only 13 in the nation. I wrote papers with faculty members. I still have copies of some of those papers, written by Gensamer, Pearsall and Smith. Our names appeared in alphabetical order.

While I was on this job, I got a master's degree. I went to night school for six years. I was working all day and, besides, women could not enroll in the day school in engineering and science. I was the only woman in those classes, surrounded by curious males. When I completed my course work largely in metallurgy, they decided to give me a degree in chemistry because the engineering departments would not grant engineering degrees to women. So I have an M.S. in chemistry from the College of Engineering and Science.

Parent's or Guardian's name ___Mr. L. T. Pearsall___

Address of same ___14___ ___Oakwood Rd.___
House No.   Street

___Crafton Br.___ ___Pittsburgh___ ___Pa.___
City   State

If previously registered, in any Department at the Carnegie Institute of Technology, state the

Course ___Science___ Class ___Senior___ Year ___1930-31___

Do you expect to earn part of your expenses during the coming year? ___Yes___
Yes or No

If so, what part? ___All___

I got married at the end of World War II. I used to play chess with another lab assistant at lunch. Howard Hartner, who worked in another wing of the building, heard about our game and came over to join the chess matches; at least that was his excuse. I saw a lot of him and we fell in love and married. During the war, he joined the merchant marine and then the air corps.

After the war, I worked for a while in Bell Labs. Then we went to State College where Howard got his degree while I worked at Penn State as an electron microscopist until our son, David Carl, was born. While Carl was growing up, I worked from home, writing chemical abstracts and articles for scientific journals. After we returned to Pittsburgh to be near aging parents, I had several jobs including one for the National Aeronautics and Space Authority at the University of Pittsburgh.

Today [Spring, 2001] I keep busy volunteering at the Carnegie Museum and helping to plan my class's seventieth reunion. I have kept in touch with Margaret Morrison and Tech—now Carnegie Mellon—over the years. I spend leisure time with Carl, my daughter-in-law Carolyn, granddaughter Karen, and my sister, Jocelyn Pearsall Harrington, MM '36.

Elizabeth (Pearsall) Hartner*
General Science '31, M Chemistry, MCS '37

Education

B.S. 1931   **Science,** Margaret Morrison Carnegie College, Carnegie Institute of Technology. Analytical, Physical, Organic, Physiological Chemistry; Biology, Histology, Bacteriology, Mathematics.

M.S. 1937   **Physical Chemistry,** Graduate School, College of Engineering, Carnegie Tech. Electrochemistry, Thermodynamics, Phase Diagrams, Chemical Instruments, Seminar, Differential Equations.

Experience

1942-1943   **Research Engineer,** in Metallurgy, Timken Roller Bearing Company

1943-1944   **Research Engineer,** in Metallurgy, Westinghouse Research Laboratories

1944-1945   **Member of the Staff,** Metallurgy, Bell Telephone Labs

1952-1953   Digest Writing for Metal Progress

1956-1958   **Member of the Staff,** Physical Metallurgy, E.C. Bain Research Laboratory, United States Steel Corporation

1960-1962   **Junior Fellow,** Mellon Institute, Physical Metallurgy

Selected Publications

Mechanical Properties of the Isothermal Decomposition Products of Austenite, with M. Gensamer and G.V. Smith. Trans. American Society for Metals, 1940.

The Tensile Porperties of Pearlite Bainite and Sheroidite. with M. Gensamer, W.S. Pellini, and J.R. Low. Trans. American Society for Metals, 1942.

New Electron Metallography, March 1962.

"Electron Microscopy Across the World," *Metal Progress,* June 1963.

An Introduction to Automated Literature Searching Marcel Dekker, Inc. New York, New York, 1981.

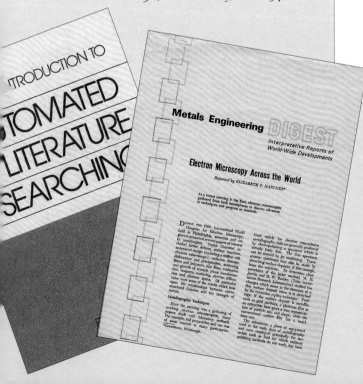

Top right:
Elizabeth's resume

Bottom left:
Elizabeth wrote chemical abstracts and articles for scientific journals.

* Deceased, 2002

The Way We Were:

From Margaret Morrison to the Women's Army Corps

Mary Louise Milligan
Pittsburgh,
Pennsylvania

- *Secretarial Studies '32*
- *Secretarial Club*
- *Student Council*

Mary Louise with her
mother and two brothers

My mother's example and Margaret Morrison's demanding education launched me on a career that included leadership in the Women's Army Corps (WAC) and several philanthropic endeavors. My mother, who was born in France, had strong emotional ties to her homeland. I can remember as a child that she sent packages to relatives in France during World War I and again, when I was a grown woman, during World War II. She believed that women shared wartime responsibilities with men, a lesson I learned from her example.

My father died when I was 12, leaving mother with three children. Fearing that the schools in East Pittsburgh where we lived were inadequate, she paid tuition to send me to high school in nearby Turtle Creek. On weekends she often took me to art lessons, exhibits and concerts at the Carnegie Institute, just down the street from Carnegie Tech. I always wanted to become a Tartan. Tech had an excellent reputation as a college with high standards and demanding entrance requirements. I wanted to be able to get a good job when I graduated so I applied and was accepted into secretarial studies at Margaret Morrison.

Mother had moved to Edgewood by the time I entered Margaret Morrison. Like most of my classmates, I commuted by streetcar to campus, often carrying my lunch to save money. I remember vividly the long hours I spent huddled over my books. I used to study in the Hut, the wooden library building on the end of the Cut across from the Fine Arts building. During warm weather when the windows were open, music from Fine Arts flooded the library, but I soon learned to ignore, and then to enjoy, the distraction.

I was particularly fond of two faculty members. Edith Winchester, a young secretarial studies teacher who later became dean of the college, was unforgettable. She made everyone feel important and at home, and she had a rare capacity to make us study hard and like it. Elizabeth B. Demarest, a taskmaster who set high standards, made the study of history fascinating.

I also learned my craft by working as a part-time secretary for the Home Economics Department. Commuting and this demanding schedule prevented me from taking part in many activities except for the Secretarial Club and the Student Council. At Margaret Morrison, I learned to schedule my time and to work hard, traits that my later work in the WAC demanded.

I graduated in 1932, three years into the Great Depression, but I got a job immediately as secretary to the principal at Forest Hills High School. I had to pass a rigorous screening by both the principal and members of the school board, my first experience with a job interview. While I was at Forest Hills, I studied for a master's degree in school administration at Pitt, attending school at night and during the one-month summer vacation. After graduation from Pitt in 1941, I became assistant supervising principal of the Forest Hills school district and the first woman to become a member of the Allegheny County Principals Round Table.

Then came World War II. Like my mother, I thought that women should serve in the war effort. When the government announced the pending formation of the Women's Army Auxiliary Corps, I applied, beginning a protracted screening process that ended in Baltimore before a battery of

I have always kept in touch with Carnegie Mellon. My brother, Malcolm J. Milligan, was a 1937 graduate of the Drama Department and became an actor in the Pittsburgh Playhouse and later on the New York stage. He died in 1957, and in his honor, we gave funds for the student lounge and lobby in the Purnell Center for the Arts.

I received an Honorary Doctor of Laws degree from Carnegie Mellon in 1959, served as co-chair of the Homecoming Committee in 1982, and received a Merit Award from the Alumni Association. My husband and I also established the Mary Louise Milligan Rasmuson Scholarship fund before he died in December 2000. Although I am now in my nineties, I hope to see Carnegie Mellon's beautiful new campus for myself one of these days, even though it is far away from both my summer home in Alaska and my winter place in the California desert.

Mary Louise (Milligan) Rasmuson
Secretarial Studies '32
Honorary Doctorate, College of Fine Arts '59

generals and psychiatrists. I was one of the 440 women who made the grade out of the many thousands who applied.

We were sent to Fort Des Moines in Iowa for our basic and officer training, and I emerged with a rank equivalent to a second lieutenant. We were not granted army commissions until we became the Women's Army Corps and dropped Auxiliary from our name. I became the head of the WAC training center and remained in this position until the end of the war in 1946 when I was asked to come to Washington to work on legislation to make women a permanent part of the regular army, and I became the Deputy Director of the WAC.

From 1952 to 1956, I was stationed in Heidelberg, Germany, as an adviser to the Commanding General of the U.S. Army in Europe. In 1956 I was appointed Director of the Women's Army with the rank of Colonel. I retired after 20 years of service in 1962.

A year before I retired, I married Elmer E. Rasmuson, a civilian aid to the Secretary of the Army. We moved to his home in Alaska, where he was Director and Chairman of the National Bank of Alaska in Anchorage and served for a time as the city's mayor. My husband and I worked to organize a museum in Anchorage. I chaired the Anchorage Historical and Fine Arts Commission for 23 years, after which I chaired Anchorage Museum Foundation. I became an officer of the Rasmuson Foundation which assists non-profit organizations in Alaska. I still serve with both of these foundations.

Top:
Mary Louise with her mother, Alice Milligan, when she became WAC Director

Bottom:
Elmer and Mary Louise Rasmuson, June 2000

The Miracle on Morewood Avenue

One of the high spots of Tech's 1948 Homecoming Week, I am sure, was the "open house" staged by that miracle on Morewood Avenue, the new women's dormitory, Morewood Gardens.

The huge apartment house, which Carnegie Tech purchased two years ago and re-vamped, through architects Fisher and Schmertz (also Tech grads!) into a four-towered dormitory with a dining room for freshmen students, is an innovation on the Tech campus. For the first time in Tech history, all women dormitory students are now housed under one roof.

The furnishings of the new dormitory will delight the heart of any co-ed. Tech furnished its new building with an eye toward beauty as well as utility. Eight carloads of furniture, consisting of good, plain modern design wooden beds, dressers, chairs and cots make the place exceedingly attractive. So do the thick carpets and the drapes and lighting fixtures in the lounge rooms. Color and airiness have chased away all vestiges of rooming house gloom.

At Morewood Gardens, a new generation is starting its college life. There is an inter-room phone system. There is a penthouse and a sundeck on the roof. There are now 350 co-eds in residence, and the dormitory is capable of housing 400.

—*Carnegie Alumnus,*
December 1948, p. 4

Chapter 3

1929–56
Margaret Morrison During Its Middle Years

Margaret Morrison Carnegie College faced a number of challenges between 1929 and 1956. The Great Depression beginning in 1929, followed by America's role in World War II (1941–46), reduced the resources of all the colleges at Carnegie Tech, including Margaret Morrison. This financial crunch and competition from other colleges forced Margaret Morrison to phase out two of its programs, Nursing and Social Work. On the other hand, both Home Economics and Secretarial Studies held their own, while General Studies grew steadily. In addition, Margaret Morrison alumnae forged successful careers in a dozen areas, and their alumnae organization strongly supported the school.

Margaret Morrison's two deans, Dr. Charles Watkins (1929–47) and Edith Winchester Alexander (1947–56), faced four major problems: a changing student body; inability to get sufficient resources for buildings and equipment; the rise and decline of two new majors and the revision of curricula in the two traditional Margaret Morrison disciplines, Home Economics and Secretarial Studies; and the development of student norms that conflicted with some of the administration's rules. In 1956,

Dr. Margaret LeClair, Professor of English, succeeded to the deanship, symbolically marking an unofficial transition from a vocational college to a growing orientation to the liberal arts, a development that was to culminate in phasing out the college in 1973.

Who Were the Students?

The following table lists Margaret Morrison students by their majors at commencement:

MMCC GRADUATES AT FIVE YEAR INTERVALS, 1930–1955

	1930	1935	1940	1945	1950	1955
Costume Economics[1]	11	9	8	9	0	0
Household Economics[1]	15	10	18	6	0	0
Home Economics	25	13	15	16	59	48
Secretarial Studies	36	33	60	7	50	48
Social Work[2]	11	9	7	4	11	0
General Science/Science	4	8	7	8	12	13
General Studies	0	11	20	15	42	23
Nursing[3]	0	2	9	9	0	0
TOTALS	**102**	**95**	**144**	**74**	**174**	**132**

[1] Consolidated into Home Economics, 1945

[2] Phased out, 1953

[3] Phased out, 1949

The sign on the walkway before Skibo, the old Langley Aeronautical Building

Why Some MMCC Students Failed

Observation over a period of several years leads to the conclusion that most of the failures on the part of our students are due to a lack of ability, to poor health or to poor preparation. Idle and frivolous young women are rarely found in the student body of the Margaret Morrison Carnegie College.
—*Margaret Morrison Carnegie College, Annual Report* 1930–31, pp. 1 and 2

Margaret Morrison remained a small, local college. During most of this period, enrollment fluctuated between 450 and 566, as the accompanying sidebar shows. Throughout these years, most Margaret Morrison students lived within commuting distance of campus—in Pittsburgh and, to a lesser degree, the rest of Allegheny County. For example, 47 percent of Margaret Morrison's 495 students in 1931–32 lived in Pittsburgh. Another 27 percent lived in Allegheny County outside Pittsburgh's city limits, while an additional 20 percent came from the rest of Pennsylvania. Only six percent resided in states other than Pennsylvania, and none came from abroad. The percentages had changed somewhat by the 1944–45 academic year: 56 percent Pittsburghers, 12 percent from the rest of Allegheny County, 20 percent from Pennsylvania outside Allegheny County, 12 percent from the remainder of the country, and still none from abroad.

Religious affiliation data for the 1937–38 academic year indicate that 76 percent of women students at Tech were Protestant, 13 percent were Jewish, and 11 percent Roman Catholic. In 1955, the figures were 58 percent Protestant, 30 percent Roman Catholic, and 9 percent Jewish, with a scattering of other faiths in both years.

Most Carnegie Tech students commuted to campus during this period. Among all women students in 1930 (we have no exclusive figures for Margaret Morrison), only 28 percent lived in the dormitories and the remainder commuted either from their homes, the homes of relatives, or rooming houses. Ten years later, the percentages remained about the same: 26 percent in dorms and the rest commuters. No wonder that the trauma accompanying commuting remains so vivid in the minds of Margaret Morrison alumnae. A new dormitory, Morewood Gardens, completed in 1948, provided better and more abundant dormitory space. The percentage of dormitory residents among women rose to 50 percent in 1954.

Commuting and poor preparation played large roles in the low graduation rates of Margaret Morrison students. For the entire decade of the 1930s, for example, an average of only 54 percent of the students who entered as freshmen graduated four years later. Many students dropped out during the freshman year when the strain of two to three hours on streetcars every day proved overwhelming for beginning students, many of whom were poorly prepared. Well over 50 percent of all the students who applied for admission during the 1930s and 1940s were accepted and registered for classes. During the 1950s, the introduction of a course in remedial math and the institution of orientation programs substantially reduced dropout rates throughout the college. In addition, the reasons for leaving school seem to have changed as the report from the dean indicates (see page 44).

Dropouts were replaced in part by two other groups. About 30 students with advanced standing transferred to Margaret Morrison from other colleges each year. In 1937, the 35 transfer students came from 29 different colleges. Most of them left academic programs to seek vocational training at Margaret Morrison. In addition, in a typical year 25 students who had already graduated from college enrolled at Margaret Morrison to study for a single year. In the first 15 years of this program, these students came from 52 different colleges, including seven students from Mount Holyoke, eight from Wellesley, and 11 from Smith. Most of them entered Secretarial Studies, leaving with a unique combination of a B.A. in liberal arts and a B.S. in Secretarial Studies that prepared them for excellent careers.

Maintaining Standards in Margaret Morrison

There was a time when the atmosphere in Margaret Morrison was that of a women's college, characterized by neatness and orderly conduct on the part of students going from one classroom to another. At present, change of classes resembles a factory at the noon hour, and a visitor strolling through our corridors might well mistake this for a man's school, with a few coeducational students enrolled. Gradually, more and more sections of men have been scheduled in this building. As these young men have become better acquainted with this building, they conduct themselves in a manner that is not conducive to good discipline among our students. In spite of conspicuously placed signs, the men smoke in the corridors of the building, discarding their cigarettes without a thought of the appearance of the floors of the corridors and classrooms. Furthermore, they do not leave the building promptly after a class has ended, but loaf singly or in groups for considerable periods of time chatting with the girls....The laboratory classes in the department of General Science and the classes in dictation in the department of Secretarial Studies have been constantly interrupted by gun fire (from the ROTC rifle range) in the basement of this building. Gun fire of this type is almost as completely out of keeping with a woman's [sic] college as the housing of athletes (locker rooms for football players) which for a number of years has contributed a source of annoyance.
—Annual Report of the Dean, 1939

At Last, a Modern Dormitory in 1948

In 1938, Carnegie Tech released architects' drawings for a newly designed campus that included seven new buildings. In addition to a student activities building, the plans included a new dormitory for women and an addition to the Margaret Morrison building. None of the plans for this extensive renovation reached fruition. Neither did a bequest of $200,000 from the will of Mrs. John L. Porter, widow of a Tech trustee and benefactor. She designated the money to build a women's dormitory, but the money was eventually used to improve the original Industries Hall. Tech then renamed it Porter Hall. Such was the fate of elaborate building plans proposed in the midst of a depression.

Margaret Morrison's deans advanced requests for relatively minor renovations in their annual reports. Year after year during the depression period, they asked the Tech administration, in vain, to pave the tennis courts next to the Margaret Morrison building in order to prevent dust from fouling laboratory equipment. They also deplored the drab appearance of the Forbes Street end of the Margaret Morrison building. Their pleas to have ivy planted at the base of the walls went unanswered. Each year, however, Tech made a few renovations

in the Margaret Morrison building, including painting and repairs to the plumbing. The only major renovation in the building during this period took place in 1941 when the old recreation hall on the fourth floor was turned into a much-needed classroom for Secretarial Studies. Requests to maintain the building for the exclusive use of women students, however, went unanswered.

Several improvements to campus facilities did, however, benefit Margaret Morrison students. In 1932, Tech opened Thistle Hall, an addition to the gymnasium, as a recreation center for the campus. It included a large dance floor that immediately became the site of weekly tea dances, a smoking room, and the Black Cat Grill where light refreshments were served.

Refreshments were served between dances in this lounge in Thistle Hall. Students designed the decorations and furniture.

New Dorms Needed

Better living conditions, better recreational facilities and an infirmary are insistent needs of our group. Modern living conditions for the women seem no nearer than when I came six years ago, and we cannot hope for a larger resident enrollment until our living quarters are better. New housing plans for the new dormitory need to provide not merely a place for room and board but also adequate facilities for the development of wholesome recreational, cultural, social and moral life.
—*Annual Report of the Dean of Women, 1931, p.7*

In 1939 Tech purchased the Schiller Mansion on a plot of land that extended from Devon Road to Beeler Street along Forbes Street. Renamed the Carnegie Union, it became the social center of the campus for both students and alumni. It featured a game room, log-burning fireplaces, three dining areas, rooms for student publications, and rooms where sororities could hold their weekly meetings. Margaret Morrison students loved it.

After World War I ended, Tech changed the Langley Aeronautics building into a new Skibo, contributing to the confusion that this often-used name produced for later generations of students. Although the sign on the walkway said Skibo (see page 40), students often called it the Beanery or the Commons. The building became a cafeteria serving the entire student body, and, like every earlier building named Skibo, became notorious for hamburgers, fries, cokes, and endless bridge games in which many Maggie Murphs became proficient.

Tech finally began to pay attention to facilities specifically designed for Margaret Morrison College after World War II. In 1922, the Carnegie Corporation had promised to make a gift of $8 million to Tech if the school would raise $4 million by 1946. Under a vigorous new president, Robert E. Doherty, who took office in 1936, Tech launched a fund drive that met this goal. The arrival of a check for $8 million set off waves of rejoicing on the campus. This freshet of money enabled Tech to purchase Morewood Gardens, a seven-story building enclosing 59 apartments on Morewood Avenue, and to renovate it as a women's dormitory, opening in September 1948. In 1950, Tech opened a new wing attached to the building that featured a dining room to serve 500 students. At long last, Tech had responded to the pleas of both the deans of women and the deans of Margaret Morrison for a modern women's dormitory.

Top:
Exterior and interior of The Carnegie Union

Bottom:
Sketch for the Addition to Morewood Gardens by Alfred D. Reid Associates Architects

In 1950, Tech also renovated a house at 5143 Margaret Morrison Street to use as a nursery school for the Home Economics Department. This building, located near the Home Management House, educated a whole generation both of home management students and of the children they taught. It was moved to a new wing added to the Margaret Morrison building in 1962. Today the lineal descendant of this program that began in Margaret Morrison is the Center for Early Childhood Education, a part of Carnegie Mellon's distinguished Psychology Department.

The Curriculum

Chapter four consists of the reminiscences of Margaret Morrison alumnae who attended Tech during the period between 1930 and 1956. These delightful, personal accounts reveal far more about the college and its departments than any summary statement could convey. A brief account of developments in the entire college and in each department within the college, however, may serve to provide a context for these comments.

In *The Doherty Administration, 1936–1950,* (Carnegie Press, Pittsburgh, Pa., 1965, pp. 163–164), Dean Glen U. Cleeton of the Division of Humanities and Social Studies identified the following five educational changes made at Margaret Morrison between 1936 and 1950. They were: *"(a) liberalization of all programs of instruction, (b) broadening opportunities for the pursuit of general education objectives, (c) revision of basic courses to place greater emphasis on analytical thinking, (d) revision of existing curricula to*

meet changing professional opportunities for women, and (e) reorganization of the departmental organization of the college." Cleeton also pointed out that the tradition of giving each student individual attention continued throughout this period.

The basic objectives of the college, however, did not change, as the 1949–50 Annual Report of the dean, p. 44, made clear. *As inspired by the college motto— 'To make and inspire the home'—our curricula are designed to prepare women not only for professional careers but also, either as an adjunct or as part of their training for the professions, for homemaking. Thus, our graduates have three courses open to them: a professional career, a homemaking career, or some combination of the two. They have been successful in finding excellent opportunities in the professional field of their choice, with homemaking continuing to be the most popular career."*

Home Economics

Home Economics, often in several sub-departments, dominated the curriculum of Margaret Morrison for decades after the founding of the college in 1906. In 1930 there were three majors in the field, each with its own department head. They were Costume Economics, Household Economics, and Home Economics Education. An attempt to combine them into one department during the 1930s failed when alumnae, students, and faculty members protested. When enrollment fell during World War II, however, Dean Watkins consolidated them into a single Home Economics Department. At the same time, new emphases in the profession promoted changes in opportunities for employment

Attracting Students

Since the expense involved in attending Margaret Morrison Carnegie College is now equal to or greater than the outlay necessary for attending other institutions available to the young women of this district, more thought should be given to what the school can offer in addition to a well-rounded education. If this college is to attract a large group of young women, it must offer dormitory accommodations, food, and recreational facilities equal to the offerings of other institutions in this vicinity. —*Annual Report of the Dean, 1944–45, p. 2* (Note: Tuition was $320 in 1940 and rose in stages to $500 in 1946 and $700 in 1956.)

Top:
Miss Miriam Weikert, the nursery school's director, greets a student

Bottom:
A Home Ec student uses the Fade-Ometer, which subjects fabric to light as intense as any sun rays.

as teachers, clothing designers, dieticians, buyers, and commercial testers for the food, textile, and clothing industries. At the close of Dean Winchester's administration in 1956, Home Economics was the largest department in Margaret Morrison, followed by Secretarial Studies and General Studies.

Secretarial Studies

Secretarial Studies usually had the second largest enrollment during this period. Like Home Economics, it offered a broad general education, taught largely by faculty from other colleges, combined with professional courses, such as typing and shorthand. Its graduates were always in high demand. As early as the teens, Secretarial Studies majors could elect a minor in English, a program that eventually led to a new Department of General Studies. Beginning in 1918, Secretarial Studies opened a new program in which graduates with a Bachelor of Arts degree enrolled for an additional year at Margaret Morrison to learn secretarial skills and earn a Bachelor of Science degree.

Top left:
A secretarial studies student uses a mimeograph machine.

Top right:
A nursing student with a patient

Bottom:
Students learn to type.

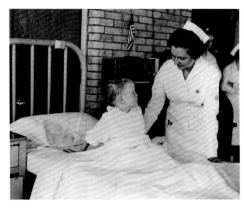

Nurses Training

Margaret Morrison inaugurated a Nurses Training Program in 1930 to prepare women for teaching and administrative positions in hospitals. During the first two years of the program, students took all their classes in Margaret Morrison. Then they spent two full years, as well as the intervening summers, at West Penn Hospital. They returned to campus for a fifth year to complete their Tech requirements and upon graduation received a B.S. from Margaret Morrison and a diploma from the West Penn Hospital. The number of students enrolled ranged from 16 to 30 during this period. The small enrollment and the establishment of similar programs in nearby schools caused Tech to discontinue the program. Its last two students graduated in 1949.

Library Work

Between 1919 and 1922, the Carnegie Library School, a part of the Carnegie Institute, established academic affiliations with Carnegie Tech and other local colleges. In this program, Margaret Morrison provided three years of academic courses and the Carnegie Library School provided a year of technical training in library work. A total of 88 Margaret Morrison students received degrees in library work between 1922 and 1934.

In 1930, the Carnegie Library School was transferred to Carnegie Tech as a separate school, and in 1934 became a graduate school only, requiring a four-year undergraduate degree for admission. Margaret Morrison undergraduates could take a pre-library track in the General

Studies Department, and some female graduate students of the Carnegie Library School lived in Tech's dorms. In 1962 the Carnegie Library School was transferred from Tech to the University of Pittsburgh.

Social Work

Margaret Morrison had established a Department of Social Work in 1914, but its enrollment was always small. To increase enrollment, a two-year graduate program leading to a master's degree was established in 1937. Although the department experienced a temporary spurt in enrollment, the number of students in both the undergraduate and graduate programs declined steadily thereafter until both programs became economically unfeasible. The last five students graduated in 1953.

The Sciences

Dean Breed, who was trained as a scientist, introduced science courses into Margaret Morrison's general curriculum from the beginning of her administration. She also opened a new major in general science, but the average number of degrees awarded in this program from 1915 to 1935 was only four. Dean Charles Watkins (1929–47), who had been head of the General Science Department since 1917, continued this emphasis. After a wartime spurt in enrollment, the number of students declined steadily, however, annually graduating a dozen or so students. The name of the department was changed to Biological Science in 1956 and then in 1962 to a new Department of Natural Sciences in which the courses were taught by faculty from the College of Engineering and Science.

General Studies

In 1915, Dean Breed gave Professor of English Frank P. Day responsibility for coordinating instruction in general studies for Margaret Morrison students. After World War I, he became director of a newly-established Division of Academic Studies that had grown out of the English Minor option in Secretarial Studies. Within Margaret Morrison, the number of General Studies majors increased steadily until by the end of Dean Edith Winchester's administration in 1956, it was the third largest department in the college. Students in General Studies majored in English, history, social studies, or modern languages and were taught exclusively by faculty members from outside the Margaret Morrison faculty. Two factors temporarily inhibited the growth of this department. For many years, Margaret Morrison women were not admitted to advanced courses in the other colleges, limiting their choice of electives. In addition, low enrollment in modern languages caused Tech to abandon all fourth-year language courses and to eliminate Italian completely.

Two developments associated with all of these programs brought severe financial problems to Margaret Morrison, problems with which the administration of Carnegie Tech had to deal. Small class size—one of the most important advantages of a Margaret Morrison education—was expensive. In 1925 President Baker had called attention to the large number of classes enrolling fewer than 10 students. That situation continued, even in Home Economics in which several majors, such as foods and nutrition, homemaking, or costume economics, each required advanced courses for majors.

Left:
After graduating from MMCC, some alumnae studied at the Carnegie Library School in Oakland.

Right:
Dean Charles Watkins

ACADEMIC DEGREES HELD BY MMCC FACULTY

Degree	1930	1956
Bachelors	20	4
Masters	9	25
Doctors	2	10

Top:
Dean Mary Watson Green

Bottom:
The Home Economics Faculty in 1946:

First row:
Elias, Barrick, Crow, Van Sycle, Hyde

Second row:
Richards, Weikert, Marshall, Caster, Myers, Parisi

The second development was the proliferation in other colleges of new programs in social work and nursing. Small and decreasing enrollments in these fields eventually led Tech to phase them out when their economic costs became excessive and near–by institutions offered similar programs at lower tuition rates. Both Home Economics and Secretarial Studies were to meet the same fate, and for the same reasons, when the decision was made in 1969 to phase out Margaret Morrison.

The Faculty

The academic quality of the Margaret Morrison faculty increased steadily through this period, as the accompanying table illustrates. As they had in the past, faculty members devoted their lives to teaching. In their reminiscences, alumnae cited name after name of teachers whose instructional skills, personal interest in their students, and high professional standards had helped to shape their lives. In addition to their teach-

ing assignments, faculty members played increasing roles in the community, serving on commissions and committees, giving speeches to community groups, and reading papers at meetings of professional groups. Few of them, however, produced research. Short lists of publications that appeared intermittently in dean's reports were usually not based on research. Margaret Morrison had begun to look out-of-place at Carnegie Tech, particularly after the research-oriented Graduate School of Industrial Administration was founded in 1950. Faculty members in other colleges and divisions were increasingly engaged in research or, in the case of the College of Fine Arts, creative works.

By 1956, faculty members from the College of Engineering and Science (E&S) and the Division of Humanities and Social Sciences played a large role in the education of Margaret Morrison students. E&S faculty often taught MMCC's basic math and science courses and, increasingly, admitted women into advanced electives. Students in General Studies often had only one or two courses, if any, taught by members of the MMCC faculty. Instead, professors from history, English, psychology and social studies taught these courses. This situation came to a head in the late 1960s when the number of women enrolled in general studies and science and taught by faculty from other colleges far outnumbered those enrolled in the traditional Margaret Morrison fields.

Student Life

Margaret Morrison provided many aspects of a rich student life throughout this period. As seen, however, the school was handicapped by a severe shortage of satisfactory dormitory space. As a result, until Morewood Gardens was built, more than half the students commuted to campus, thereby limiting their access to the full campus culture. The commuters' organization, the Citcom Clan, meeting occasionally in the evening, attracted few Margaret Morrison students, making it an inadequate substitute for the camaraderie of dormitory life.

For many decades, even though sororities flourished in the College of Fine Arts, Dean Breed forbade Margaret Morrison women from joining them or developing their own. Sororities could have provided a way to build social ties across departmental lines and to develop close personal ties. After Dean Breed retired, Tech gave permission between 1929 and 1934 to organize six local sororities. Requests by students to permit these sororities to become branches of national organizations were consistently rebuffed until the resignation in 1940 of Dean Mary Watson Green, a staunch foe of national affiliation.

Rather than sororities, the deans preferred that Margaret Morrison students join departmental clubs or religious organizations. Each Margaret Morrison department had a club that most of its majors joined. The members met with faculty and visiting speakers to discuss recent developments in the field and to enjoy each other's com-

pany, blurring the class lines that so often kept sophomores, juniors, and seniors apart. Honorary societies, such as Mortar Board and Phi Kappa Phi, crossed departmental lines. So did seven religious organizations that included men and women from all classes and colleges at Tech. Margaret Morrison's deans were particularly fond of the YWCA and commented on its value year after year in their annual reports.

Margaret Morrison deans, aided by the school's faculty, established strict rules for the behavior of students. Margaret Morrison women were expected to dress modestly and properly. They were required to obey college rules governing their life on and off campus, as the accompanying excerpt from the 1956–57 *Morewood Gardens Handbook* illustrates. They abided by the rules set up by their Student Senate and enforced through an Honor System in which students pledged to report themselves and anyone else who broke the rules. Trials conducted by student courts could then mete out a variety of punishments for violators. After World War II, the Honor System was abandoned at Margaret Morrison without a word in any of the Annual Reports of the Dean about its demise.

Top:
Dean Edith Winchester Alexander

Center:
Telegram announcing election to Mortar Board

Bottom:
Margaret Morrison Senate party, 1947
Left to right:
Audrey Wilkins, Peg Brown, Phyllis Grant, Peg Gautch, Justine Garnic

Dormitory Rules for Women at Carnegie Tech

Each girl is to make her bed before she leaves the dormitory in the morning

Shorts, slacks, bluejeans, jodphurs, and curlers are not to be worn in the dining room during dinner, with the exception of Saturday when curlers may be worn if they are covered by a bandana. These clothes are not to be worn in the lounge on Saturday or Sunday after two o'clock unless the girl is entering or leaving the dormitory.

Men may be received on the first floor only.

Quiet hours are to be observed during the following hours:
Sun–Thurs, 7:30PM–8:00AM
Fri–Sat, 11:00PM–9:00AM
—*The Morewood Gardens Handbook*, 1956–57, p. 3

Top:
Calendar girl,
Irene Warne, *The Scot*,
December 1953

Center:
Scotch 'n' Soda, *The Thistle*, 1954

Bottom:
Homecoming Queen candidates: Jimmy Lang, Kitty Morgenthaler, Betsy Suesserott, Dottie Dugan, Barb Waddell, Lou Hanson, Pat Andrews, Carole Siefert, Pat Dimling, *The Thistle*, 1954

Side by side with this formal culture of the college, women from Margaret Morrison developed their own norms of behavior. They attended dances frequently enough to generate strident protests from their deans, particularly about dances in off-campus fraternity houses or hotel ballrooms. Rather than obey a strict dress code, some Margaret Morrison women posed for calendar art published in *The Scot*. They organized Varsity Varieties, scantily clad song and dance shows at Spring Carnival. Their competitions for the annual Queen Campaign at Spring Carnival sent them from frat house to frat house in costumes that violated both the letter and spirit of the Morewood Gardens' dress code.

Some of them played bridge for hours on end, smoked cigarettes, and drank at parties. Over time, the official rules changed. Women students got smoking rooms. Dress codes were abolished. Tech established the same rules for its men and women students. Co-ed dorms began in 1969. In the long run, the norms of college students dictated the nature of the official rules, but that day was far in the future at Margaret Morrison during the three decades after 1930.

Alumnae Affairs and Careers

Margaret Morrison alumnae continued to join together socially and to support Carnegie Tech financially. In 1955, 20 percent of engineering graduates contributed to the alumni fund, followed by 17 percent of Margaret Morrison alumnae and 12 percent from the College of Fine Arts. Each class, beginning with the charter class of 1909, had a representative who gathered information for class notes that appeared in *The Carnegie Alumnus*. They organized women's clans in three cities: Pittsburgh, Philadelphia, and Youngstown, and joined Tech clans in other cities. The class notes carried news of marriages, births, changes of address, new jobs, and meetings of various alumni groups, particularly the Pittsburgh clan. That clan held teas, luncheons, bridge parties, anniversary reunions at homecoming, theater parties, visits to art exhibits, and fashion shows. Most of these events raised money for scholarships for deserving students.

Margaret Morrison alumni played distinguished roles in World War II. At least 152 Margaret Morrison alumnae served in the WACS, WAVES, SPAR, Marines, Red Cross, or USO during the war, many of them as officers. They had majored in every Margaret Morrison department where their technical training equipped them for a wide variety of wartime jobs. Like their fellow male alumni, they were vital, contributing members of the Great Generation.

And many of them forged successful careers. Carnegie Mellon's University Advancement Alumni Database contains fragmentary reports of the careers of Margaret Morrison alumni. Many entries, however, list only the name of a company or an institution rather than a specific occupation. The records contain 730 entries for this period. Four hundred entries fall under the general heading of education:

57 college/university professors, 165 secondary or elementary school teachers, and another 185 identified only by an institution's name, but most of them were surely teachers. Health professions came next with 65 entries, followed by 56 individuals who were self-employed or owned their own businesses, and 30 librarians.

Some entries contain titles that indicate successful careers, largely in business: President, Vice-President, Supervisor, Partner, Manager, Physician, Lawyer, Executive Director, and Treasurer. Almost all of these 730 women were married. Clearly a Margaret Morrison education prepared its graduates for careers both as homemakers and as professional women.

In Retrospect

Dr. Charles Watkins inherited a thriving technical college when he succeeded Dean Mary Bidwell Breed in 1930. Its programs in both home economics and secretarial studies were well established, and two additional programs—social work and nursing education—were soon to join them. In addition, two departments originally established to service the rest of the college would soon expand into science and general studies departments. Falling enrollment and competition from less expensive schools, however, closed the two new programs and forced the others to reorganize.

Margaret Morrison's students were overwhelmingly residents of the Pittsburgh area, and, until Morewood Gardens was opened in 1948, more than half of them commuted from their homes. Long commutes, poor preparation, and early marriage prevented more than half of entering freshmen from graduating with their classes until the 1950s. A thriving student culture grew up to challenge the entrenched, conservative ways of the administrators and much of the faculty. Nevertheless, Margaret Morrison alumnae, many of them successful professional women or homemakers, rallied around their school, establishing alumnae associations and contributing money to scholarship funds.

Our Competition

We are in keen competition with Penn State and Seton Hill in the home economics area and with PCW (now Chatham) and Pitt in general studies, science, and secretarial studies. Our recruiting efforts must be increased to acquaint prospective students with the opportunities for careers which exist in Margaret Morrison Carnegie College. We should continue advertising to let the public know that Margaret Morrison is a part of Carnegie Institute of Technology and not just a women's college which happens to be located strategically near C.I.T.
—*Annual Report of the Director, 1935, p. 2*

Top left:
Officers of the 1943 Pittsburgh Women's Clan: *President,* Irene (Quinn) Harnack, M' 09 (center), *First Vice President,* Charlotte (Schaffner) Young, M' 10 (left), and *Secretary,* Christine Leighou, M' 33 (right).

The Way We Were:
A Fine Tech Romance

Hilda L. Rugh
Bolivar, Pennsylvania

- *Nursing Education '38*
- *Cwens*
- *Gamma Rho Beta*

I grew up in Bolivar, Pennsylvania, a small town near Pittsburgh. I went to a small high school, but received a relatively good education there and graduated second in my class. I was the youngest of six children. My father owned the Garfield Refractory and was able to send all six of us to college. I wanted to take a three-year nursing course, but Dad insisted that I get a college degree, so I entered the five-year nursing program at Margaret Morrison in September 1933.

What an experience! Nine of us joined the program at the same time. We became very close, almost like sisters, and we stayed in touch for many years after graduation. Small classes and personal attention from the faculty helped us to learn and to enjoy our classes at the same time. It was a small, intimate school where everyone got to know their classmates, and we loved it.

I had excellent teachers, particularly Dr. Schultz in chemistry. He had high standards, and gave me a failing grade in my first chemistry class. I was crushed. I complained to my father about it, and he told me to stick with it and take an F as a difficult lesson. That was good advice. My work improved so much that I was elected to Cwens, the sophomore honorary.

During my freshman year, I lived in Birch Hall, the renovated stable on the hill behind the old Mellon mansion. Dad wondered why he was paying so much money for his daughter to live in a stable, but I enjoyed it. Then I moved to Cedar Hall on Forbes Street for my sophomore year. We had a very strict housemother, Miss Myers, who made us toe the line. I loved the tea dances every Friday and remember fondly being served formal dinners by male students.

We nursing candidates spent the following two years at West Penn Hospital. It was a strictly regimented program taught by nurses who had earned advanced degrees. In addition to attending classes, all of us worked on the wards, wearing distinctive white uniforms so that patients would know we were students. We lived at the hospital, where each of us had a private room so that we could study. The rules were much less strict at the hospital, to our delight—no housemother, for example.

We moved back to campus during our senior year to finish our academic program for the B.S. degree. We also got a certificate from West Penn. The major event of my senior year, however, was dating Libbus Lewis. Lib was the son of a Syrian immigrant who had come to the United States as a teenager to escape persecution from the Turks. He worked in a steel mill in Washington, Pennsylvania, but the family had little money. Lib, however, won a football scholarship, and he arrived at Tech with only a cardboard box and one suit of clothes.

These were the great days of Tech football. During the 1920s and 1930s Tech won five victories over Pitt and three over Notre Dame. Both students and the alumni went mad over Tech football. Lib Lewis was one of the heroes in the 1934 Notre Dame game when he caught the winning touchdown in a renowned 7 to 0 victory. Later in life, I confess, I sometimes got tired of football. Lib could attend a high school game on Friday, a college game on Saturday, and a pro game on Sunday. "Enough," I sometimes shouted.

Right:
The 1933 nursing class

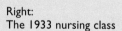

Lib claims that he had spotted me when I was a freshman, but then I disappeared for the two years at West Penn. When I returned as a senior, he was living with four or five other guys in an apartment over the drugstore at Forbes and Margaret Morrison Streets. We had a wonderful campus romance—tea dances in the gym, plays in the Little Theater, and all the other activities on campus. We married on March 13, 1942, when I was 26 and he was 30.

After graduation, I served as an instructor in pediatrics at West Penn and then as a school nurse until the war. During the war, I served as head nurse in Victory Memorial Hospital in Waukegan, Illinois, while Lib was stationed in the navy nearby. After the war, Lib turned to truck sales, and in 1957 started the Connecticut White Truck Company in New Haven. The business flourished. Lib was a highly competitive, goal-driven man, characteristics that stood by him both on the football field and in business. I busied myself entertaining for the company and doing volunteer work. After Lib retired at age 74 and sold his company, we moved to Florida.

Since we had no children, we were able to use our money to give to our extended family as well as to Carnegie Mellon. Carnegie Mellon was the second great love of our lives. Both of us were grateful for the wonderful education we received at Tech. We donated funds to build the Hilda and Libbus Lewis Alumni Lounge in the University Center. I also chaired the Class of 1938's 50th reunion effort. Before he died, Lib and I set up a life income plan with Carnegie Mellon. Tech gave us each other, as well as a beautiful background for life, and we have tried to repay the school in some small way.

Hilda (Rugh) Lewis*
Nursing Education '38

* Deceased, 2003

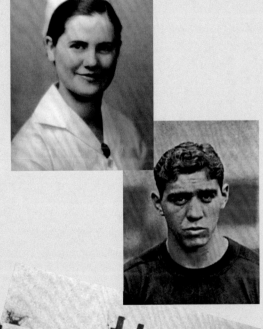

Top:
Hilda and Lib at home

Center:
Hilda and Lib as students

Bottom:
Tech students advertise their menu choice.

Somewhat chastened by their rather poor showing the preceding Saturday, Captain Stewart and his mates entered the third game of the season— Notre Dame—with a wealth of determination. The result is history. The famed Harpster surprise attack clicked in the first three plays of the game, when, on the third play, Bevino passed to Lewis for a touchdown. Score: 7 to 0. From then on the Tartans sat back on the defensive and defied their rivals to cross the goal.
—1934 Thistle

The Way We Were:
Margaret Morrison as an Education for Life

Betty J. Yagle
Buffalo, New York

- *Secretarial Studies '41*
- *Gamma Phi Sigma*
- *Intersorority Council President*
- *Thistle*
- *The Scottie*
- *Freshman Social Chairman*
- *Cwens*

1941 Intersorority Council:

Front row:
Weatherwax, Squitiere, Gup, Layton

Back row:
Yagle, Crumpton, Richards, Hirsch, McCullough, Young

I grew up in Aspinwall, a small community near Pittsburgh. There were about 100 students in my high school graduating class. My father, a construction engineer, had attended night school at Carnegie Tech, and he encouraged me to enroll in Margaret Morrison in the fall of 1937 as a secretarial studies major.

As I think about it, three parts of my life at Margaret Morrison stand out. The curriculum in secretarial studies prepared me very well for my first two jobs. The courses in typing, shorthand, and business practices were thorough and demanding, and the faculty, both in their classes and as role models, set high professional standards. Many of the classes, however, failed to challenge me intellectually, so I decided to supplement the standard curriculum with courses in art history, advertising, and Spanish, among others.

College life outside of class also helped to shape me. I commuted from home for two years, and at the end of my freshman year, I joined Gamma Phi Sigma, one of the three local sororities. Tech had seven sororities then, four in Fine Arts and three in Margaret Morrison. The sorority enabled me to make friends with girls from all the Margaret Morrison majors. Since most of us were commuters, we held our meetings in the homes of sorority members or in the meeting rooms in the Student Union, the lovely old mansion on Forbes Street.

I was president of the Intersorority Council during my senior year. Both the Margaret Morrison and the Fine Arts sororities belonged to this organization, giving all of us a chance to make friends outside of our college. The Council made plans for participation in Greek Sing and for our annual dance, two of our most popular events.

In my sophomore year, I was elected to Cwens, the sophomore honorary. This was a second chance to meet girls from other majors, many of whom shared my wider interests. We helped the freshmen feel at home, helped transfer students adjust to Tech through the Twin Sisters movement, and sponsored dances, teas, and even a luncheon for the Pitt Cwens before the Tech Pitt football game. Several of us drove to Lexington, Kentucky, to attend a Cwens convention at the University of Kentucky.

Thirdly, at the end of my sophomore year, my family moved to Buffalo, and I moved onto campus. My parents wanted me to go with them, but I wanted to continue at Tech. I had been saving money from Christmas presents for many years, so I had some resources to help defray expenses. I moved into Whitfield Hall, another renovated mansion on the edge of campus. I loved it. There I got to know girls from all of the arts, particularly Lil Dorsey [later Margeson] my roommate from drama, and Polly Jensen [later Heidt], an art/design major. Like the sorority and Cwens, living in a dorm opened my eyes to a much wider world than I had known in high school.

Although some of the secretarial courses were routine, they gave me the skills I needed for a variety of careers. I first got a job during World War II as an executive secretary with Bell Aircraft in Buffalo. As the war ended, I went to work for the federal government in England and Germany. I worked for the U.S. Technical Industrial Intelligence Committee, not as a spy, but again in a very interesting secretarial position.

While I was stationed in Hoecht, Germany, I met two Carnegie Tech friends, Captain Art Burleigh and Major Thomas Riley. In that devastated country, it was comforting to have friends from home. On returning, I worked in Washington, D.C., and then returned to Buffalo to work for the Cornell Aeronautical Laboratory, where I also learned to fly. Then I met an MIT aeronautical engineer, Clifford Muzzey, and we married in 1948.

I have had a happy and varied life since then, thanks in large part to the excellent education I received at Margaret Morrison and the confidence that my experiences there gave to me. Cliff and I settled in Buffalo. We both loved sailing, so we sailed the Great Lakes together as well as the waters of Cape Cod, the Caribbean, and the Mediterranean. I have taken continuing education courses in anthropology and contemporary women authors. I even edited a book about the contemporary art in Buffalo's Albright Knox Art Gallery. Through the years, I have kept busy with volunteer work. In Buffalo, I edited a Voters' Guide for the League of Women Voters and did volunteer work at Buffalo's Roswell Park Cancer Hospital. In Portland, Maine, I chaired two piano competitions, and directed Youth Activities for the Symphony. In Florida, I deliver Meals on Wheels.

I have kept in touch with my roots at Carnegie Tech—with Lillian Dorsey, with members of the class of 1941 when I served as class correspondent, as a volunteer for the Carnegie Mellon Admissions Council, and as an active member of the Alumni Association. A 1986 '41 Class Reunion luncheon brought memories of Margaret Morrison flooding back to me. At a meeting in Lexington, Massachusetts, I had heard a voice with a pronounced New England accent that reminded me vividly of another New Englander, Margaret Morrison's Dean Edith Winchester Alexander. To my surprise, I learned that the stranger was the dean's sister, Ruth Morey. This happy accident led to a luncheon meeting in 1987, with just the three of us, a few months before the dean died. Dean Alexander regaled us with Margaret Morrison stories. She had an encyclopedic memory for the hundreds of students and scores of faculty members with whom she had worked. What a delightful day! What a wonderful way to recall my life at Margaret Morrison!

Betty (Yagle) Muzzey
Secretarial Studies '41

Top:
1941 graduates from Whitfield Hall celebrate:
Left: Betty (Yagle) Muzzey
Janet (Stover) Quirk
Lillian (Dorsey) Margeson
Elizabeth (Moyer) Eyer
Hilda (Horner) McCreight
Polly (Jensen) Heidt
Frances "Penny" (Taylor) Adkins

Bottom:
In government service in Germany 1945–46:
Left, Capt. Arthur Burleigh, CIT'40; Center, Betty; Right, Maj. Thomas Riley, CIT '42

The Way We Were:
Working My Way Through Margaret Morrison

Margaret Carver
Hanover, Pennsylvania

- *General Science '43*
- *Gamma Phi Sigma*
- *Phi Kappa Phi*
- *Sigma Xi*
- *Cwens*
- *Student Council*
- *Margaret Morrison Senate*
- *Athletic Association*
- *Dorm Council*
- *Dorm Bagpiper*
- *Glee Club*

I grew up in Hanover, Pennsylvania, where my father was in retail and my mother was a homemaker. I knew early on that I wanted to be a doctor like my uncle, who would take me along on house calls in his green Model A Ford, and unlike my sister who was a teacher. During high school, there were dreams of college, but prospects were poor since my father's business had failed when Montgomery Ward and Sears came to town. I read in the Carnegie Tech catalogue that the General Science program in Margaret Morrison served well as a pre-med education. So I went to Harrisburg, 40 miles away, took some sort of test, and was awarded a Brashear scholarship—full tuition for two years if my grades warranted. What a windfall! After those first two years, I had other scholarships, but still needed to earn money for room and board.

I had never been to Pittsburgh and had certainly not seen the Carnegie Tech campus before I arrived to register. Over the ensuing months, I came to appreciate that here was a semi-secluded campus in the midst of a big city, a wonderful situation. We had the mansions along Forbes with their lawns and foliage, Margaret Morrison Street, Schenley Park, the Phipps, the Cut, real tennis courts, Panther Hollow, and the quad between Fine Arts and Machinery Hall. And we could walk to the drugstore, the movies, a museum, a famous library, the Greeks, or to a street-car that would take us to the downtown city with all its attractions. What a bonanza for a small town native!

My first job on campus was in the Coal Research Lab, where I worked with chemicals, spilled sulfuric acid on my arm, and had to go to a prom swathed in bandages from shoulder to wrist. I don't recall that it spoiled the fun. Later on I worked for Professor Clara Douglas, who was doing research on vitamin C, using rats as subjects. My job was to remove the adrenal glands from the rats.

I've often wondered whether there was any link between that job and my future work as a gynecologist. Anyway, I've never regretted having to work outside of my classes and other activities.

My years on campus included our country's entry into World War II. From then on, there was a palpable difference in our lives. An undercurrent of seriousness developed. This, however, did not keep us from having fun and participating in campus activities. There were the famous big bands at Spring Carnival, Greek Sing, the last of the big intercollegiate football games, and dormitory life. At first I lived in Birch Hall, the renovated stable behind the old Mellon mansion, and then in Cedar Hall along Forbes Street, and finally in Whitfield Hall, the elegant mansion on the hill overlooking the campus. Residents of these halls had their meals in Mellon Hall and were served by male students attired in white jackets. It was all very posh.

I was involved in a lot of organizations while I was a student: Cwens, the sophomore women's honorary; Margaret Morrison Senate; Dorm Council; the Bagpiper, a dorm newspaper; Glee Club; the Athletic Association; my sorority, Gamma Phi Sigma, which became Delta Gamma once MMCC allowed affiliation with nationals; and in my senior year, Phi Kappa Phi and Sigma Xi. I am still on the national roster of Sigma Xi as a member of the Carnegie Mellon chapter. I do not recall much about student government actions or dorm council except that we had few problems to cope with during the war—mainly little things like girls who

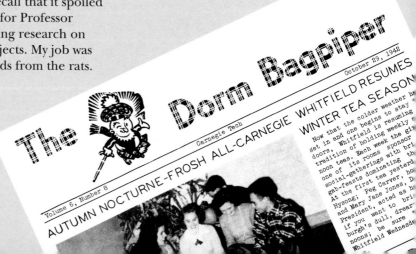

1943 Women's Glee Club:

Front row:
Weise, Ellman, H. McKean, Schwartz, Atkinson, Taylor, McBurney, Sandlin

Center row:
Miller, Schadel, Zimmerman, M. McKean, Fisher, Thompson, Young

Back row: Chetlin, Reed, Bowman, Skeehan, Carver, Saul

stayed out after curfew. I do, however, have fond memories of the glee club—wonderfully relaxing after work and study—and of the delightful, competitive times we had in sorority and Greek Sing.

After graduation, I worked at Linde Air Corporation in Tonawanda, New York, in its research labs. Then I married a classmate from Printing Management. When his Air Force training took him to Texas, I went along and worked at Sunoco labs while he did 50 missions over Europe. When he was assigned to ferry planes all over the world, I went back to Pittsburgh, intent once more on seeking admission to a medical school. My application was too late for the 1945 term, so I went to see Dean Jessie Yon, a lovely and concerned lady who got me a job as a lab instructor in general science classes in MMCC. When I went off to med school at Pitt the next fall, I became assistant housemother in Mellon Hall for a year while I looked for another job. Meanwhile, my husband was discharged, and thought that medicine was no profession for a woman, so we divorced amicably, went our separate ways, and always remained friends. In fact, he sought my professional advice on several occasions.

After graduation and internship, I began to practice in Uniontown, Pennsylvania, close enough to Tech that I could easily stay in touch. Seven years later, I did an additional three years of medical training and became certified in Obstetrics and Gynecology, which I practiced until my retirement in 1997. During those years, I joined the Andrew Carnegie Society and also set up a scholarship fund to which I continue to contribute. This is my way of repaying Carnegie Mellon for both an excellent education and the financial help that made that education possible.

My trips to campus are curtailed now that I am visually impaired, but I was able to attend the grand opening of the Interdisciplinary Science Laboratories in October 2002. The labs are incredible! I am pleased that the Mellon College of Science and the College of Humanities and Social Sciences continue to claim an interest in us Maggie Murphs.

Margaret Carver
General Science '43

Every Monday afternoon and Thursday evening the halls of Margaret Morrison are filled with the harmonious sound of women's voices—the Women's Glee Club at its regular rehearsals. This organization is under the leadership of Mrs. Harriet Kurtz, and provides a medium of expression for many students interested in music. The glee club performs its varied programs of both popular and classical music for many local organizations. Its season is climaxed by the annual home concert sung with the Men's Glee Club.
—1943 Thistle

SIGMA XI
THE SCIENTIFIC RESEARCH SOCIETY

Living It Up at Skibo

Gretchen Goldsmith
*Pittsburgh,
Pennsylvania*

- *General Studies '43*
- *The Scottie*

L ike many other Margaret Morrison students, I commuted from home. My family lived at 5700 Bartlett Street, just a few blocks from campus. My father, a physician, often dropped me off at school and sometimes picked me up in the evening. He usually found me in Skibo. By Skibo, I mean the original Skibo, the shack at the bend in Margaret Morrison Street across from where Donner Hall is today.

I entered Margaret Morrison in September 1939 as a General Science major interested in science and math. I took all the psychology courses I could find and also built up a major in mathematics. Since Margaret Morrison's math offerings were limited, I enrolled in math courses in the engineering school, where I was the only woman student at that time. I took math in the engineering school throughout my undergraduate years.

In the early 1940s, Carnegie Mellon had limited student facilities, to put it mildly. We commuters had to eat lunch somewhere. Some commuters brown bagged it. Of course there was Skibo, originally the Langley Aeronautical Building built during World War I and remodeled to become a student cafeteria. We also occasionally patronized the Carnegie Inn, once Carnegie Tech's field house on the site of today's Donner Hall, later remodeled to provide food service. Once a month, we could eat on the third floor of Margaret Morrison, where the household economics majors served an excellent, inexpensive lunch.

For my friends and me, however, Skibo, "the Shack," was the place. Just before World War I, two architecture students had built a 20' x 20' ramshackle building just off campus to serve food to Tech students at odd hours. It passed through a series of owners, many of whom built additions without benefit of an overall plan or architectural advice. By 1940 there were about 20 booths at one end and a few at the other along with a row of pinball machines and a counter, where hamburgers, french fries, hot dogs, and coffee were the staples. We loved it, particularly we commuters. It was our home away from home.

My brother, Bill Goldsmith, preceded me at Tech and introduced me to the delights of Skibo. It was my social life. I was very busy there playing bridge with my friends. I almost always ate lunch at Skibo. I could always find a bridge game, and I quickly learned to shuffle cards greasy from hamburgers and fries. I'd also go there late in the afternoon after classes to wait for my father to pick me up for a ride home. Now and then I'd play with the Skibo's cat, Mrs. Andy. Skibo was better than a sorority. It was handy, attracted both men and women, and was always open. A lot of football players and dramats—Gary Davis, Al Checco and Audrey (Botkin) Roth among them—hung out there. Many a romance bloomed over greasy fries and hot dogs.

Top:
Skibo

Bottom:
Carnegie Inn

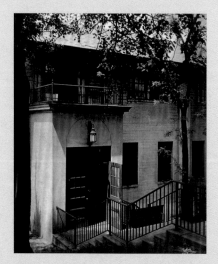

Some of my friends who lived in the dorms would sign out and stay at our house for the weekend. My brother Bill's girl stayed there most of the time. Mother and Dad welcomed our friends, who were delighted to get out from under the strict parietal rules and the watchful eyes of housemothers. One evening some of my friends who were Jewish told Mom that Dean Mary Watson Green had told the Jewish girls that they should keep a low profile during sorority rush. None of the sororities admitted Jewish girls and that cut many women out of a key element of the school's social life. Mother was furious and she descended on Dean Green and several other administrators to complain. Green resigned in 1940 to be succeeded by Mrs. Jessie Yon, who encouraged Jewish girls to form their own sorority. But Skibo was better than any sorority. It attracted all kinds of people and—of course—included both men and women. It was home to me.

After graduation I worked at the Metals Research Lab and at National Tube doing quality control work. Bill Lankford and I got married and he worked on a government research project that took him to Penn State until the war ended. We returned to Pittsburgh, and soon afterward I became a full-time mother of four children. I became involved as a volunteer for a number of organizations, such as Citizens for Better Schools, the PTA, the School Boards Association, and Friends of the Library. Through these years, both my brother Bill and I stayed in touch with Tech. We served on alumni association projects and were early members of the Andrew Carnegie Society. Then after my husband died in 1986, I entered the School of Urban and Public Affairs (SUPA) and earned a master's degree. I met Steve Calvert, assistant vice president for alumni relations, in 1992 when the Academy for Lifelong Learning was being developed, and became the founding president. ALL has brought me to campus almost every day during the last ten years. I now eat in the splendor of the new University Center, where the food is more varied and nutritious than we ate at Skibo and laptops seem to have replaced bridge games as student recreation.

Nothing at Carnegie Mellon approaches the Shack. The O in the University Center serves hamburgers and mounds of french fries, but the Center also serves a wide range of healthful foods, including salads. Students, faculty and staff eat at handsome tables and chairs, some overlooking the swimming pool. A few pinball machines line the back wall; that's Skibo-like, but no one smokes, and I have never seen a card game there. For me, something is missing.

Gretchen (Goldsmith) Lankford
General Studies '43, M HNZ '90

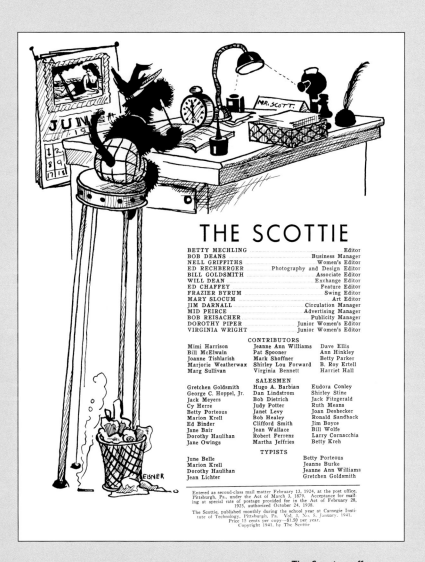

The Scottie staff in 1941

The Way We Were:
Hanging Out at The Tartan

Louisa J. Saul
*Pittsburgh,
Pennsylvania*

- *Household
  Economics '44*
- *Tartan Editor*
- *Cameron Choir*
- *Alpha Epsilon Phi*
- *Pi Delta Epsilon*
- *I. R. C.*
- *Glee Club*
- *Publications Committee*

The Carnegie Tartan
staff in 1944

I was a native Pittsburgher, born and bred in Squirrel Hill near the Tech campus. Neither of my parents had gone to college, but my mother, a career woman, wanted both of her daughters to receive an excellent education and have a career. My family could not afford to send me away to school and I didn't want to attend Pitt, so I chose nearby Margaret Morrison. My parents pointed out that Foods and Nutrition was a wonderful career choice for a woman, so in the fall of 1940, I enrolled in Household Economics, though I really wanted to be a journalist.

When I arrived on campus, I promptly made my way to the offices of *The Tartan,* where I became a cub reporter. I hung out at *The Tartan* all the time; in a way, *The Tartan* became my unofficial academic minor. I worked my way up the editorial ladder. It was the war years and not a lot of guys were on campus, so I seized the opportunity. By the second semester of my junior year, I was managing editor on half scholarship and received a full scholarship during my senior year when I became editor. During the last part of my senior year, a unit of the Army Specialized Training Program (ASTP) came

The Carnegie Tartan

Carnegie Institute of Technology, Schenley Park, Pittsburgh 13, Pa.

PHONE MAYFLOWER 2600   PHONE SCHENLEY 4557

PRESENTED FOR NATIONAL ADVERTISING BY
National Advertising Service, Inc.
College Publishers Representative
420 MADISON AVE.   NEW YORK, N.Y.
CHICAGO • BOSTON • LOS ANGELES • SAN FRANCISCO

After Office Hours Call
Editor-in-Chief . . . . EM. 9424
Business Manager. . . . . .SC. 8951

Entered as second-class matter in the Pittsburgh Post Office under the Act of March 3, 1879
Published weekly during school year, except holidays and examination periods.
Subscription Price $1.10 per year.

Editor. . . . . Louisa Saul
Military Editor . . . . Cpt. Allan E. Van Patten
Business Manager . . . . .Merle Wolff
Managing Editors . . . . Elaine Levin, Gerry Edelson
Assistant Military Editor . . . . .P. f. c. L. M. Van Deusen
Makeup Editors . . . . .Sy Corwin and Al Perry
Sports Editor. . . . . .Wally Ellman
Assistant Business Manager. . . . . .Merle Wolff
News Editor. . . . . .Ernie Lowenstein
Feature Editor . . . . .Jerry Brickman
Headline Editor. . . . . .Wally Ellman
Printing Editor. . . . . .Adeline Herlick
Copy Editors . . . . .Marshall Nuremberg, Nick Georges
    Reporters: Alma Weinberger, Lucille Emmel, Jeane Boltey, Dorothy Caplow,
Jo Svirman, Miriam Frankel, Hellen Miller, Ruth Tisherman, Clara Herron, John Regal
Anita Newell, Georgette Paljug, Rosemarie Lang, Mary Jane Horridge, William Gladstone,
Mary Jane Ferguson

to campus. A lot of these GIs worked and hung out at *The Tartan*. We used to stay up all night downtown at the printers on Thursday to proof the weekly paper and to put it to bed. I still have a file. I can't believe I wrote some of that sophomoric stuff.

After graduation, I became the editor of the Alpha Epsilon Phi magazine, the journal of the national Jewish sorority. That's another Carnegie Tech story. Tech had only local sororities during the 1940s, and none of them accepted Jews. So during my freshman year when Jewish girls felt left out of the excitement of rushing, we went to see Dean Jessie Yon and told her we wanted to start a sorority. She told us to go ahead, so we did. Then at the end of my junior year, we were invited to join the nationally affiliated Jewish sorority, Alpha Epsilon Phi. We approached Dean Yon again and she told us, again, to go for it. So we did; we were the first nationally affiliated sorority on campus.

Since I was a commuter, I didn't have to live by the parietal rules in the dormitories. I walked back and forth to home, even late at night from *The Tartan*. I got a taste of dorm rules, however, when I lived for five weeks in the Home Management House on Margaret Morrison Street. Home Economics majors all had to live in that house for a few weeks during their senior year. I was not enthusiastic. The housemother who lived there never seemed to give me messages when I had phone calls. She used to sneak up on us to see if anyone was smoking and forbade us to take food to our sleeping quarters upstairs. Each of us even had to plan a dinner conversation a week in advance and submit our plan to her for approval. I guess she thought she was preparing us to give dinner parties when we married.

Since I edited *The Tartan*, I was allowed out at night after the 9:00 curfew. The men from the ASTP used to walk me home, to our mutual delight. Some of them lived in the men's dorm directly across the street from the Home Management House, so we decided to communicate by Morse code. I assembled my housemates. The GIs started sending messages by flashing their lights on and off. We responded with a lamp. Wonderful, innocent fun. But Miss Weikert caught us. "Louise

Saul, pull down that blind," she ordered sternly. We knew something was in the works when she failed—for the first time—to turn up for breakfast. Sure enough, she went to the administration and asked to have us expelled. Happily, common sense prevailed.

I have many happy memories of my years at Margaret Morrison. As a freshman, I went to the Tea Dances in the gym on Friday afternoons. They really did serve tea. When I wasn't at *The Tartan*, I hung out at the old Skibo along Margaret Morrison Street. Lunch there meant a hand of bridge, french fries and cigarettes, with smoke swirling in clouds around our heads.

After graduation, I worked for four years as a dietician at Montefiore Hospital. Then I married, had two children, went to Ohio State on weekends during the 1980s to study landscape design, and started my own landscaping business. I became reattached to Carnegie Mellon when I joined the Academy for Lifelong Learning and began to attend the Margaret Morrison lecture series. Old Skibo and the Home Management House are gone, but a new and expanded *Tartan* is now in splendid quarters in Carnegie Mellon's magnificent new University Center.

Louisa (Saul) Rosenthal
Household Economics '44

Editor's Armchair

To the End That We May Remember

One Friday in a past November, we strolled nonchallantly into the pigeon roost that is the Tartan office, sank back into a red leather swivel chair, propped our pumps on the editor's desk, and before our King Size had tapered to ashes, we had lost our identity. Gone were those blissful "I" days. For the duration of our college career, our personality was to be strictly "We." We became a multiple being responsible no longer only to one person. Ours was to be the power behind a voice that would speak for an entire student body. In our heart we couldn't help but feel just a little proud, for we had come a long way, from the curly headed little six-year-old who wrote poetry about the snow and dreamed of starving over a typewriter in an attic.

Now as we look forward to being thrust roughly back into our individuality, we can not hide an oversized regret. It isn't easy to blot four years out of one's life, four years of heartache, of fascinating personalities, of inner satisfaction, of creative expression...

... With a reluctant tear, we bid a sad farewell to the most vital force in our college life.
—*L.S., March 21, 1944*

The Way We Were:
A Lifelong Research Chemist Discovers Kevlar®

Stephanie Kwolek
*New Kensington,
Pennsylvania*

- *General Science '46*
- *Phi Kappa Phi*
- *Science Club Secretary
  and Treasurer*
- *Newman Club*

M y father died when I was ten years old. He was a naturalist by avocation and passed on his love of science to me. We spent many hours in the woods near my home in New Kensington, Pennsylvania, where we searched for wildlife, studied wild plants and collected leaves, seeds, etc. to put in my scrapbooks.

My mother was one of a small number of women who worked outside of the home in the 1930s. In addition to me, she reared my brother, Stanley, who entered Carnegie Tech in 1944 to study Chemical Engineering. Like most engineering students at Tech, his education was interrupted by a draft into the army. After basic training, he was sent to the University of Kentucky for further engineering training. After the war, he returned to Tech, received credit for his wartime studies and graduated in 1948. We are a Tech family.

I joined Margaret Morrison Carnegie College in 1942. At the time, undergraduate women interested in science were not admitted to the College of Engineering and Science. However, they could take courses in chemistry and other sciences taught there. I lived both on the campus (Forbes Hall) and at home in New Kensington. When I lived at home, I commuted by train. The 45-minute ride was spent either in study or in conversing or playing bridge with the many students traveling to Tech, the University of Pittsburgh and Duquesne University. The Tech students walked from the Shadyside Station via Morewood Avenue to the campus. The best I can say for that hike is that it kept us in good physical shape.

While at Tech I had use of both a Carnegie scholarship and a Pennsylvania State scholarship. I majored in chemistry with a minor in biology. At the time, my interests were in chemical research and medicine. Since the advanced chemistry classes had small numbers of students, it was possible to get considerable attention from the faculty, particularly from professors Dr. Clara Miller and Clara Jane Douglas. A classmate, Catherine Brosky, and I also took some advanced chemistry classes under Dr. Guido Stempel in the College of Engineering and Science.

With so many laboratory classes, I did not have much time for socializing; I did, however, participate in the Science Club, Newman Club and Carnegie chapter of the honor society, Phi Kappa Phi. During the summers, I worked in biochemical research at Pitt and as a chemist at Gulf Research and Development Company in Harmarville, Pennsylvania.

I graduated in 1946 still interested in medicine; but being a realist, I knew I had to start earning money. The DuPont Company made me an offer in polymer/fiber research that I could not resist. As with other companies, universities and government agencies, the opportunities for professional women in those days and for some time to come were limited, but the university atmosphere, large library, generous financing of research, an excellent technical support system for research and a good opportunity to make significant discoveries in polymers and fibers were very important to me. I was hooked and remained for 40 years. After four years in the DuPont, Buffalo, New York laboratory, I was transferred with a large group of technical people to the newly built Textile Fibers Pioneering Research Laboratory at the DuPont Experimental Station in Wilmington, Delaware.

The 1946 Science Club:

Front row:
S. Kwolek, C. Brosky,
D. McBurney, M. Brown

Back row:
J. Lowe, J. Streicher,
R. Flannagan, A. Wilkins,
M. Rapach

Property of DuPont Co.

Here I began scouting low temperature processes for the preparation of condensation polymers. (A polymer is a very long chemical molecule made up of many repeating smaller units. It can be spun into fibers or made into other products.) The low temperature processes made possible the preparation of polymers that were unmeltable or thermally unstable and found application in the future large-scale preparation of Lycra® spandex fiber and Nomex® and Kevlar® aramid fibers, registered trademarks of the DuPont Company.

In 1964, I began a search for the next generation, high performance fiber. This work resulted in the unexpected discovery of liquid crystalline solutions of synthetic extended-chain (rigid rod) aromatic polyamides and their super strong and super stiff fibers. This technology is the foundation of the Kevlar® fiber. I then worked with other DuPont scientists to turn the fiber into a commercial product. Kevlar®, which is used primarily as a composite, is five times stronger than steel on a weight basis. Today, Kevlar® has more than 200 end uses. It is found in military helmets, clothing and equipment; in bulletproof vests worn by policemen and women and even police dogs; in spacecraft, boat hulls, fiber optic cables, anchor lines for large sea vessels, hoses, ropes, gloves, skis, tennis rackets, brake shoes (replacing asbestos), airplanes, helicopters, etc.

When I retired from DuPont, I held 16 patents, nine of them jointly with colleagues, and had published 30 technical articles. As a result of this lifetime of work, I have been the recipient of many honors and awards. A few of these are: American Chemical Society Award for Creative Invention in 1980, DuPont Lavoisier Medal for Technical Achievement in 1995, Induction into the National Inventors Hall of Fame in 1995, National Medal of Technology given by President Clinton in 1996, Perkin Medal given by the Society of Chemical Industry in 1997 and the Lemelson–MIT Lifetime Achievement Award in 1999.

Over the years, Carnegie Mellon has honored me with the Alumni Association Merit Award in 1998 and the honorary Doctor of Science and Technology in 2001. In 1996, I gave an undergraduate symposium entitled "An Adventure in Polymer Chemistry" for 50 chemistry majors at Carnegie Mellon, followed by a dinner for 25 faculty members and students. I continue working with students, have served as a mentor for women scientists and have participated in a number of programs introducing young children to science.

I am proud of the achievements of women from Margaret Morrison Carnegie College.

Stephanie L. Kwolek
General Science '46
Honorary Doctorate, Mellon College of
Science '01

Property of Lemelson/MIT Found., Boston, Mass.

Top:
Stephanie L. Kwolek with chemists Dr. Paul W. Morgan and Dr. Herbert Blades at the DuPont Textile Fibers Pioneering Research Laboratory Experimental Station in 1976

Bottom:
Stephanie L. Kwolek holding a model of an aromatic polyamide.

The Way We Were:
Margaret Morrison as a Window on the World

Evelyn L. Alessio
*New Kensington,
Pennsylvania*

- *General Studies '57*
- *Delta Gamma
  Vice President*
- *Undergrad Advisory
  Committee*
- *Campus Chest
  Chairman*
- *Panel of Americans*
- *Mortar Board President*
- *Cwens*
- *Phi Tau Gamma*
- *Phi Kappa Phi*
- *Pi Delta Epsilon*
- *Tartan*
- *Student Handbook
  Editor*

Margaret Morrison opened a window on the world for me. I arrived on campus at age 18 in 1954 after spending my freshman year at Seton Hill, a small Catholic school in Greensburg, Pennsylvania. I wanted a women's school that was part of a more comprehensive college in a city that could offer a wide range of opportunities. Hence, Margaret Morrison. I enrolled in General Studies with a major in English. What a revelation! Among my favorite professors were Margaret LeClair, Erwin Steinberg, and Fred Sochatoff. Professor Sochatoff taught Latin Literature in Translation, a lively, tightly structured class. All my classes were small, usually under 20 students, and the professors employed Socratic methods: asking questions, probing our answers, keeping us on our toes. And they had high standards, demanding assignments and lots of papers.

In my junior year, I added a second major in the History Department, where professors such as Paul Ward and Ted Fenton challenged us in similar ways. Seven women were enrolled in both the English and history seminars. All of us went straight to graduate school. After Margaret Morrison, the academic work at Harvard, where I earned a master's degree in Counseling Psychology, was easy.

Dorm life opened other doors. I lived in Morewood Gardens, where we dined in refined splendor with white tablecloths and a dress code befitting the proper young ladies we were supposed to become. Many of the women on the floor were graduate students. They included Ann Dreselly, the first woman to earn a degree from GSIA, and a number of dramats including Mike Pollock. They helped to introduce me to the wider university and to an intriguing range of life styles.

I belonged to a number of organizations on campus. During my senior year, I was president of Mortar Board, which carried on some of the traditions such as the President's Reception at orientation as well as events for Fine Arts freshmen and transfer women. These helped a little to connect women across departments and colleges. Among other things, we worked with the administration and Omicron Delta Kappa, the men's honorary, on issues raised by student government, giving us a perspective on the whole campus.

Left:
Programs from the May Beegle Concert series

Right:
1957 members of Mortar Board, the honorary society for senior women:

Front on floor, Evelyn Alessio; second row on bench, Marjory King, Mary Lauten, Stephanie Mackay, Joyce Bernini, Jean Walker, Carol Schler, Nancy Gardner; top row, Eva Lu Spears, Anne Elder, Hannah Oppenheimer, Betsy Kuhn, Alma McCloud

In my junior year, I chaired Campus Chest, a campaign to raise money among students for a variety of organizations such as World University Service and the United Negro College Fund. Both organizations opened worlds far beyond Forbes Avenue. The Panel of Americans had a similar impact. This organization sent a faculty member and five students—a Catholic, a Protestant, a Jew, an African-American, and an international student—to talk about inter-group living on campus to groups in the community. I made my first visit to Terrace Village, a segregated African-American housing project in Pittsburgh's Hill District, as a member of the Panel. A real eye opener.

The Pittsburgh Symphony played in Oakland's Syria Mosque, a few blocks from campus. Student tickets were inexpensive. The Mosque was also home to the May Beegle series of concerts, plays, ballet performances, and similar events. Now and then I'd go to a play at the Playhouse or a movie at the Schenley Theater. Tech offered a host of cultural opportunities to any interested student. Not that I was always serious. The Greeks, our hangout on Forbes Street just across the hollow, took care of that. I dated interesting guys. Most of them were graduate students in GSIA or the sciences, particularly physics. I met undergraduate men and a few graduate students in elective humanities courses. I remember Bob Worsing, Jim Langer, Hugh Young and Ed Feigenbaum, all of whom have gone on to distinguished careers.

After I left graduate school, I took a job as a counselor at Mount Lebanon High School. After I married Regis Murrin and we began our family, I interrupted my career for about twenty years while I cared for our growing brood of four girls. During that time, looking forward to resuming my career, I did advanced graduate studies and was fortunate to occasionally find part-time positions. I was even more fortunate to continue my career as a school psychologist with the Upper St. Clair schools, where I had many wonderful colleagues including Mary (Prezioso) Wilkins '55, who had been my sorority big sister.

Margaret Morrison helped to prepare me to lead a full life. Since I retired in 1994, I became active again in the community, particularly with a League of Women Voters local government project for elementary school students and as a trustee of the Pittsburgh Child Guidance Foundation. My work with Pennsylvania Peace Links has taken me back, after forty years, to Terrace Village where we are piloting a violence prevention curriculum, funded by the Alcoa Foundation, for families with infants and toddlers. That project and others have led us to international exchanges in early childhood education and global peace. Now, more than ever, I appreciate the world view that opened up for me in Margaret Morrison.

I was not particularly distressed when Carnegie Mellon phased out Margaret Morrison. I had been a General Studies major and the university expanded the departments in which I had studied (English, history and psychology) in the new College of Humanities and Social Sciences. Alongside pride in the superb university that Carnegie Mellon has become, I retain fond and grateful memories of Margaret Morrison, the founding stone of women's education at Carnegie Mellon.

Evelyn (Alessio) Murrin
General Studies '57

Evelyn's expense book
from 1954-55

The Way We Were:
I Joined Everything

Joanne Lacey
Euclid, Ohio

- *General Studies '58*
- *Kappa Alpha Theta First Vice President*
- *Cwens*
- *Phi Tau Gamma*
- *Mortar Board*
- *Phi Kappa Phi*
- *Campus Chest*
- *Junior Panhellenic Council President*
- *Scotch 'n' Soda Executive Board*
- *Student Congress President*
- *Undergraduate Advisory Committee*
- *WRCT*
- *YWCA*
- *Women's Dormitory Council Vice President*
- *Newman Club*
- *Scot*

I filled in my appointment calendar every night before I went to sleep. During my years at Margaret Morrison, I belonged to at least 15 organizations—not all at once, of course. I'm most proud of the four honoraries, Cwens, Mortar Board, Phi Tau Gamma, and Phi Kappa Phi, but I also had a lot of fun and led several student organizations. I was a prop mistress in Scotch 'n' Soda and a member of its Executive Board. My photo appeared as a calendar girl in the 1957 *Scot* and again as my sorority's candidate for Spring Carnival queen. I was on the Advisory Committee of Campus Chest, and was a member of radio station WRCT, the YWCA and the Newman Club. At different times, I was vice president of the Women's Dormitory Council; vice president of my sorority, Kappa Alpha Theta; president of the Junior Panhellenic Council; president of the Student Council; and chair of the Undergraduate Advisory Committee. And I had a boyfriend. I couldn't have survived without an appointment calendar.

I had enrolled in Margaret Morrison because I won a scholarship to Tech from the Elks Club in Euclid, Ohio, where I lived. I was the valedictorian in a class of 360 students at Euclid High School, and the scholarship was my reward. It paid half of my tuition for two years.

I knew next to nothing about either Margaret Morrison or Carnegie Tech when I won the award, and I had never been to campus, but I decided to come anyway, encouraged by my father who was delighted with the scholarship money. In retrospect, I could not have made a better decision. For the last two years, I was awarded a full-tuition scholarship from the Southern Women's Club of Pittsburgh.

I took a train to Pittsburgh to meet my forthcoming roommate, Nancy (Rohl) Napoleon. She showed me around. We ate lunch in Skibo, the old Langley Aeronautical Building on Frew Street. Like the rest of Tech, Skibo was homey and friendly, and I soon felt comfortable in my new surroundings. Nancy and I roomed together in Morewood Gardens for all my four years on campus

My father advised me not to major in mathematics because, he said, there were no jobs in math for women, so I enrolled in the Psychology Department. Before I graduated, I had taken all the undergraduate psychology courses in the catalogue, including one night class in which most of the students were already employed. I also took several graduate courses in the department and filled out my schedule with home ec courses that have served me well as a wife and mother.

1958 Women's Dormitory Council:
Front row: Ruth Vysoky, Jo Lacey, Mrs. Green
Second row: Jan Cargill, Mary Doyle, Jan Madden, Peg Ford, Barb Krack, Sherry Moulton, Sally Schwerzler, Gail Garvin, Jan Natopolos

I loved Carnegie Tech courses. I was accustomed in high school to classes where we memorized facts and regurgitated them on exams. Tech was different. The Carnegie Plan emphasized problem solving rather than regurgitation, and I took to it. My first semester, however, gave me a real shock. I took The Development of Western Civilization from a young history instructor, Ted Fenton, who is now authoring this book. When I got a C at the end of the first semester, I went to see him, telling him that I had always had straight As. He told me I was lucky, that it was a very low C, and I should be thankful. I learned. Earned an A in the second semester.

I graduated in 1958 and promptly married Delmar Ritchie, a 1957 Industrial Management graduate and we settled down in Sherwood Forest, Maryland, where we still reside. We had met at the ATO house in 1956, and the relationship flourished. Our names were in the headlines of the same edition of *The Tartan* in 1957, his as intramural athlete of the year and mine as president of the Student Council. Our kids think the pictures are a hoot.

Del took a job in Baltimore with Poole and Kent (mechanical contractors) and is still with them almost 46 years later. I worked as a social worker for two years until the first of our three children was born. I never returned to full-time work as raising the children kept me fully occupied. Today I am busy with seven grandchildren, a Bible study group, and as a sponsor/mentor for men

enrolled in the United States Naval Academy. They have become almost like family to Del and me, with continuing relationships with them and their families.

Del and I are devoted to Carnegie Tech/Mellon, even to having his (CIT ATO) and her (CIT KAT) vanity license plates. We attend homecoming each year, dividing our time between campus events and partying with old friends. We sponsored refurbishment of a room at Skibo Gymnasium in honor of Clarence "Buddy" Overend, Del's grandfather. Buddy Overend was a member of the first class of the Carnegie Technical Schools and Director of Athletics from 1923 to 1952, a period that included the golden years of Tech football. Keeping in touch with over 70 old Tech friends has given us joy over the years. In recent years, we have tried to repay Margaret Morrison and Carnegie Tech for our debt of gratitude by contributing through charitable gift annuities. We have many fond memories of the hard work and the fun we each experienced during the four precious years at Carnegie when we were young, had few responsibilities, and our lives seemed to stretch endlessly before us.

Joanne (Lacey) Ritchie
General Studies '58

Top:
1954 Homecoming Queen and her court. Joanne is third from the left, second row.

Bottom:
Joanne and Del on their wedding day

Carnegie
ALUMNUS

VOLUME 29   JUNE 1944   NUMBER 4

Chapter 4

1929–56
Memories from Maggie Murphs

I n response to invitations from Mary Phillips, Director of the Margaret Morrison Carnegie College Program, 200 alumni submitted reminiscences of their days as students at Margaret Morrison. They came in many forms: handwritten, typewritten, computer processed, e-mail, and phone interviews. We read them all—over and over again—and emerged much better informed than if we had depended for information solely on documents preserved in Carnegie Mellon's excellent archives. A few individuals also sent memorabilia—newspaper clippings, photographs, and personal effects—many of which have enlivened this book.

We wanted to use something in the book from everyone who responded to our invitation, but two problems emerged. First, most of the reminiscences contained far more material than a short book could accommodate. Some letters were several pages long, recalling a host of memories of a vital period in a woman's life. Therefore, we chose shorter passages from each document. The reminiscences were, without exception, a pleasure to read, and we will deposit all the original entries in their entirety in the archives when we have finished mining them.

Second, we found many similar comments about most topics. Commuting can serve as an example. Five individuals wrote about the adventure of commuting from Mt. Lebanon to campus, sending in different words approximately the same message. "I took a streetcar from Mt. Lebanon to downtown and transferred to another streetcar to Tech. Then I walked across the Cut, often in bitterly cold weather. I reversed this process in the evening, spending two hours a day in transit." Rather than repeat similar passages, we numbered them, placed the numbers in a hat, and pulled one. We used this lottery system many times for many subjects.

Reminiscences from alumni have helped to shape the entire volume. Knowing what alumni remembered helped us to identify topics to emphasize in the text. We are grateful to all the alumni who submitted reminiscences, even though some of you are not represented by name in this chapter or in chapter six. A full list of alumni who responded to Ms. Phillips' appeal for reminiscences appears on pages 126 and 127. We are greatly in your debt.

Finally, we have tried to check information—dates and spelling of names, for example—in this chapter's reminiscences as well as throughout the book. We apologize for errors we may have made.

Left page reading clockwise from upper left corner:
1st Lt. Nancy McKenna, M'39, Marine Corps Reserve; Ensign Katherine Palen Ritchey, M'31, Coast Guard Reserve; Pfc. Bernice Shine, M'28, A.A.F. WAC; Lt. Elizabeth E. Bitzer, M'31, Dietitian, Army Nurse Corps; Ensign Marjorie Weather-wax Woodside, A'43, Naval Reserve; Capt. Charlotte M. Shuman, A'22, WAC; Lt. Agnes C. Glunt, M'41, Army Nurse Corps; Lt. Eleanor I. Johnston, M'40, Dietitian, Army Nurse Corps; Mrs. Naomi J. Thompson, A'40, American Red Cross; 1st Sgt. Marjorie Bandman, A'40, WAC; Ensign Elizabeth Leaman Kingcome, M'37, Naval Reserve; Pvt. Ann E. Konstan, M'42, WAC; Ensign Carolyn Eggers, A'28, Naval Reserve; Lt. Edna B. Stewart, M'42, Navy Nurse Corps

Memories:
Home Economics

*D*r. Calla Van Syckle was head of the department. She had a wonderful sense of humor, but she was very strict. I remember that you didn't run in the halls and you observed a certain decorum. You came to class dressed properly and didn't talk in class unless you raised your hand and were recognized. Lab sessions, however, were much less formal. You did your work and you were allowed to talk to and help one another. When you walked into a Van Syckle class, you knew that serious business was going on.
Phyllis (Grant) Silverman
Household Economics '48

In the Spring of our senior year, five of us from the Costume Economics Department had several Friday afternoon meetings with President Doherty in an effort to save the department from rumored extinction. Although he let us know in advance that his mind was made up, Dr. Doherty was open to any discussions on the subject and these meetings became extremely interesting. Even more than that, they became frustrating to us as we could see the handwriting on the wall. Within a few years, the Costume Economics Department sank into the annals of history.
Alberta "Bertie" (Rosendahl) Walker
Costume Economics '45

The class that I really remember was a class with Hazel Parezzi. She taught us dressmaking and introduced us to *Women's Wear Daily.* I also enjoyed Virginia Alexander's classes in costume economics.
Margaret (Johnston) Thomas
Costume Economics '42

Top right:
Costume design

Bottom center:
Meal planning and
preparation

In nutrition class, we were required to taste yogurt for the first time. Can't remember anyone liking it. It was new to most of us.
Dolores (Walker) Fullerton
Home Economics '52

Kudos to Miss Abbott, Miss Hyde, and Miss Glendon in the Home Economics Department for preparing me so well for the outside world. Upon graduation in 1935, I was immediately employed by the Pittsburgh Public Schools in the School Lunch Department. Jobs were hard to come by in those days.
Mary Frances (Nichol) Dana
Home Economics '35

During my senior year, the ongoing Great Depression caused a great change in my life. My father, David Gustafson, lost his professorial job as head of the CIT Department of Printing. His salary had been paid by the Pittsburgh printing industry. My family had to move to Illinois to live with my grandmother, and the college let me stay on in the Home Management House a short time until graduation. The Depression played a significant role in the lives of many students.
Ruth (Gustafson) Johnson
Home Economics '35

My course of study was Costume Economics, *not* Home Economics. There were departments of Costume Economics (clothing), Household Economics (food), and Vocational Home Economics (teaching). During our senior year, we worked one day a week at Kaufmann's Department Store in all capacities needed for merchandising. While we had been taught to drape, for a fashion show we used patterns furnished by Kaufmann's and modeled the finished products. My favorite memory is of getting together with classmates the night before a senior project was due. We sewed all night, making winter coats from scratch, washed our faces, and reported to class the next morning. (For the record, sewing all night was not approved of by our professors!)
F. Irene Thomas
Costume Economics '37

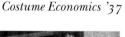

Memories:
The Home Management House

H̲ome Ec majors were required to live in the Home Management House on Margaret Morrison Street for five weeks during their senior year. Five girls assumed the jobs generally found in a family home: hostess (wife, mother, lady of the house), cook, housekeeper, marketing, and meal planning. The jobs rotated weekly. Each student occupied a single bedroom in the three-story, brick-and-stucco house. Each year students gave a dinner for their parents, who were very proud to eat a meal planned, cooked, and served by their daughters.
Maxine (Shermer) Slesinger
Home Economics '38

The weeks in the Home Management House were a wonderful learning experience but also a lot of fun, particularly for those of us who were commuters. While I was in residence there, my fiancé was a frequent dinner guest, seated in the place of honor at the table where he received the warmest dinner plate. Occasionally the campus pyracantha was pruned late at night to make a centerpiece for the table. Meals were rated on taste, color in the presentation, service, and the centerpiece that counted for 50 percent of the meal rating. Why so much, we always wondered.
Janice (Yent) Saibel
Home Economics Education '55

Perhaps because I was a commuter, the five weeks in the Home Management House were the best weeks of my college years. They gave me a taste of what campus life was like. When I was hostess for a dinner party for the mothers of the other girls in the house, I received a beautiful centerpiece for the dinner table from the man I was dating. Dick and I were married in 1941 and have had 60 happy years together.
Betty (Ogilvie) Kehew
Home Economics '40

After dinner coffee in the Home Management House

Another memory of the Home Management House concerns our evening meals. Regardless of how much homework we had, or how many tests to study for, or what time dates were due to arrive, we had an hour of "table conversation" after dinner! You can't know how much college girls could squirm at the dinner table unless you can find a way to see us squirming each evening.
Mary (Roe) Condio
Home Economics Education '53

I was married my senior year, living in a third floor, furnished, walkup apartment. I was not exempt from Home Management class, and was informed that my grade would be based upon a visit by the teacher. I'd heard the stories: The brass must be polished weekly, never serve an all white meal such as fish, mashed potatoes and cauliflower, and, "She moves the lamps and checks the shades to make sure I dusted everywhere." What a flurry of cleaning there was in anticipation of her visit. I vividly remember that I served chicken salad on a bed of lettuce, sliced tomatoes, homemade rolls and strawberry shortcake, thus a colorful meal. Got an "A" too.
Barbara (Kinner) Ekiss
Foods and Nutrition '58

I was a cook one week along with Marilyn (Franklin) James. It was April Fool's Day, and we had a beautiful table set with flowers and candles. We presented Miss Mabel Stoner with crusts of bread for her dinner. She was noticeably disgruntled with our prank and we thought we might get a bad grade, but Marilyn and I survived with a high mark.
Lois (Campsey) Stauffer
Home Economics '54

We had a very limited budget and when my turn came to plan menus at the Home Management House, I was determined to treat us to a steak dinner. The trade-off for this feast was an economical meal the night before: jelly omelettes. Everything went well until we added the grape jelly. Then the chemical reaction occured: the eggs turned a bright green. I was shocked. We had twelve people and a guest waiting for dinner. When the platters appeared—carried overhead to hide their green hue as long as possible—the looks on the diners' faces were hilarious. Still, no one laughed as we were graded on good manners. I'll never forget all these people politely nibbling on the green eggs while I sat making small talk.
Patricia (Mitchell) Devoy
Home Economics '57

Memories:
Secretarial Studies

The secretarials were always ready—pen in hand—as Mrs. Ely entered the shorthand classroom dictating as she came. We spent free moments between classes completing the required number of shorthand pages assigned each night.
Jean (Guthridge) Francis
Secretarial Studies, '46

A student practices using the dictaphone.

In the depth of the depression in 1936, Miss Winchester was busily molding us into ideal private secretaries, using her distinctive combination of wry comments on our personalities and stress on our technical skills. In our senior year, we spent one day a week working in downtown offices. My company was Harbison-Walker Refractories, and they pared down their secretarial staff so low that on one day there I typed the weekly output of specifications in the department to which I was assigned. During the great flood of 1936, my department had to set up temporary headquarters in the engineering building at Tech. I went down several days to help out. They paid me! It was the first money I earned as a secretary.
Lucile (Meyer) Hutchins
Business Studies '36

My instructors in the Secretarial Studies Department were both inspirational and helpful. Dean Alexander, a very special person, taught Business English. I still have "My Teaching Hope Chest" that Elsie Leffingwell helped me to compile and which I used when I began to teach. Margaret Ely, my shorthand teacher, was my advisor during my student teaching days at Westinghouse High School. Grace Patterson taught me all I ever needed to know about filing records. Laura Hayes and Betty Jane Lloyd prepared me well both for teaching and for a successful business career. Carnegie Tech's reputation opened doors for me throughout my career.
Shirley (Herman) Townsend
Secretarial Studies '51

Everyone reaches out for people trained as secretaries because they can type. During the second semester of my freshman year, I typed for the head of the night school when there were more night than day students at Tech. Later I typed two books for one of the professors, and I worked part-time for the rest of my college years. We became good friends, my type-writer and I.
Virginia (Morgan) Obrig
Secretarial Studies '30

I was a graduate of Indiana State Teacher's College in Indiana, Pennsylvania, when I enrolled in Margaret Morrison's graduate course in Secretarial Studies in 1946. Our classes were intensive (shorthand and typing twice a day, five days a week), but we really learned to be excellent secretaries and had our pick of the best jobs in the Pittsburgh area. Our class had to work for a year before Tech granted us a degree, so I am listed as a graduate of the class of 1948.
Barbara (Woods) Craig
Secretarial Studies '48

I enrolled in the secretarial course at Margaret Morrison because it was one of the best in the country. I was fortunate to be elected Campus Queen and represented Tech in the Sugar Bowl game. My office practice took me to U.S. Steel, where I was hired immediately after graduation. I worked there three years, served in the Women's Marine Corp for three years, and then returned to U.S. Steel. I've enjoyed the many reunions I have attended at Tech.
Nancy (McKenna) Murrin,
Secretarial Studies '39

The 1944 Secretarial Studies faculty: Patterson, Cranna, Fisher, Hays, Chaman, Ely and Winchester

Memories:
Nursing Education

I graduated from high school in the depression and my father couldn't afford to send me to college. I went to West Penn Hospital, and when Miss Bowers, the directress, saw my grades, she offered to lend me the money to go three years to college and two to nursing to get both degrees. I said I would love to go. While we studied at West Penn, we could live in the nurses' home, a large building on Friendship Avenue. We ate our evening meals there and studied in our rooms. We had private rooms because we were going to college and needed privacy to study. We could stay up much later than girls could do in Tech dorms. West Penn was a mile or so from campus, and we used to walk back and forth or, if we had a streetcar token, ride a streetcar.
Alice (Thompson) Volkwein
Nursing Education '35

I loved my years at MMCC. I was one of a small class of five-year nursing students who entered MMCC in 1940. At that time, we were an oddity because the majority of nurses were graduates of the three-year hospital courses. My first two years at MMCC, the two years following that at West Penn Hospital Nursing School and then the fifth year back at MMCC gave me an education and experience that I have always valued. Our professors were always the best and our contact with them was close. Due to the war situation, all of our classes, as well as labs, were taught by professors; we had no experience with grad students. However, because we were the "five-year students" in the nursing school, we were also expected to assume more important duties than the three-year students. Those teaching experiences could not have been better.
Jean (Metzger) Harris
Nursing '45

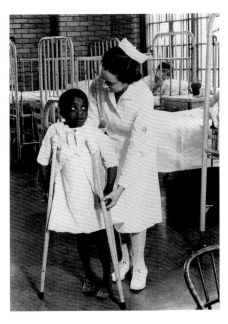

The Margaret Morrison nursing curriculum was only a few years old when I enrolled in 1938. It was a wonderful blend of hands-on nursing and baccalaureate classes. While we were at West Penn, we had full-time training in all the specialties, such as surgery, obstetrics, pediatrics, public health, psychiatry, the diet kitchen, and the out-patient clinics. They shortened our training in only two services: nursing care and surgical patients. As a result, we graduated with all the practical training of three-year hospital nurses and with additional teaching and management skills that we learned at Tech.
Sally (Ray) Keaton
Nursing Education '43

I was in college during the war years. The government organized a program they called Cadet Training. If you signed up, they paid your way through nursing school. In return for promising to stay in essential nursing until the war ended, the government gave us uniforms and a monthly stipend. I think it was 15 dollars. We thought we were rich!
Jeanne (Hecht) Steele
Nursing Education '47

Practical nursing experience at West Penn Hospital

I was enrolled in the nursing program from 1934 to 1939. In the midst of the depression, everyone seemed to be poor. I couldn't afford to live in a dormitory, so a relative in Blawnox took me in for $5 a week, and I rode the train to Shadyside station and then walked to school. Late classes or work often had me running to the station just in time to see the train pulling out. As soon as I entered school, I began to work in the National Youth Administration program. I worked between 35 and 50 hours a month for the first three years. In my senior year, I went to see Dean Green to ask for financial aid and received $50 from the scholarship fund.
Mary Margaret (McCaslin) Robinson
Nursing Education '39

I was one of only seven students in the nursing program, class of 1940. I received a degree in nursing education after five years of study. I became a professor of nursing at a large university. Although I have seen many nursing programs, I still feel that our CIT program provided us with the most well-rounded, professional education in nursing I have seen.
Rita (Schmidt) Caughill
Nursing Education '40

Thanks to Carnegie Tech and the five-year nursing program, I was provided a background that gave me 41 years as a nursing instructor in four different cities. And the entire cost to my parents was $5,500! Those five years were "hit the books" but certainly worth it. The professors were excellent, real taskmasters but willing to help you when needed. Dr. Lang, head of our program, was especially helpful.
Virginia (Wade) Schalles
Nursing Education '41

Memories:
Social Work

Going to Margaret Morrison changed my entire life. Not knowing what to study, I chose to major in social work. We were taught, supported, nurtured and given a social conscience. We had found our lifelong careers and passions.
Elaine (Levin) Budd
Social Work '44

I was a natural to enroll at what was then Carnegie Tech. Three relatives had graduated from the school. I wanted to major in social work and Margaret Morrison had an excellent major in the field. I had an undergraduate experience that few others could rival. In our junior and senior years, there were four students and four social work faculty. Our close involvement with our professors was unrivalled. In addition to our academic courses, we had two field placements. One of my placements was with the Department of Public Welfare in Wilkinsburg; the other was at Soho Settlement House. Three of the four of us later earned our Master's of Social Work degrees and worked professionally until our retirement. All four of us celebrated our 50th and 55th Homecomings at CMU.
Ruth (Taubman) Glosser
Social Work '44

My mother, Lorine Hertz, had so many stories of MMCC. This is one she told often: Andrew Carnegie came to their class and gave a talk, and at the end he said, "Now I hope you all leave here and find good husbands!" She would laugh and say, "How times have changed."
Lorine (Friedman) Hertz
Social Work '18
Submitted by her daughter
Nancy (Hertz) Muskin
Secretarial Studies '45

One of the most vivid memories of my time at Margaret Morrison was our library. It was a YMCA hut left over from World War I and was located directly across Margaret Morrison Street from the fine arts building. The collection was adequate to support Margaret Morrison's curriculum. Engineering and fine arts each had its own library. By today's standards, the hut would be considered primitive—just study tables, good lighting, one librarian and stacks for the books. I spent many happy hours there.
Lillian (Udman) Weitzenkorn
Social Work '43

My father, Ralph Merrill, was in the first graduating class in 1908; and when a friend of his called the women's school 'Maggie Murphy' and he repeated it in *The Tartan,* the name Maggie Murphs stuck. That isn't why I went to MMCC, however; it just sort of happened. We studied quite hard because Tech was hard. But we lived for the weekend. The fraternities and the Dragons, the men's senior honor society, had black tie parties all the time, with big name bands. In our senior year, we went to the Chatter Box, the nightclub downstairs at the William Penn, one of the nicest places to have a party.
Jane (Merrill) Mason
Social Work '38

After returning from army experiences during WWII, I graduated from Clarion State University of Pennsylvania in January 1950. I then took a nursing assistant position at Warren State Hospital, where I met Nelson Johnson, who was Chief, Social Work Services, and Tom Donaldson, a social worker. Both of these men had MSWs from Carnegie. In discussions with them, I arrived at the decision to seek admission to Carnegie/MMCC and was accepted.
William Scheafnocker
Social Work M '53

There were four of us in social work courses—Ruth (Taubman) Glosser, Elaine (Levin) Budd, Kay (Kinley) Sillins and me. We became good friends and still keep in touch.
Helen (Johnston) Martin
Social Work '44

Social Work students leading a class in group games and dances

A laboratory class in chemistry

*B*ecause of the war, Tech expedited general science majors during the first semester of their senior year in 1943. We spent many hours together in the science laboratories that resulted in a close comradeship among us. For our last semester in the fall of 1943, Janet (Denslow) Landerl and I were asked to serve as laboratory assistants under the direction of Dr. Clara Miller. It was a delightful and rewarding experience. With the assistantship, the department gave each of us a desk in an office we shared. I cherish that memory of Margaret Morrison above all others.
Joy Swan
General Science '44

Sex Education was nonexistent. However, the only course in which we studied reproduction was physiological biology. Out of 180 women in Margaret Morrison, only we four science majors took this course: Shirley (Karfiol) Bernstein, Ruth (Brantlinger) Debusschere, Norma (Squitieri) Rocchini and myself. This is humorous when we consider today's "Bare it all!" on TV.
Joanne (Tishlarich) Luther
General Science '42

Hugh Clark, the rector of the Episcopal Church of the Redeemer in Squirrel Hill, sponsored a student Canterbury Club. On Thursday mornings, he would drive up Morewood Gardens' circular drive to pick up any woman student who had hung something white out of the window, meaning she was ready to go to Canterbury House on Margaret Morrison Street before classes for juice, roll, coffee, and a short service. It was here that Wil Rouleau, an engineering student, and I met. After MMCC, I went to Carnegie Library School for an M.L.S., continuing to live in Morewood Gardens, where many library students lived while attending classes in the main Carnegie Library in Oakland. After working a year, I returned to Pittsburgh where, three days after Wil received his Ph.D., the Rev. Clark married us, and Wil began his 45 years of teaching in the Mechanical Engineering Department. Rev. Clark, who began at the local church in 1936 and served four years in the Philippines as an air force chaplain during World War II, continued as rector through 1970.
Ruth (Osborne) Rouleau
General Studies '52
M.L.S., Carnegie Library School '53

On weekday visits to the Chemistry Department as a young child, I'd invariably see "Miss Miller" and "Miss Douglas." They always came to our house for a special Christmas dinner. Only later did I realize that they were Dr. Clara Miller and Professor Clara Jane Douglas, both professors of chemistry and colleagues of my father, Dr. Lawrence H. Schultz. The long, narrow stockroom for the lab's chemicals and apparatus supplies stood between their two offices. When I came to Margaret Morrison as a student, I entered familiar territory.
Margaret (Schultz) Tsiang
General Science '53

In November 1948, the presidential election dominated the news for political types like me. I was too young to vote, but I was campaigning for Henry Wallace, the third party candidate. Pundits agreed that Thomas Dewey was sure to win, but Harry Truman was re-elected in a famous upset. My history teacher, Dr. Lambert, who had kept his sympathies to himself during the campaign, could not restrain himself. Instead of holding class, he took all 15 of us to breakfast in Skibo to celebrate. Social Relations classes were like that— small enrollments, excellent teachers, and warm personal relationships.
Celeste (Silberstein) Behrend
General Studies '49

I lived at Whitfield Hall because Jeanne (Ditzler) Dodds, who was a senior and president of the student association, had first choice of the rooms at Whitfield. She asked me, although I was only a sophomore, to share the room with her. I can remember that the dean used to eat dinner with us and she would caution us, "Before you speak, think: is it kind and is it necessary?"
Jean Flegal
General Studies '43

When I entered Carnegie Tech in 1948, I was not sure what I wanted to do as a profession. Teachers such as Melva Bakkie inspired me to be a teacher. Even today at my advanced age, I tutor young people. Although I was disappointed when MMCC closed early in the 1970s, I continue to think fondly of CMU and its progress.
Mary (Waite) Florida
Home Economics Education '51

Things were quite different when I enrolled in MMCC in February 1930. Yes, February. I had been awarded a half-tuition scholarship upon graduation from Schenley High School on the condition that I enroll in the college of my choice immediately. MMCC okayed my application. My chemistry lab instructor was Dr. Warner, later president of Carnegie Tech and my friend forever. Most of the classes for General Science were in the MMCC basement. Among our wonderful teachers were Clara Miller, Clara Douglas, Martha Eggers, Dr. Lang and Dr. Schultz.
Frances (Brown) Newhams
General Science '33

Of the many fine teachers at MM during my time, Professor Norman Dawes of the History Department stands out. He made history both interesting and fun. When he talked about early man, he used his own head to illustrate Cro-Magnon man, turning his head sideways so that we could see the profile. Sure enough, just like the profile in the book! His lectures were always a pleasure, so well organized and clear that note taking was easy
Eleanor (Bright) Bice
Social Work '39

This is belated tribute to a teacher in the Household Economics Department, Mrs. Marshall. I transferred to Margaret Morrison from a liberal arts college in the middle of my sophomore year. Few of the courses that I had taken during my first year-and-a-half of college counted toward graduation at Tech, but I was determined to graduate with my class in 1941. By taking a course overload, going to night classes and taking inorganic chemistry one summer at Pitt, I was able to take every required course but one, a course in experimental cooking that Mrs. Marshall taught. In order to enable me to graduate, she offered to teach the course to me, a lone student, during the summer of 1941. It was a kindness I did not appreciate fully at the time, but I hope that this public acknowledgement will help to make amends for my youthful self-centeredness.
Helen (Zimmerman) Liversidge
Household Economics '42

Ruth Marshall, Household Economics faculty member

I would like to salute some great teachers: Norman Herbert Dawes, History; Ethel Spencer, English; Clara Emily Miller, Chemistry; William Frederic Kamman, French and German; and those poor professors in the College of Engineering who were somewhat astounded to find GIRLS who elected to take math, physics, and chemistry in their heretofore totally masculine classes.
Janet (Denslow) Landerl
General Science '44

Through the years, I have kept in touch with the head of the Secretarial Department, Edith Winchester Alexander, and visited her often after she retired. She was an inspiration to her students and the recipient of many honors.
Martha (Chersky) Orringer
Secretarial Studies '41

Professor Margaret LeClair is someone I will never forget. Her course in Modern Literature opened new worlds to me. She broadened my world by teaching me to look beyond the surface of what was written, to look at the power of words, and to expand my understanding of what it is to live a life with passion, compassion, and a sense of justice. One rainy day, walking across the Cut in my yellow slicker, bobby sox and saddle shoes as a young woman of my times, I realized that Professor LeClair was guiding me to change my expectations of myself. I suppose she never knew just how profound an influence she had on me, but I still think of her often, and with gratitude.
Eileen (Cerutti) McConomy
Business Studies '56

Memories:
Commuting

I regretted at the time, and still do, that I didn't live on campus. Living at home did have advantages, but living on campus should be part of college life.
Mary (Crago) Benson
Costume Economics '30

Commuting wasn't all bad. The transit system went on strike during my sophomore year. I picked up a ride with a student who had posted a notice offering a ride from my area. Four years later I married him and he is still driving me around at times.
Theresa (Pepine) Doerfler
Home Economics Education '55

I commuted from Mt. Lebanon. I took a streetcar downtown, getting off at the clock before Kaufmanns and transferred to another car to get to Tech. Passes cost ten cents. I joined the Citcom Clan, an organization for commuters, but I was unable to attend regularly because my parents did not want me to come home at night after the meetings. Just knowing that I was a member of something at Tech, however, gave me a sense of belonging, and that helped.
Ruth (Young) Langkamp
Household Economics '43

I commuted daily by streetcar and bus from East McKeesport, Pennsylvania, so campus life was at a minimum. I can't forget the long walk across the Cut every day from Forbes Street to Margaret Morrison. And I have a vivid memory of standing in front of my locker in the basement of Margaret Morrison eating my lunch. I always loved to study, so that is what I valued most at Margaret Morrison.
Martha (Wainwright) Jones
Nursing Education '44

The Citcom Clan, 1946
First row: Young, Knoer, Meloy, Weikel, Forsythe, Aronson, Kutchukian, Abrosi, Stewart
Second row: Teasdale, Winter, Noll, Seiner, Klier, Sedney, Colnos, Riehl
Third row: Gibel, Sapsara, Pearlstein, McPherson, Fry, Evans, Stoner

Girls who commuted to Carnegie Tech used to bring brown bag lunches and eat them in the rec hall on the fourth floor of Maggie Murph. They discussed their classes and sometimes finished their Friday English themes. Most of these girls were able to attend Carnegie Tech during the depression because they earned partial scholarships in high school. They commuted by trolley using round, brass tokens with a diamond cut in the middle. Some rode the Pennsylvania Railroad and walked up Morewood Avenue from the Shadyside station near the J. A. Williams warehouse.
Louise (Wunderlich) Manka
Business Studies'37

That first year as a transfer student (1953), I lived with my sister Elsie, A '53. As two country girls loose in the big city, we did daring things— took in racy movies at the Art Cinema and went to plays at Center Avenue. Once during a streetcar strike, we even hitched rides.
Mary (Houston) Shaffer
Foods and Nutrition '55

Sixty-odd years later, what I remember most was the daily commute by streetcar—into town from Mount Washington and out again on Forbes Street, then scurrying across the Cut to make an 8:30 class. All too frequently the streetcar would detour into the Craft Avenue car barns for no apparent reason, while the minutes sped by.
Eleanor (Duffy) Kasehagen
Secretarial Studies '33

I was a commuter so going to college meant going from one world to another. My best memories are of walking to classes with my friends, especially Vivienne (Spitzer) Podolsky; eating in the Beanery and studying in the Hut, which had a lovely fire in the winter (imagine a library in a temporary wooden building, which has a fireplace and a fire); going to the Friday matinees in the Fine Arts Building—talking, talking, talking in the Handcraft Room on the first floor—and just feeling that I was in college and the world was ahead.
Edith (Swartz) Zober
Social Work '38, M'45

We all wanted to live in Whitfield Hall, the brick women's dorm that stood on a knoll high above Forbes Avenue. To get to it, we either walked through the front gate in the wrought iron fence and then strolled up the long, curving driveway, or climbed the 106 stairs from the backyard to the campus. Inside, a baby grand piano and a huge fireplace with a carved oak mantle graced the living room. My roommate and I had a large, marble bathroom to ourselves. The shower stall had circular water pipes that sprayed us from head to foot. What luxury! Originally, Whitfield House was the old Brown mansion that CIT acquired in 1932.
Virginia (Wade) Schalles,
Nursing Education '41

Before we went home for the holidays, the cook in Boss Hall prepared a wonderful dinner for the girls. We dressed in our best clothes. The tables were set with linens, candles, flowers, silver, and china, but best of all, the waiters dressed in tuxedos. When I saw a handsome fellow in his tux, it was love at first sight. I chased him for seven years until he caught me, and we are still together after 49 years and five children.
Elsie (Pestner) Kostyo
Home Economics '51

The telephone was out of order on the second floor of Laurel Hall in 1947. We freshmen were told by our housemother to stay in our rooms, and that the only repairman allowed in the dorm had to be over 50— and a family man. I peeked. He was!
Shirley (Gill) Fedor
Home Economics Education '51

When we lived in Whitfield Hall, our housemother, Mrs. Hespenheide, had definite rules for male visitors. We entertained our dates in the downstairs living room, and Mrs. H, as we called her, would look through a crack in the door to make sure that all four feet were flat on the floor as we sat on the couch. As long as our feet were flat, she knew no nonsense was going on. She was right.
Jane (McCann) Cody
Clothing and Design '49

As a freshman at Carnegie Tech in 1947, I was one of 11 students, including a house mother and a senior proctor, in Laurel Hall. We became a very close group and somehow managed with two bathrooms and one telephone. We thought we had gone to heaven when we moved to Morewood Gardens the next year.
Jane (Connor) Wiseman
Social Work '51, M '53

We were the first class to go into Morewood Gardens. We had fireplaces and mantles in some rooms and everything was newly furnished. This was my first time to live away from home, and it was a real adventure. Girls from all over Tech lived on the same floor: Maggie Murphs, dramats, architects, music majors, artists— everyone. Hearing what they had to say and what they did was truly exciting for a freshman girl. All freshmen were in B tower, where we had our own dining room where the waiters were fraternity men. So there you were at seven o'clock in the morning, ready to go to breakfast in full make-up and your hair combed—looking just great—because you wanted to impress the fraternity fellas.
Kathryn (Ditty) Updike
Costume Design '52

Three of us shared a triple room in Forbes Hall. Our room in this old mansion had a bay window, three beds, three desks, three dressers, a chaise, and large closets. In our senior year, the three of us decided that we were not going to graduate without getting drunk, so we got some gin, crackers and cheese, and maraschino cherries and we drank. I'm almost sure that our housemother, Mrs. Parsons, knew what we were doing, but she didn't interfere. What could be safer than three girls in their own room, even if they were drinking? I remember that after a few drinks, I couldn't balance on one foot when I tried to put my pajamas on. My two roommates—Jean (Wiekofsky) Miller and Eileen (Caplan) Siegel—and I are still friends.
Ruth (Neiman) Winer
Secretarial Studies '43

Whitfield Hall

The touring company of "This Is the Army," a show written by Irving Berlin, whose cast was made up of singers and dancers from the armed forces, came to Pittsburgh's Nixon Theatre. Our sorority invited them for a spaghetti dinner at Whitfield Hall. They loved it, and they loved Pittsburgh because people here were so friendly. One Maggie Murph met one of the cast, kept in touch throughout the war, and finally married him.
Janet (Chetlin) Rosecrans
Foods and Nutrition '44

The fall of 1951 was full of excitement for sophomore girls who wanted to rush one of the seven sororities on campus. There were many activities, particularly open houses that were held in various fraternity houses since there were not yet any sorority houses on campus. The coveted bids were handed out, and we were given a dink with the Greek letters of the sorority we intended to join sewed on the front. Pledge weeks over, the winter culminated in initiation ceremonies in the spring of 1952. Each sorority had an assigned room for Wednesday night meetings in the beautiful mansion sitting on the bluff overlooking Forbes Avenue and Beeler Street. After sorority meetings, some of us walked down Forbes to The Greeks, a popular name for the University Grill on Forbes near Craig. These were nights of great loyalty and friendship for those of us who joined a sorority, and we all felt and displayed an exuberant camaraderie.
Lydia (Reiber) Strehl
General Studies '54

SORORITIES

For Spring Carnival, each sorority or campus organization that wanted to participate chose two members to be candidates for campus queen or members of her court. Each group developed a skit to present their candidates and sell them to the student body. I was one of the two chosen by my sorority. We created a dance to the tune of "The Man with a Golden Arm" and danced to that tune at each frat house and campus event during the week before voting. When the votes were counted, my sorority sister was chosen Queen and I was chosen as a member of the court. Talk about the thrill of a lifetime; that was a 10.
Barbara (Moore) Ramsey
Home Economics Education '56

Sorority was not an option for me. Dean Mary Watson Green did not permit a sorority for Jewish girls, nor were we to be invited to join any others. While I did not aspire to become Homecoming Queen, this was socially isolating, since only sorority girls were in the inner circle of activities.
Phyllis (Klein) Levy,
Home Economics '40

For the 1954 Spring Carnival, when I was to be dressed as Queen Elizabeth, Mary Michael Pollock made a helmet of masking tape painted silver with aluminum paint and sprinkled with silver glitter. The helmet had to dry on my face overnight, and in the middle of the night it began to shrink. I dragged an unwilling, sleepy Michael out of bed at 2:00 a.m. to cut off the helmet, hoping she wouldn't also chop locks off my hair. It was worth it. We won first prize among the sororities and made the five o'clock news.
Barbara (Bulger) Barr
Merchandising '55

Margaret Morrison was my campus family. The sororities went national in my sophomore year, and as a commuter, that was a great way to develop friendships with students in all majors. We also had the Cut, Senior Fence, the Hut, and Skibo—all very special to each of us.
Rhoda (Mears) Hussey
Business Studies Education '46

For our required gym classes, we were suited up in green romper-like outfits, and for swimming we wore pea-green tank suits. I still have friends I made while we played field hockey games on the Cut.
Ruth (Templeton) Jones
Household Economics '44

In the fall of 1944, when all the servicemen on campus were called to duty, Tech opened the rifle range to women as an extracurricular activity. I remember that when I shot from a prone position, the sling was so tight that it broke the blood vessels in my upper left arm. I was a sight, even though my sight on the target remained good. About ten of us practiced once or twice a week, and we learned to break down and clean our rifles when we finished shooting.
Carol (Ford) Cooney
General Sciences '45

Many a day I crawled through the dirt in a low passage under Margaret Morrison to get to the rifle range so that I could learn to shoot. For extra gym credits, I went to the archery court, an outdoors area with targets for archery.
Frances (Timms) Busler
Household Economics '33

I remember how I hated to wear those bloomers to play hockey on the Cut. On a couple of occasions as my classmates and I walked in our bloomers past the art school, architecture students leaned out of the windows shouting, "Hey fellows! The circus is in town. Here come the elephants." Not content with these insults, they would drop bags of water on us. They called it fun.
Agnes (Cancelliere) Campbell
Business Studies '35

Gym was required once a week. You could take regular gym classes, swimming, modern dance, archery, rifle. We had a very good women's rifle team. At Spring Carnival, men had buggy races and sororities had roller-skating teams, with four of us on a team. It was very competitive. I have a picture of the roller skating races going past our old library, an old relic from WW I.
Adelaide (Aschmann) Brady
Household Economics '38

In our freshman year, we were required to take gym, which included field hockey, about which I knew nothing. But I remember it was great fun running up and down the Cut with a hockey stick.
Pauline (Clyde) Gaffney
Foods and Nutrition '50

WOMEN'S RIFLE TEAM

Historians may claim that man is superior over woman, but we at Carnegie are inclined to disagree. We have seen some very fine men's rifle teams, but never have we seen anything that compares with the 1937 women's team. The girl marksmen broke the long-standing world's record by scoring 2993 out of a possible 3000. They weathered the season undefeated and untied, to annex the Women's National Championship.

The mainstays of the rifle team are Katherine Thomas and Martha Waterman. Martha Waterman is the finest girl marksman to come to Carnegie, and although only a freshman she holds the national championship for individual shooting, having scored a perfect target—not a miss all season.

1937 Thistle

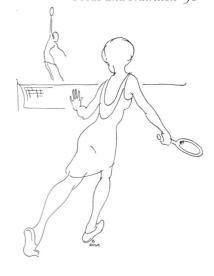

Memories:
The War Years

World War II overshadowed our college lives. On the bright, sunny September day in 1939 on which I set off in my red plaid suit to register for my freshman year at Carnegie Tech, Hitler's army invaded Poland. On a gloomy, dark December day in 1941, we gathered in the fine arts building to listen to President Roosevelt's Day of Infamy address to Congress and his declaration of war against Japan and Germany. On another gloomy December day in 1942 when we were awarded our degrees, most of the men in the class were only days away from induction into the armed forces. And so a pall was cast over all our days at Carnegie Tech.
Lucille (Orr) Crooks
Business Studies '43

The presence of uniformed men on campus brought the war close to our consciousness. We saw them struggle with the obstacle course where they trained each day, watched the military drills on the Cut, and hosted the tea dances that soldiers attended along with civilian students. We were filled with emotion when the soldiers were ordered to leave for Indiantown Gap, a large military installation. Within a few weeks, they were on the battlefields of France.
Mary Vincent
Costume Economics '46

I was in the class of 1943, graduating from MMCC with a degree in home economics that required four years of chemistry. Florence (Gessler) Minifie, a costume economics grad, and I were recruited to work as chemists at the American Smelting and Refining Company. The company supplied Yellow Cabs for us when we worked the midnight shift. We Maggie Murphs were part of the Great Generation.
Martha (Sekey) Wayman
Home Economics '43

Honorary captains of the Tech ROTC salute under the old Spanish naval rifle in Schenley Park.
Front row: Dorothy Piper, Marjorie Maple, Madeline Forsythe, Peggy Johnston, Virginia Bennet, Joanne Tishlarish, Peggy Stuchell, Molly van Ameringen and Marisse Forbes;
Back row: Alice Woods, Isabelle Gup, Peggy Young, Betty Shanor, Jean Howard and Jeanne Ann Bradley.

When I arrived on campus, we were still involved in World War II. Many navy boys were housed in several campus dorms. They were awaiting the completion of their LST boats that would take them to their posts. The fellows would parade up and down Margaret Morrison Street. We were really proud of them, even though their appearance on campus called for some restrictions on our part. All the girls on campus were alerted to walk in pairs or groups if we went out after dark because some of the boys had become a little overly flirtatious.
Norma (Maurhoff) Pickard
General Studies '48

I was married in the middle of my senior year. I had a week with my husband who had just returned from two-and-a-half years overseas before he left for Okinawa. After he left, as part of my training, I was working in a cafeteria where the jobs circulated so that all of us could experience every part of the operation. I was making rolls, and Mrs. Marshall, whom all of us loved, commented that the rolls were not quite right. I started to cry and ran up to the rec hall. She came after me: "Rea, they weren't that bad," she said. I replied, "Mrs. Marshall, I haven't heard from my husband for 45 days," and she cried with me.
Rea (Simon) Elias
Home/Costume Economics '45

In 1943, Maggie Murphs were "expedited," along with the architects and engineers. We went to school during the summer and graduated early. The campus resounded with the Hup, two, three, four of the over 600 ASTP (Army Specialized Training Program) boys studying at Tech. There was something fishy about the army staff; it included Col. Bass, Lt. Pickerel, and Sgt. Oyster. If a platoon marched past an unsuspecting female, the "Eyes Right" command often sent self-conscious girls scurrying into the nearest doorway. By late December 1943, most of the ROTC members had been called to active duty, and the ASTP students transferred to various army bases. Many from both groups landed in Normandy in June 1944; some never returned.
Margaret "Judy" (Skeehan) Lackner
Business Studies '44

Hot dog and Hurrah! World War II was over! It was September 1945, and the campus would be full of returning G. I. Joes. Under the G.I. Bill of Rights, all veterans had the right to pursue higher education with the approval and support of Uncle Sam. The admissions office was inundated; the girls were delighted.
Diana (Kutchukian) Thomasian
Social Science '49

Memories:
Career Preparation

"Maggie Murph" was a wonderful, eye-opening experience for a country girl in 1949. From my point of view it was huge, as I had 20 in my high school graduating class and attended elementary school in a one-room schoolhouse. I was not overwhelmed though. Living in Morewood Gardens and having most of my classes in Margaret Morrison gave me a sense of belonging. Because they cared, I received extra instruction on how to study. I was on probation my first semester, then graduated on the Dean's List. My degree in Foods and Nutrition gave me the opportunity to work in many fields: home service representative for a utility company, dietician for Joseph Horne Co., school cafeteria dietitian, research dietitian for Wear-Ever Aluminum, and home economics teacher for the Pittsburgh Public Schools. Without the four years at Margaret Morrison, I would not have accomplished so much in my lifetime. "Thanks, Maggie Murph!!"
Barbara (Myers) Nightingale
Foods and Nutrition '53

Even though I did not work after my marriage to Alex McCulloch, I feel that my degree from Carnegie Tech contributed to my being able to help raise our four children—a school teacher, a surgeon, a dentist, and an IBM computer expert.
Helen (Brackemeyer) McCulloch
Secretarial Studies '43

After driving on campus about three weeks ago, I realize in spite of the many changes (the Cut filled with buildings, MMCC's name gone), it's the stability of the university and the foundation that prepared me to become a fashion coordinator, a teacher, a principal, a wife and mother that is important in this changing world of uncertainties.
Mary Ina (Hill) Jones
Merchandising '53

Sales experience in a business class

I will never forget Virginia Alexander with her beautiful hats (she was a fantastic clothing design professor) and Professor Demerest with her high-necked dresses and beautiful Russian Orthodox cross. My Home Ec education and my time at Maggie Murph have served me well. I taught 32 years, did dietetics for 12 years and now am a volunteer Catering Coordinator and Hostess for Albertina Ker Centers. Incidentally, for sit-down dinners, I find myself still using my thumbnail to measure the distance of the silver from the edge of the table!
Lois (Speed) Gruver
Home Economics '38

Wonderful education—mostly wonderful teachers—Miss Alexander (English), Mrs. Meyers (Home Ec—especially nutrition), etc. Never felt that I was behind when I went on to get my internship certificate in dietetics or my Master's at Penn State. We may not have had the fancy equipment of some of the Land Grant Colleges but we had the teachers. We had basics hammered into our heads.
Natalie (Nathan) Krasik
Foods and Nutrition '45

Margaret Morrison gave its students a subtle push toward a career of some sort. There were women role models in the college and also a sense that one had to earn a living just in case one did not capture an engineer. I know three women from my era (1943–47) who long ago achieved professional status in the job market: a home ec major who became a manager at Heinz, a secretarial major who became an editor at the *Pittsburgh Post Gazette*, and a dietitian who became director of all of Kaufmann's dining services. So despite the message over the entrance to the building, the college tried to do for women what engineering did for men.
Lois (Shoop) Fowler
General Studies '47
Professor of English, Emerita

I began in Fine Arts at Carnegie Tech. In my sophomore year, I transferred to Margaret Morrison, where I got excellent career preparation in Business Studies. After marrying a Fine Arts grad, I completed a master's degree in English at West Virginia University where he was working. I taught business in high school, and later went on to teach for many years at WVU.
Mary Lou (Campbell) Clarkson
Business Studies '40

After graduating from college, I returned and obtained my master's in Social Work from MMCC. Although I married and had four children, I had a long and rewarding experience as a professional social worker until my retirement at the age of 69. I only wish that my 16-year-old granddaughter, Natalie, can have a well-rounded education that will help her grow—such as I had during my years at MMCC. Needless to say, like my grandmother, I am encouraging Natalie to find her own rewarding, professional place in the world.
Catherine (Kinley) Sillins
Social Work '44, M '47

I remember how daring it was for Margaret Morrison girls to take classes with the engineering students in "their" building. I took Commercial Law there, not really expecting to learn a lot about that subject, but expecting a real charge from being in a class with so many males. It was also a big lift to have engineers come to Margaret Morrison classes; ostensibly they came to study languages.
Ruth (Siegle) Easley
Business Studies '38

A classmate of mine was a brilliant mathematician. She wanted to take more advanced classes in math and science, so she appealed to the dean for permission to take these classes in Engineering and Science. The answer was unequivocally "no." After she graduated, she entered graduate school and later became a full professor of mathematics at the University of Manchester in England.
Reva (Lipman) Swartz
Nursing Education '38

I thoroughly enjoyed Margaret Morrison. It was very difficult. I did secretarial work for a department head while in college, and that kept me busy. I was thrilled to get to $15 a month. I applied it all to my tuition because things were difficult with the Depression and I had sisters at the University of Pittsburgh.
Charlotte (Savage) Friedheim
Household Economics '38

I entered MMCC on the GI Bill after active duty in the WAVES, where I taught sailors how to use a special device for anti-aircraft guns. I was a commuting student, trying my best to help my parents, and studying in the evenings. I fondly remember some outstanding professors: Miss Ethel Spencer, who was also my advisor, Austin Wright, and Fred Sochatoff.
Rosalyn Mervis
General Studies '50

I was a freshman student enrolled in the Secretarial Studies Program, and as an elective, I chose the highest mathematics course offered in Margaret Morrison. To my disappointment, I had studied most of what the course offered in high school and ended up tutoring many of my classmates. Since I was not registered as a science major, I was not permitted to take math courses in the engineering school. I went to Dean Edith Winchester to ask her if there was some way I could take advanced math courses without switching majors. She went to bat for me. The head of the Math Department agreed to let me take solid geometry, and, if I made a C or better, admit me to a calculus course. Fortunately, I made the grade and was able to get the necessary math credits to become certified to teach high school math.
Sylvia (Linder) Mason,
Secretarial Studies '43

I commuted by bus and trolley car and sometimes it was very cold, but it was all worth it because I graduated with honors. I was also involved in the student government, was elected to Mortar Board, and then to Phi Kappa Phi, which was quite an honor for me. When I graduated, the dean sent a lovely letter to my father, which I still have, saying that they were proud of me. It's a nice thing to have.
Dorothy (Magnuson) Leeper-St. Clair
Costume Economics '38

A Bachelor of Science degree in English? Yes. That's what Margaret Morrison Carnegie College awarded me in 1947 through the General Studies program, with a minor in Secretarial Studies. Required subjects completed, I literally wrote my own schedule, taking every English and American literature course available on campus, many with superb faculty members such as Donald Goodfellow, Ethel Spenser, Norman Dawes, and Dr. Lee Gregg. I was able to take courses in both arts and engineering and work on several campus publications, receiving a first-rate liberal arts education with a touch of business training.
Mary (Keefer) Henneberger
English '47

I commuted from Avalon, one and a half hours each way, taking a streetcar and a bus; it gave me a chance to do some of my homework. I liked Dr. Fred Sochatoff very much; he taught comparative literature. It was a very happy time in my life. In order not to run out of money, I completed my degree in three years. Then I was able to study for another year at Carnegie Library School for my M.L.S. After graduation, I came here to New York and worked in the New York Public Library and elsewhere, being active in the New York Library Club.
Eve Thurston
General Studies '50
M.L.S., Carnegie Library School '51

"And the whole wonderful idea came to me during a home-management lecture at Margaret Morrison."

Memories:
Pot Pourri

The weekly tea dances attracted fellows from Pitt. I met my first husband, Herman Laub, at a tea dance. At our big formal dances, we enjoyed big bands led by Glen Miller, Tommy Dorsey, and Harry James. Of course we enjoyed Spring Carnival, Scotch 'n' Soda, and performances in the Drama Department. Between classes we would study in the MM library located in the Hut, often falling asleep because we had studied late at night. MM once had a talent show in the fourth floor rec hall, and I was part of a quartet that sang "Blue Moon."
Louise (McCullough) Laub
Secretarial Studies '41

THE UNIVERSITY GRILL
The Only Place with a TECH Atmosphere

A VARIETY OF LUNCHEONS AND DINNERS
Meet Me at the Grill
4605 FORBES STREET

Carnival to Open With Dorsey's "Sweet Swing"
Orchestra Features Frank Sinatra
Plus Harmony Quartet
The Carnegie Tartan Tuesday, April 23, 1941

The year 1942 was a magical time when I began my freshman year at Tech. In addition to CIT students, the campus was host to several diverse groups of service men, such as French naval officers and ASTP trainees. I wish I could say that my thoughts were always on academic life, but they were not. My recollections of that first fall on campus include dancing in the gym to Artie Shaw's band, meeting friends at Skibo, or lunching in the Beanery. I remember falling in love week after week when I was a freshman. For a young girl, it was a magical year in a magical place.
Anne (Sweeney) Hasley
General Studies '46

I loved everything about college. Dorm life was great. I felt I belonged! Being called to CWENS and Mortar Board. Welcoming incoming freshmen as president of Margaret Morrison Senate. Being part of Scotch 'n' Soda. Best of all, being blessed with a roommate like Genevieve "Gee Gee" (Straessley) Kopriva.
Mary (Yorke) Gibson
Home Economics '38

One of the funniest things was the dinkies all freshmen had to wear. They were beanies, but they were scotch plaid and had yellow tassels. Everyone knew you were a freshman. That caused lots of conversation.
Marjorie (Aronson) Ravick
Home Economics/Retailing '49

Since our dorm, Birch Hall, only housed nineteen, a dorm advisor, and the housemother, Mrs. Wilson, we certainly were destined to become a close-knit group. Our livingroom was quite spacious, and to my delight we even had a piano. This was a bonus for me while I was learning to play bridge during our "captivity" after dinner. When I was dummy, I excused myself from the table to pursue another challenge. To the chagrin of my new friends, I struggled for many weeks to play "Stardust," a top tune on the Hit Parade at that time.
Barbara (Miller) Trellis
Home/Costume Economics '51

Memories of Tech, '35–'39. Gathering before the fireplace at the Grill just to talk or after the agony of the blue books. Field hockey on the Cut. Study and research at the Hut, Tech's library. Christmas chapel at Kresge Theater. Men's spring panty raids on Forbes Hall, and our housemother Mrs. Patty's concern. Dances at the gym and the big bands at Spring Carnival.
Ruth (Lauffer) Cost
Home/Costume Economics '39

My World History class met on the Tuesday, Thursday, Saturday schedule. One cold Saturday morning, a large, brown dog wandered into class and made himself comfortable in the front of the room. The professor proceeded with his lecture, but midway through it, the dog began to snore. We giggled; the professor stopped for a moment; then he went on as professors do no matter what.
Ruth (Steinman) Blumberg
Household Economics '43

For the King of Hearts campaign in 1950, Wes Kenney and his supporters, running for the Independents, ingeniously placed a mattress on top of the Margaret Morrison peristyle where Wes vowed to stay, day and night, until the election. All of us were amused, entertained, and amazed at this election gimmick. He did have covert substitutes, although we never knew it at the time. Of course, he won the contest and reigned happily as King.
Patricia (Snedden) Drischell
Secretarial Studies '51

I can still see the smoking room at MMCC, so packed with gals we could hardly move and smoke so thick it was all a blue haze. Can we imagine this today!?
Carolyn (Smith) Leighton
Costume Economics '43

I had an interesting job as an interviewer for a psychology professor, who was writing a paper on drinking habits. Two of us students went together to question upper-income-level people on what they drank and when. There were definitely milk drinkers and heavy liquor drinkers. This was a high-paying job—I got $1 per interview.
Helen Pollis
Business Studies '45

When I went there, it was during the war and most men were still gone and didn't start returning to campus until 1946. So we'd see lots of movies. We dyed and bleached lots of heads of hair. We bleached me blond, with regular peroxide and ammonia. What did we know? The solution was so strong that when they tipped my head backwards so they could sponge the stuff into my hair, it bubbled the paint on the window sill.
June (Haskell) Farrahy
Costume Economics '48

And then came the turning point of my life. My 'big sister' Pat (Hoyer) Horine and I walked over to the Skibo. In walks Pat's boyfriend and his ATO fraternity brothers. I had been a very quiet, shy, reserved high school student. Never dated. The ATOs included me in all their Rush Week activities and I began dating, received my first kiss, made many new friends. Had a ball.
Sandra (Hammers) Samuelson
Home Economics '57

While I was the cook for a week in the Home Management House, I made pea soup in a pressure cooker, and it blew up. I cut classes all day to clean soup from the stove and ceiling.
Mary (Sperring) Davis
Foods and Nutrition '54

Scotch 'n' Soda's 1950 "Too Much"

As a freshman, I thought the dorm cafeterias gave small portions of food and I seemed to be always hungry. So every night we freshman were allowed out of the dorm for 45 minutes between 7:30 and 10:00, and my engineer boyfriend would take me to Scottie's Diner for two poached eggs on toast. He figured he had so much invested in me that he married me.
Dorothy (Gerlach) Nemy
Home Economics Education '54

It was my sister Margaretha (Lang) Neu, now deceased, who encouraged me to enter Carnegie Tech. She told this story many times. She was a Home Ec major in teacher training, and all seniors had to spend six weeks in the Home Management House. Her turn came in March at the time of the '36 flood in Pittsburgh. Miss Abbott, the professor, made the girls fill all the bathtubs with water for emergencies and wouldn't let them take baths. So one girl would keep Miss Abbott busy while another would take a bath and then fill the tub again.
Margaretha (Lang) Neu
Home Economics '36
Submitted by her sister
Jeanne (Lang) Schlicht
Textile Research '49

THESE ARE WOMAN'S HIGH PREROGATIVES ❧ ... AND INSPIRE THE HOME ❧ TO LESSEN SUFFERING AND INCREASE HAPPINESS ❧ TO AID MANKIND IN ITS UPWARD STRUGGLES ❧ TO ENOBLE AND ADORN LIFE'S WORK HOWEVER HUMBLE ❧

Chapter 5

1956–73

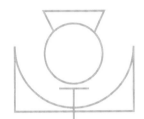

Phasing Out
Margaret Morrison

Margaret Morrison Carnegie College engaged in a losing struggle to survive in the face of increasing societal and institutional odds during the seventeen years of the Margaret LeClair and Erwin Steinberg deanships. Far-reaching changes in the roles of women in society marked these years. For example, several national studies focused attention on the changing roles of women in both the workforce and the family, and women students turned increasingly to careers in the liberal arts and sciences. Rather than focusing on homemaking as a profession, home economists increasingly emphasized research in their disciplines. Research in the field, however, required many faculty members trained as researchers and expensive laboratories filled with new equipment. Public colleges offered both the space and the research opportunities—and at lower tuition costs to students—posing a threat to the home economics programs at Margaret Morrison.

Changing circumstances at Carnegie Tech and in nearby colleges also challenged Margaret Morrison. The rapid rise to national prominence of the Graduate School of Industrial Administration (GSIA) increased the already important role of research at Tech. Margaret Morrison's attempts to develop a business program that would meet GSIA's high standards failed, a threat to another Margaret Morrison professional program. In addition, local colleges opened two-year secretarial studies departments that cost far less than Tech. The steady increase in enrollment in the natural sciences and general studies persuaded Tech's administrators to merge Margaret Morrison's science programs with those in engineering and science and to develop both a Bachelor of Arts degree in the liberal arts and sciences and new graduate programs in these fields. Then in 1967, Carnegie Tech merged with the Mellon Institute of Science to form Carnegie Mellon University, with an independent College of Humanities and Social Sciences. Once students in science, the humanities and the social sciences were incorporated into the new university structure, Margaret Morrison was left with two departments—Business Studies and Home Economics—both diminishing steadily in number and with a faculty near retirement age and largely uninvolved in research. After almost a full decade of study, Carnegie Mellon decided to phase out its women's college. Chapter 5 analyzes these developments.

Women to Fill More Jobs Here

"A record number of women will swell the nation's labor force in coming years," Dr. Erwin R. Steinberg said yesterday, and he added: "Most of them will be highly educated women with special skills. Society will have to make some radical adjustments to use them effectively." Dr. Steinberg is dean of Margaret Morrison Carnegie College, the women's division of Carnegie Institute of Technology, which is sponsoring a nationwide meeting on the changing role of women in the United States. Dr. Steinberg said more women are getting jobs because they are marrying earlier, having children at an earlier age, and are free of the responsibilities by the time they're in their early forties.
—Henry W. Pierce for the *Pittsburgh Post Gazette*, May 16, 1964

A Balanced Program

The chief implications of the changing pattern of women's lives for their educations are these: a reaffirmation of the values of a liberal education, the obligation of the college to include preparation for a job in the undergraduate curriculum, and the need to strengthen our counseling and guidance services. All the arguments for a liberal education gain cogency when applied to the woman as wife, mother and citizen. Since the fact of central importance for most women is their contribution to the family, primary emphasis during college years should be placed on a balanced program in the humanities, sciences, and social sciences.
—Margaret F. LeClair, "The Girl, the School, and the World," *Carnegie Alumnus,* September 1959, p. 7

The Societal Setting

In 1957, a year after Margaret LeClair became dean of Margaret Morrison, the National Manpower Council published *Womanpower,* a report that focused on the changing roles of women and their present and future contributions to the labor market. It trumpeted one major conclusion: women were an indispensable source of both manpower and brainpower outside the home. *Womanpower* spurred society's growing interest in the status of women and their vocational roles. It implied that if women were to combine marriage, families and careers, they and their husbands and children would need to change family patterns. It also recommended a new emphasis on volunteer activities by women. Six years later, The Report of the President's Commission on the Status of Women reinforced the conclusions of the earlier report.

In an article published in 1965 that drew on these and similar studies, Dean Erwin Steinberg called attention to the changes in roles that typical college-educated women would face in the future:

Age range
21–22 graduation from college
21–23 employment, marriage
22–30 child bearing
22–40 child rearing; community volunteer work
38–45 part-time employment;
*   community volunteer work*
40–   full-time employment

This profile suggested that, instead of focusing heavily on courses to prepare women for immediate employment, college education for women should emphasize the intellectual skills, information and self-esteem that would be useful as they entered the full-time labor market 20 years later. A sound education should also prepare women for their roles as wives and mothers and for additional roles as volunteers in community organizations. Finally, excellent education should prepare women to continue learning both informally and in future work in colleges if they decided in their forties to catch up with developments that had taken place during the 20 or so years since they graduated.

Both Dean LeClair and Dean Steinberg took these reports seriously. The reports also indicated trends in the choice of major fields of study for women, trends that had already become evident at Margaret Morrison and were destined to escalate sharply.

These trends also had clear implications for a new program at Margaret Morrison. In the spring of 1961, the administration sponsored a survey of Margaret Morrison alumnae to determine if they wished to return to campus for professional or graduate study on a full-time or part-time basis. The findings revealed that many MMCC alumnae, like women nationwide, were entering a second work cycle to renew skills, acquire new ones, or enhance intellectual and cultural growth. Beginning in 1962, alumnae began to meet with faculty members to work out individual programs suited to their needs, particularly in home economics, business studies, technical writing, or teaching. Margaret Morrison was responding to new societal needs. In a decade, the program attracted 136 students, many of whom earned M.S. degrees, but decreasing enrollments and the decision to phase out Margaret Morrison ended the program in 1973.

The Administration

The appointment of Dr. Margaret LeClair as Dean of Margaret Morrison in 1956 marks a turning point in the history of the college. A member of the English Department, she was a distinguished scholar who had won the Dustin Prize in Short Story and Essay Writing, the Wheeler Prize in Poetry, and the Slocum Prize in Scholarship. She had joined the Carnegie Tech English

Right:
Dean Margaret LeClair

Courses Scheduled, 1960

	BIOLOGICAL SCIENCES	BUSINESS STUDIES	HOME EC	TOTAL
Electives	0	2	2	4
15 students or over	4	9	15	28
Under 15 students	5	2	8	15
TOTALS	**9**	**13**	**25**	**47**

Department in 1946 and had been head of Margaret Morrison's Department of General Studies since 1955. In 1960 when she resigned the deanship to accept an appointment elsewhere, Tech chose a promising scholar, Dr. Erwin Steinberg, as head of General Studies. He had also been a member of the English Department since he joined the faculty in 1946. Both deans brought with them aspirations and standards derived from their long associations with scholars from the wider university. In 1958, Betty Jane Lloyd of the Department of Secretarial Studies became assistant to the dean, then assistant dean (1963–71), and finally associate dean, a position she held until her retirement in 1983.

Before she left the campus in 1960, Dean LeClair submitted to President Warner a careful study of class size in three Margaret Morrison departments, showing that one-third of its classes had fewer than 15 students enrolled.

In order to remedy this situation, she estimated that the optimal enrollment at Margaret Morrison would have to total about 630 students. Given the attrition rates of the first three years, the senior enrollment would then total 137, ideally distributed as follows: Biological Sciences, 15; Business Studies, 25; Foods and Nutrition, 24; Home Economics Education, 24; Clothing and Textiles, 24; and General Studies, 25. These

enrollment figures would require additional faculty in Home Economics Education and Biological Sciences. General Studies would present no problem, she argued, since it was expanding rapidly and was taught by faculty from the Division of Humanistic and Social Studies. Here was another warning shot across the bow; as it had been for many years, enrollment in the professional options at Margaret Morrison was too low.

John C. Warner was Carnegie Tech's president from 1950 to 1965 when Horton Guyford Stever succeeded him. After receiving the report from Dean LeClair, Warner appointed a commission in 1960 to make recommendations about the future of Margaret Morrison. Its members, all men, included only one Margaret Morrison faculty member, Erwin Steinberg, the head of the Department of General Studies and soon to be Margaret Morrison's dean. In a memorandum entitled "The Future Development of Margaret Morrison Carnegie College," Warner noted that entering SAT scores of Margaret Morrison students were improving steadily and that their grades were higher

Professional Training

To provide a woman with a good general, liberal education and at the same time prepare her to do something useful are not mutually exclusive goals. Indeed professional training, approached in the fundamental way the Carnegie Plan calls for, can and should be an essential part of a liberal education.
—John C. Warner, "The Future Development of Margaret Morrison Carnegie College," unpublished paper, p. 2

Top:
The dean's office

Bottom:
Jake Warner with Campus Queens

than those of Engineering and Science students in joint classes. He recommended the development of Bachelor of Arts degrees in the humanities and the social and natural sciences. These new degrees should have clear professional, as well as liberal-general, education components. The difference between this degree and the Bachelor of Science, he wrote, should be one of kind and level not of standards or quality. Simultaneously, he declared, both Home Economics and Business Studies should re-define their professional and liberal-general studies programs.

Warner identified several short-run implications of these plans, designed overall to develop Margaret Morrison into "a front-rank college with a unique program for women's liberal-professional education." They included special efforts to recruit more students of even better quality, finding ways to reduce the large number of classes with enrollments under 15, and instituting joint appointments with the Division of Human-istic and Social Studies, the College of Engineering and Science, and the College of Fine Arts. Warner was attempting to reform Margaret Morrison in an attempt to save the college.

MORTAR BOARD

Who Were the Students?

The data in the accompanying table dramatize the changes taking place in the Margaret Morrison student body. Except for graduate work in home economics educa-tion, the number graduating in both Home Economics and Secretarial/Business Studies declined more or less steadily while enroll-ment of both undergraduate and graduate students in General Studies/Humanities rose dramatically. By 1969, the year that Tech made the decision to phase out Marga-ret Morrison, the undergraduate enrollment had fallen to 114 in Home Economics and 31 in Business Studies. This small enrollment produced a large number of small classes. This distribution pattern meant that most classes beyond the common freshman year enrolled fewer than 15 students, some fewer than ten. The two Margaret Morrison pro-fessional disciplines were no longer attract-ing enough students to sustain their pro-grams at reasonable cost to the university.

The quality of Margaret Morrison's student body, however, had increased stead-ily. For example, median scores on the SAT exam for entering freshmen rose from 915 in 1956 to 1,164 in 1964. Students in science had the highest scores, followed by those in the humanities. Margaret Morrison had raised its admission standards through-out this period.

CHANGING ENROLLMENT 1956–73

	1956–57	1957–58	1958–59	1959–60	1960–61	1961–62	1962–63	1963–64	1964–65	1965–66	1966–67	1967–68	1968–69	1969–70	1970–71	1971–72	1972–73
HOME ECONOMICS																	
Undergraduate	205	139	149	144	141	113	131	106	119	117	NA	144	114	122	78	42	15
Graduate								1	4	6	NA	30	30	52	23	20	5
SECRETARIAL/BUSINESS																	
Undergraduate	116	68	72	49	60	122	113	116	138	129	146	25	31	30	21	13	3
Graduate												8					
ALL SCIENCES & MATH													Transferred to E&S				
Undergraduate	41	25	25	34	40	75	58	68	74	69	63	63					
Graduate						5	3	1	11	5	8	6					
GENERAL STUDIES/HUMANITIES														After Joining H&SS			
Undergraduate	112	102	106	101	134	193	212	180	232	226	255	286	462	562	586	683	689
Graduate									58	62	91	181	174	206	186	183	194

PHI KAPPA PHI

UNDERGRADUATE ENROLLMENT
HOME ECONOMICS AND BUSINESS, 1968–69

	FRESH	SOPH	JR	SR	GRAD	SPEC
Business Studies	7	4	10	9	0	1
Foods and Nutrition	5	5	6	0	1	0
Home Ec. Education	6	10	13	14	30	0
Textiles & Clothing	16	13	8	11	0	0

This improvement in entering scores rapidly improved performance in the classroom. Although verbal scores in MMCC trailed verbal scores in E&S, MMCC students earned grades from a third to a half grade higher than their E&S peers in classes where students from the two colleges were mixed.

Dean Steinberg's Annual Report for 1964–65, p. 23, summarized the situation succinctly.

Obviously, MMCC is getting a different kind of student from the kind it attracted ten or eleven years ago. Their interests are broader and less narrowly vocational, they are smarter and better prepared (in some areas they are even out-performing the E&S students), they come from a much higher socio-economic stratum in society, they have higher aspiration levels, and they tend to be urban in background and relatively sophisticated.

This "different kind of student" preferred the liberal arts to either home economics or business.

Among this "different kind of student" were 125 graduate students attending Master of Science and Master of Arts degree programs newly opened in 1965—in home economics education, natural sciences, history, and English. Forty-two of the 125 were men. Previously, of course, Margaret Morrison had a graduate degree program in Social Work with 40 of 92 degrees granted in the 1946–53 period going to men.

When Margaret Morrison was phased out in 1973, the master's program for Home Economics Education closed. The master's programs in English and history were transferred to the new College of Humanities and Social Sciences and the degree in natural sciences to the appropriate departments in the Mellon College of Science. There they all remain, a legacy of Margaret Morrison Carnegie College.

Student Life

Carnegie Tech women from both Margaret Morrison and Fine Arts spent much of their leisure time in the company of Tech men. The names of thousands of Tech couples appear on the alumni rolls. No surprise there. Getting to the altar, however, involved overcoming or avoiding a galaxy of obstacles. In an article in the September 12, 1958 *Tartan*, a student, Dave Kamons, gave the following advice on this matter to men and women students alike.

Naturally every guy's first thought is the girls in Morewood Fortress. There are all kinds of little problems in logistics involved: having no car, no money, and/or no names, addresses and phone numbers being most common. Transportation problems are eased with the help of Pittsburgh's Finest Bus Line. Oakland (go to Warner Hall, turn left, keep walking) is just a stroll away. Shadyside, Pittsburgh's own Village, and Squirrel Hill also make a convenient walk. There's nothing like a quiet stroll to establish that vital rapport.

Finding a girl requires more ingenuity. The Orientation Committee provides the initial push with the Freshman Mixer. The man with real guts may even pick a phone number at random from the C-Book and take his chances. The entire procedure isn't necessarily recommended, but anything is better than cuddling with a Calc book.

"Turfing" in Schenley Park

Inciting the Boys to Action

Incited either by a lack of anything better to do or perhaps, as Dean Ellis put it, by spring fever, or maybe as a protest against the impending tuition raise, a small group of highly imaginative Carnegie Tech freshmen attempted a panty raid on Morewood Gardens. [Administrators] aided by the Security Police somehow managed to keep the students across the street. The girls, however, apparently disapproved of these measures because they were inciting the boys to action by throwing various articles of lingerie out the windows, lowering ropes, and [indulging in] other pleasantries.
Carnegie Tartan, April 22, 1964, p.1

Top:
Panty raid

Bottom:
Lounge in Morewood
Gardens

The girls have it easy. All you have to do is sit back and wait for the phone to ring. In an average evening there will be about fifteen minutes total time when someone isn't already on the phone, giving something like a one-in-twenty-five chance of a call getting through. And there are fraternity mixers, and those evil, evil fraternity men perched like vultures across the street. If you really want to be well-known on Fraternity Row, don't close your curtains, a formula guaranteed not to fail.

Privacy on a date is the number one premium. Donner and Morewood lounges are comfortable and nice in an institutional way, but they're fishbowls. The obvious solution is Schenley Park. On a warm, dry evening, turfing under the stars and smog is great.

Curfew at Morewood is the best time of all. No girls should miss the hundred yard dash to the sign-out book. The most popular feature of curfew time is the traditional Super-Kiss. Starting time is shortly after the five-minute warning bell rings.

The prime center of activity during the long year is the Skibo snack bar. The name of the game is people watching. The total scene can go on forever: TGIF on Skibo Patio, underground flicks, even demonstrations. But the real scene is more the attitude than the action. Everything has the potential for being ridiculous. Get involved, but occasionally step back, realize what you're doing, and laugh.

Some dormitory regulations attempted to ban, or at least restrict, the high jinks that enlivened student life, high jinks such as panty raids. Here are regulations under

Section D, Courtesies, from the *1966 Residence Hall Handbook*, a new edition prepared by the Association of Women Students.

Courtesies: Tech coeds should not call or talk out of windows. When being serenaded, the women [should] turn off all lights, then open curtains and listen quietly as a courtesy to the serenaders.

Demonstrations: If an unruly demonstration [such as a panty raid] should occur. All windows should be closed and blinds pulled. Encouragement of a demonstration from the windows is considered participation.

Blinds: Out of respect for yourself, all blinds should be down when you are dressing.

Dormitory regulations governed many aspects of the lives of women students. They specified quiet hours for study (Sunday–Thursday, 7:30 p.m.–8:00 a.m.; Friday–Saturday, 11:00 p.m.–9:00 a.m.) The dorm closed at 12:30 a.m. during the week and at 1:30 a.m. on Saturdays and Sundays. The rules made exceptions for "specials," cultural specials, overnights, and holidays. Women who violated these hours were subjected to one of three sets of penalties: violations that resulted in an automatic penalty, violations that resulted in a notice to appear before the Judicial Council, and violations that resulted in a written warning. For example, women had to appear before the Judicial Council for a large number of violations including:
Possession of intoxicating liquor in the hall. This is strictly prohibited. (Furthermore, beer is not permitted for a hair setting lotion.)

Coming in late resulted by far in the largest number of appearances before the Judicial Council composed of dorm residents. Cars broke down frequently, flat tires occurred at an alarming rate, and the watches of dates were often inaccurate, according to these hearings.

In 1964, Tech commissioned a careful study of both its housing for students and the regulations governing student behavior.

Proper dress in the dining room: Good grooming and neat appearance are expected at all meals. Dresses and heels are required at the Sunday noon meal and special dinners. Pin curls may be worn under a scarf to meals in the Blue

Room on Friday and Saturday nights. Food must be removed from trays at noon Sunday and at evening meals.

As a result of this study, a set of recommendations made its way through the bureaucracy and were approved by President Stever in 1965. Morewood's A Tower became an honor tower with minimal regulations for seniors, women students over 21 were permitted to live off campus if they had their parents' permission, and several floors of Morewood were set aside so that members of the same sorority could live together. In later years, similar privileges were extended to a larger proportion of women students.

These developments culminated in Tech's first adventure into co-ed housing after a vigorous campaign by both the men's and women's dormitory organizations. In 1969, 80 men and 32 women applied for places in Welch Hall. A student committee chose 33 men and 21 women from MMCC and CFA—the ratio of men to women on campus—and the experiment began in 1970 with no particular fanfare and no significant problems. The same regulations governed men and women in Welch Hall, the first example of equal treatment of the sexes in living conditions on campus.

Outside of dormitory life, there was much to do. Every year, students elected women to reign as queens at three events: Homecoming, Spring Carnival, and the Military Ball. In most years, seven freshmen competed for Homecoming Queen. They made a round of appearances at men's dormitories and fraternity houses to solicit votes. Sororities presented skits at the fraternities to campaign for their candidates for Carnival Queen. Only ROTC members could vote for the women sorority members nominated for queen of the Military Ball. *The Tartan* always carried a page of photos of the nominees.

Sororities dominated competitions at Spring Carnival. In addition to building booths for the midway, they usually competed in three events held on the quadrangle between Engineering and Administration (later Baker) Halls. The broom pull featured one girl sitting on the straw at the end of a broom while her partner pulled her by the

broom handle to the finish line. For the bottle roll, contestants placed tongue depressors in their mouths and used them to roll a large glass bottle. Finally, the sack race featured contestants hopping along— or falling down—in burlap bags.

The Women's Athletic Association provided coaches and scheduling for intramural contests in nine sports. Women's teams competed with similar clubs from Chatham, Pitt, Westminster, Indiana (Pennsylvania), Slippery Rock, Geneva, Grove City, and Seton Hill.

Women found lots to do on and off campus. A column, "This Week in Pittsburgh" appeared in every issue of *The Tartan*. It listed lectures, plays and concerts on campus, and films, symphony concerts, art exhibits, lectures, and professional sports events in the city. The administration encouraged women to attend cultural events by relaxing curfew hours.

Top:
1960 Military Ball at Hotel Webster Hall

Bottom:
Sorority high jinks at Spring Carnival

Top:
The new Skibo

Center:
Scotch 'n' Soda
program cover
circa 1960

Bottom:
Dancing barefoot
was fun.

Many organizations offered activities that appealed to a wide range of student interests. They included publications, such as *The Tartan* and *The Thistle,* and governmental bodies, such as the Student Council and the Women's Dormitory Council. There were dozens of clubs, including Cameron Choir; the Debate Club; Cwens; Mortar Board; Scotch 'n' Soda; the Home Economics Club; the Film Arts Society; both conservative and liberal political organizations; and Protestant, Catholic, Jewish, and non-sectarian religious organizations. Most of them were open to membership by both men and women, offering Margaret Morrison women a chance to both learn and socialize with students from throughout the campus.

On Friday, September 21, 1962, Tech held the first of its weekly TGIF dances in the ballroom of the new Skibo building on the edge of the Cut. Groups composed of Tech students and bands from the city played every Friday. Organized as a way to let off steam, TGIF soon became an institution beloved by undergraduate and graduate students alike as well as by students from nearby high schools who eventually became so numerous that they were banned.

Sororities played major roles in the lives of a minority of Margaret Morrison students. In 1963, for example, 265 out of Carnegie Tech's total enrollment of 923 women—more than half from Margaret Morrison—belonged to one of Tech's seven sororities, where they were joined by women from the College of Fine Arts. Sorority events provided dramatic moments throughout the year: rushing in the fall; frequent parties and dances, often with fraternities; weekly sorority meetings; skits to campaign for queen candidates; participation in Greek Sing and Greek Swing; formal dances on campus and in nearby hotels; and, of course, spring carnival with its booths, the midway, sorority competitions on the mall, and party after party. A spirit of sisterhood bound all these activities together and provided a warm and supportive environment in which a relatively small group of women students could get to know each other well and form bonds that often lasted for a lifetime. Lifetime bonds also formed between Greek men and women, symbolized when sorority members began to wear fraternity pins symbolic of serious relationships.

Facilities

By 1956, Morewood Gardens was filled to capacity and 15 students were forced to commute until space became available. The growing number of women students in both Margaret Morrison and Fine Arts seeking campus housing reached crisis proportions in the late 1950s. Therefore, Tech decided to tear down three old houses on Forbes Avenue that had been acquired in 1946 when Tech bought Morewood Gardens. In that space, Tech built a seven-story addition to Morewood Gardens that provided dormitory rooms for 220 women as well as 22 small apartments for faculty or students.

In 1963, Tech purchased the Colonial Apartments on Fifth Avenue, which provided 24 apartments for women students. In 1966, however, Tech tore down the Colonial Apartments and leased the space they had occupied to public television station WQED. To compensate for lost rooms, the Woodlawn Apartments at the corner of Forbes Avenue and Margaret Morrison Street were turned into a women's dormitory. With new housing at last available, Tech tore down the remaining houses along Margaret Morrison and Forbes Streets that had served as dormitories for Margaret Morrison women.

Tech also made dramatic improvements to the Margaret Morrison building. Then during 1958 and 1959, Dean LeClair and the department heads made a study of facilities needs that resulted in a plan for a new L-shaped wing that covered the north and part of the east walls of the building. Finished in 1962 at a cost of $800,000, this wing provided space for the nursery school, 11 new offices, three new classrooms, and six laboratories. A new entrance on the north side provided access to the building from the Forbes Avenue parking lots and completed the exterior wall that had been left unfinished when the building was erected a half century earlier. Except for research laboratories, Margaret Morrison's educational facilities had been brought up to date, another attempt to save the college.

Margaret Morrison students began to utilize two major campus renovations when they were finished in the early 1960s. In 1961 the old Skibo or Commons that had begun life as the Langley Laboratory of Aeronautics was torn down to make room for Hunt Library, a gift from Mr. and Mrs. Roy A. Hunt. Old Skibo was replaced by a new building of the same name located near Forbes Avenue. It provided dining facilities and a variety of rooms for student use, including a ballroom, the site for many years of TGIF dances enjoyed by a generation of Carnegie Tech students. Tech was becoming more attractive to prospective students.

The Faculty

Figures do not tell the whole story, but they do provide a capsule history of the faculty during these years. In 1956, the Margaret Morrison faculty numbered 26; by 1969, when the decision to close Margaret Morrison was made, it numbered 18. During the LeClair years, about half the courses taken by Margaret Morrison students were taught by faculty from other parts of the institution, particularly the Division of Humanistic and Social Studies and the College of Engineering and Science. By 1969, faculty from other colleges taught two-thirds of the MMCC courses.

In 1957–58, Margaret Morrison faculty listed a total of 12 publications for the year, eight of them by Erwin Steinberg. In 1969, the records list nine publications, two by Dean Steinberg, four by Beekman Cottrell, a member of the English faculty, one by Phillip Saunders, an economist, and three by members of the Home Economics and Business faculties. In 1956, only three members of the MMCC faculty held a doctoral degree. The proportion of faculty members with doctorates increased steadily through this period, partly because an increasing proportion of the faculty were joint appointments or transfers into Margaret Morrison from other colleges. On the other hand, few members of the Home Economics and Secretarial/Business Departments, who were tenured as associate professors, had earned their doctorates. Several attempts to hire talented young faculty failed because both industry and public colleges provided higher salaries, better laboratories, and greater research opportunities than Margaret Morrison. As the rest of Carnegie Tech increasingly emphasized research and graduate study, particularly after 1967 when Tech became Carnegie Mellon, Margaret Morrison's dwindling faculty seemed increasingly out of step.

Top:
Hugh D. Young, Head, Natural Sciences and Dean Erwin Steinberg

Bottom:
Melva B. Bakkie, Head, Home Economics and Elsie L. Leffingwell, Head, Business and Social Studies

Faculty Needed

PUBLICATIONS BY MMCC FACULTY, 1955-56 TO 1967-68

Year	No. of Faculty Publishing	No. of Publications
1955-56	2	4
1956-57	3	6
1957-58	3	12
1958-59	4	7
1959-60	6	12
1960-61	3	7
1961-62	9	16
1962-63	10	25
1963-64	9	18
1964-65	8	20
1965-66	7	18
1966-67	9	4
1967-68	9	6

As the reminiscences from alumnae in this volume attest, Margaret Morrison's faculty members maintained their reputations as excellent and caring teachers. These reminiscences praise the personal attention that faculty lavished on their students, a trait that resulted both from small classes and the values that motivated faculty members, who saw themselves as teachers and not research scholars. The reminiscences also stress the high standards that characterized the faculty both in their academic work and in the models they set for students to emulate.

In addition to their teaching, faculty members participated widely in a number of professional and community endeavors. In 1962–63, the dean's Annual Report indicates that faculty members gave 48 talks to professional organizations; organized and held five conferences at Carnegie Tech; held 29 offices or committee memberships in professional organizations; attended 41 additional professional meetings or conferences; participated in 47 college, campus or community activities; and served as consultants to 13 institutions.

Attempts to encourage research among tenured faculty, however, were only marginally successful. In 1958, Dean LeClair retained Dr. Catherine Personius of Cornell University as a consultant on research to the Home Economics Department. During two long sessions in March and April, she discussed research procedures with the staff and helped to redesign nine individual projects. Only Alberta Dodson seems to have produced publishable research despite this encouragement.

During the early 1960s, Margaret Morrison began a program of research on the role of educated women in American society. The three major researchers were Dr. Sonia Gold, a joint appointment between GSIA and MMCC's Business and Social Studies; Dr. Shirley Angrist, a sociologist; and Assistant Dean Betty Jane Lloyd. Much of this work was supported by a grant from the Scaife Foundation. This research produced a number of publications, but plans based on them to establish a permanent research center with funding from the Office of Education never materialized, particularly after Professor Gold resigned to follow her husband to Cleveland. "Three barely make a 'critical mass,'" Dean Steinberg wrote. "Two do not."

Discussions about the future of Margaret Morrison took place throughout the 1960s. This process soon revealed that six of the seven tenured members of the departments that were once known as Home Economics and Secretarial Studies would all have reached retirement age by 1973. Replacing them with young, vigorous teacher/researchers would have been exceedingly difficult and expensive, particularly in the light of falling student numbers. Margaret Morrison's core faculty was slowly fading away.

Right:
Taking shorthand

The Curriculum and Departmental Organization

Departmental organization was in constant flux between 1956 and 1973. Margaret Morrison had four departments whose students studied for the Bachelor of Science degree when Margaret LeClair became dean in 1956: Home Economics, Secretarial Studies, General Studies, and Science. None of these departments offered graduate study. By 1966–67 these departments had been reorganized into Business and Social Studies, Home Economics, Humanities, and Natural Science. In the following year, they were reorganized again into two departments: Business and Resource Management, and Humanities and Natural Sciences. In 1968 the four science programs—biology, chemistry, mathematics and physics—were transferred to the Mellon College of Science, and English, modern languages, technical writing, history, economics and psychology entered the newly-formed College of Humanities and Social Sciences. This left four programs in Margaret Morrison: business studies and the three home economics specialties of foods and nutrition, textiles and clothing and home economics education in a skeletal Margaret Morrison Carnegie College.

Two additional developments complicated this situation. In 1963, Margaret Morrison started a Master of Science degree in Home Economics Education, a program designed to serve the needs of home economics teachers from the Pittsburgh area. Most candidates studied part-time during the

summer or in evening classes, and few funds were available for student support. The number of students enrolled grew substantially during the middle 1960s; 44 of them were able to graduate before the program was closed in 1973.

A second development in graduate education in Margaret Morrison was far more successful. Members of the History and English Departments had received grants to develop Advanced Placement programs—college-level courses taught in high schools —in English and history in local schools.

Building on the success of this program, both departments won grants to establish curriculum development centers in their disciplines. Each center developed a series of courses for able students in their fields, establishing the departments as national leaders in the curriculum reform efforts of the 1960s.

In 1965, they received a grant from the Fund for the Advancement of Education to develop Master of Arts programs in English and history for teachers. Within a few years, each program was thriving, supported by grants from the Department of Education that brought to campus both experienced and prospective teachers receiving both tuition grants and stipends. Finally, in 1967 Tech organized the Carnegie Education Center funded by a million dollar grant from the Ford Foundation and offering a new Doctor of Arts degree in humanities, the fine arts, and science. The national recognition that this new venture gained stood in sharp contrast to the problems plaguing graduate study in Margaret Morrison's professional departments.

Alumnae Affairs

In October 1958, seventeen members of the Margaret Morrison charter class met to celebrate their Golden Anniversary at Tech's homecoming celebration. They were regaled at both the President's Luncheon at Morewood Gardens and the Golden Anniversary dinner at the College Club. These 17 women, all in their seventies, represented the devotion of typical Margaret Morrison graduates to the school they loved. During the previous 16 years, Margaret Morrison

Faculty Qualified for Research

To compensate for the rather large proportion of teachers on indefinite tenure at the associate-professor level, from whom we can expect little if any productive scholarship, it is essential that we continue to fill such vacancies as occur with able teachers who are also qualified for research.
—*Margaret Morrison Carnegie College Annual Report,* 1957-58, p. 21

Top:
Counting calories

Bottom:
1957 Homecoming Queen, Janis Berg pins a chrysanthemum on Carnegie's first queen, Mrs. Josephine (Whitney) Dickman, '22.

Occupations of Margaret Morrison Alumnae, 1957-73

	Gen St	Home Ec	Business	Science
Secondary Education	82	92	23	6
College Faculty and Adm.	63	28	16	17
Executive/Owner/Mgt.	59	73	28	10
Business (not specified)	12	15	27	0
Secretaries	0	2	29	0
Dieticians	0	32	0	0
Science Company	0	0	0	25
Other	173	87	70	3

alumnae had ranked either first or second in the percentage of alumni contributing to the Annual Fund.

The *Carnegie Alumnus* carried accounts of alumni meetings in every issue. Maggie Murphs joined local Clans throughout the country and formed their own Women's Clan in Pittsburgh. In 1959 they celebrated their Golden Anniversary, having held their first meeting in 1909 as the Margaret Morrison Alumnae Association. In 1937, the Clan changed its name to the Pittsburgh Women's Clan and opened its membership to all women graduates. Each year during the 1950s and '60s, the Clan sponsored a number of functions in addition to its annual meetings: scholarship benefits, Dutch Treat luncheons, Thistle Scholarship bridge luncheons, Homecoming teas, and receptions honoring distinguished guests. Each year the Clan donated $1,500 in scholarship funds to support Margaret Morrison students. The Pittsburgh Women's Clan still exists, a legacy of Margaret Morrison Carnegie College.

The fiftieth reunion of the class of 1916.

Many Margaret Morrison alumnae from the 1957–73 period have had distinguished careers. Alumni records are incomplete regarding careers, but they contain information about the careers of 982 of these alumni: 389 General Studies; 329 Home Economics, 193 Business Studies, and 71 Sciences.

A few statistics stand out, particularly the large number of alumnae who chose careers in secondary or college teaching and administration. In some years during the 1960s, fully a third of Margaret Morrison graduates found jobs in the schools. Education had always been emphasized in the two professional schools, and this emphasis increased among general studies students, particularly after the curriculum projects in secondary school English and history began. The "other" category is also intriguing. Among the occupations listed are attorney, psychologist, pastor, realtor, writer, the armed forces, librarian, welfare worker, physician, accountant, banker, computer specialist, and insurance agent. The range of occupations was particularly broad among general studies graduates, many of whom went on to graduate study. Although we have few statistics, we know that the overwhelming majority of these women were married and had children. Margaret Morrison was meeting its goals.

Tech Makes a Decision

In a memorandum to Vice President Edward Schatz, dated April 15, 1969, Dean Erwin Steinberg wrote:

"We have now reached the point where class sizes in the professional options are so small as to make these options an economic burden to the university. Furthermore, retirement patterns of the MMCC faculty now on tenure are such that, if they are to be replaced, five or six senior professors will have to be recruited in the next three or four years at considerable financial commitment if the professional options are to continue. The falling enrollment and the impending retirements suggest, therefore, that September of 1969 is the last time we

should accept students in business studies, foods and nutrition, textiles and clothing, and home economics education. Such a decision would mean that the last students on those options would graduate in June 1973."

In retrospect, a recommendation such as this one seems inevitable. Margaret Morrison had organized visiting committees for one-day visits since 1956, the first year of Dean LeClair's tenure. For a decade, the committees reported little more than the major events of the year. In 1968, both Dean Steinberg and Vice President Schatz met with the committee. It reported that the transfer of science students to E&S and humanities students to the new College of Humanities and Social Sciences had depopulated the college: "Eliminating MMCC as an educational division enrolling students may well be the logical conclusion to something that has been going on for some time," the report concluded.

In the fall of 1969, the Educational Policy Council of the Faculty Senate debated the issue, and both the Council and the Senate approved a recommendation to dissolve Margaret Morrison. In mid-November, the Executive Committee of the Board of Trustees added its approval, and the deed was done, a deed that jolted many faculty members, students and alumnae. Protests from the small groups of students who remained hardly affected the larger campus, by now indifferent to the fate of Margaret Morrison Carnegie College.

Some of Margaret Morrison's alumnae, however, were a different matter. They met among themselves and with the dean, wrote letters of protest, and complained that they had not been consulted during the decision-making process. All to no avail. Dean Steinberg conceded that the university did not handle the matter well and that alumnae should have been consulted early in the process, and he accepted the responsibility for not doing so. Instead of consulting the alumnae, Tech's officials had thought of the phasing out of Margaret Morrison as an internal problem.

Deans LeClair and Steinberg had fought a valiant, though losing, battle to save the college. They had campaigned success-fully for new facilities; retained a consultant to encourage research in the traditional disciplines; encouraged a graduate program in home economics education; carried on vigorous searches for young, research-oriented faculty; started a program for mature women who wished to return to college; organized a highly successful program in technical writing; started graduate programs in English; organized and led the curriculum development center in English; reorganized departments in an effort to keep them afloat; published widely; and represented the college vigorously in the wider university. Ludwig F. Schaefer, in his excellent history of the Stever and Cyert administrations, summarized the end of Margaret Morrison in a thoughtful paragraph:

The argument has been made that timely allocation of resources could have turned the situation around. Margaret Morrison Carnegie College might have been a leader, for example, in the area of biochemistry and nutrition on the cutting edge of science. But this argument rests on the shaky premise of imaginative planning, faculty strengths, and above all administrative support. The dean pushed for change when he deemed it possible within straitened means. The faculty on the whole were not research-minded. The cost of "revolution" was too great to make the cause of MMCC a priority for the administration. All evidence indicates that the decision was grounded on a correct assessment given the university's resources and goals. The merger provided a "window of opportunity" to take advantage of current societal tides by establishing a co-educational liberal arts college. No cohesive thought, however, seems to have been given the question of what this would mean for the future of MMCC as an autonomous entity. By essentially conducting a holding operation in the professional options where there was declining student interest, while bit by bit detaching those in science and the liberal arts where growth and prestige were promising, the administration followed a course that could only end with the disappearance of Margaret Morrison.

Margaret Morrison Carnegie College, however, left a rich legacy. This legacy is the subject of Chapter 7.

The Way We Were:
From Margaret Morrison Student to Faculty Wife

Norene DiBucci
*Pittsburgh,
Pennsylvania*

- *Home Economics
  Education '64*
- *Kappa Kappa Gamma*
- *Home Economics Club*
- *Greek Sing*

Paul Christiano
*(Norene's husband)
Pittsburgh,
Pennsylvania*

- *Civil Engineering '64
  M '65, D '68*
- *Carnegie Mellon
  Provost, 1991–2000*
- *CIT Dean, 1989–91*
- *Civil Engineering
  Head, 1986–88*
- *CIT Associate Dean,
  1982–86*

I arrived at Margaret Morrison by a roundabout route. My parents, my sister and I were all born and reared in the Italian section of Bloomfield. My father was the oldest of six children born to parents who had emigrated from Italy in the early 1900s. Like many children of immigrant parents, he left school after completing the eighth grade to go to work. He was such an avid reader, however, that he became a truly educated man. My mother was schooled by the nuns in a convent school. Both of my parents valued a solid, well-rounded education and guided my sister and me in that direction.

I attended St. Joseph's elementary school in Bloomfield and then Mt. Mercy Academy for my high school years. After graduating in 1960, I enrolled in Carlow College where I studied foods and nutrition. At the end of my freshman year, however, I transferred to Margaret Morrison so that I could get a degree in Home Economics Education. Margaret Morrison challenged me, as it did most of its students. I have fond memories of the faculty: Professor Gladys Spencer, who later became my master's thesis adviser; Professor Melva Bakkie, the head of the department; Professor Louise Bailey; Professor Alberta Dodson; and Miss Professor Carolyn Ater, who tolerated our somewhat bizarre behavior while we were living in the Home Management House. These women were strict and expected us to behave properly at all times. I also remember the rigorous schedule of science courses that supported the whole home economics curriculum that qualified us for a B.S. at graduation. And who could forget Dean Erwin Steinberg, distinguished gentleman and scholar that he was—and still is.

Like most Margaret Morrison students, I commuted to school. My family lived near West Penn Hospital about two miles from campus. I usually walked to school or took the trolley in bad weather. My friend Eileen (Mauclair) D'Appolonia, MM'65, drove to campus, and I frequently rode with her. I ate lunch in Skibo, the student center just off Forbes Street. Its snack bar served the most wonderful grilled cheese sandwiches on marbled rye bread. It's funny what we remember, isn't it?

During the second semester of my junior year, I joined Kappa Kappa Gamma sorority. Many of my friends, including Eileen, belonged and my mother encouraged me to join. Sororities played a vital role in the lives of commuting students, who otherwise missed the camaraderie of dormitory life. I enjoyed and was grateful for the friendships I developed with my sorority sisters and reveled in the excitement and shenanigans of Greek Sing and Spring Carnival. The only other organization I joined was the Home Economics Club.

Our mutual friends, Eileen and Dave D'Appolonia, CIT'65, introduced me to Paul Christiano, CIT'64, '65, '68, in the summer of 1965. Paul and I were both studying on campus, but our paths had never crossed. Paul was a full-time student working for his Ph.D. in civil engineering. I was teaching home economics in Chartiers Valley School District and studying in the evening and during summer sessions for a master's degree in Home Economics Education. We courted for a little over two years and married in November 1967.

CARNEGIE·INSTITUTE·OF·TECHNOLOGY

UPON·RECOMMENDATION·OF·THE·FACULTY·OF·THE
MARGARET·MORRISON·CARNEGIE·COLLEGE
HEREBY·CONFERS·ON
Norene Grace DiBucci
THE·DEGREE·OF
BACHELOR·OF·SCIENCE
IN·RECOGNITION·OF·THE·COMPLETION·OF·THE·COURSE·OF
STUDY·PRESCRIBED·FOR·THIS·DEGREE·IN·THE·FIELD·OF
HOME·ECONOMICS
GIVEN·UNDER·THE·SEAL·OF·THE·CORPORATION·AT·PITTSBURGH
IN·THE·COMMONWEALTH·OF·PENNSYLVANIA·ON·THE·EIGHTH
DAY·OF·JUNE·NINETEEN·HUNDRED·AND·SIXTY·FOUR

Paul was teaching Civil Engineering at the University of Minnesota when we married. I resigned from my teaching position and off we went, happy even though we had to endure the cold weather in the Twin Cities. While in Minneapolis, I worked in a home economics adult education program, teaching several classes in foods and nutrition, and I remained active by volunteering at the University of Minnesota Hospital. After our daughter Beth was born in April 1969, I continued my volunteer work and wrote my master's thesis "long distance." We are a CMU family. Paul has three CMU degrees, I have two, and our daughter, a 1991 graduate, now teaches abnormal psychology at Carnegie Mellon.

In January 1973, Steve Fenves, Carnegie Mellon civil engineering department head at that time, offered Paul a job as an associate professor. Within a short time, Paul became associate dean of CIT, then department head in civil engineering and then dean of CIT. Three years later, in 1991, newly-arrived president Robert Mehrabian asked him to become provost, the university's chief academic officer. How honored he was! He always had the good of the university at the forefront of his mind. He served as provost until July 2000.

All of Paul's appointments kept me deeply involved—delightfully so—at Carnegie Mellon. The university became our second home. We were fond of Dick and Margaret Cyert throughout Dick's administration as president, and we became very close to his successor, Robert Mehrabian and his wife Victoria. The Mehrabians and Christianos co-hosted dozens of occasions both on and off campus. We joined the Andrew Carnegie Society and had a feeling of belonging and a sense of being appreciated during that wonderful time. Sadly, Paul died in 2001 while he was being considered for the presidency of Duquesne University.

During the late 1980s, Carnegie Mellon began to pay more attention to its Margaret Morrison heritage. Steve Fienberg, dean of Humanities and Social Sciences, organized several meetings for Margaret Morrison alumnae. The College of Humanities and Social Sciences raised money from Margaret Morrison alumnae to build the Margaret Morrison Media Wing located in Porter Hall. I was active in these two efforts. Some years later, Paul and I hosted a Margaret Morrison breakfast and a hard-hat tour of the Purnell Center. Then Mary Phillips, Evelyn (Alessio) Murrin, MM'57, and I decided to continue these MMCC get-togethers, and the Margaret Morrison lecture series was off and running, with Paul acting as master of ceremonies for the first two lectures in 2000. This book, one effort of the "Mary Phillips group," is a tribute to the thousands of Margaret Morrison graduates who have made such a significant impact on Carnegie Mellon.

Norene (DiBucci) Christiano
Home Economics Education '64
M Home Economics Education '71

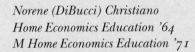

Top:
Andrew Carnegie Society pin

Bottom left to right: Four distinguished spouses of Carnegie Mellon faculty: Noël Newell, Virginia Schatz, Margaret Cyert and Norene Christiano

Opposite page: Norene's diploma and Kappa Kappa Gamma sorority pin

The Way We Were:
A Carnegie Mellon Family

Claire Rosa Ruge
*Lexington,
Massachusetts*

- *Business Studies '65*
- *WAA*
- *Delta Gamma
  Rush Chairman
  and Vice President*

Arthur C. Ruge
*(Claire's father)
Pittsburgh,
Pennsylvania*

- *Civil Engineering '25*

Carnegie Tech transformed me from a shy, diffident girl into a confident young woman. I grew up in Lexington, Massachusetts and graduated from the local high school. As an only child, I thought I needed the challenge of going to college outside of New England. My father, Arthur Ruge, was a graduate of Tech and he suggested that I apply. Looking back on those four wonderful years, I realize that it was the perfect place for me to attend college.

During a campus visit and tour, I had been shown Morewood Gardens and assumed that my room would be there. However, when the dorm assignment arrived, I was surprised and shocked to learn that it was for Schiller Hall. As soon as I reached campus, my shock turned to delight. This lovely old mansion immediately became home to all of us, nine freshmen and 13 upperclassmen. It was like a small private club and we bonded quickly. Surprisingly, I can still remember all of their names. We did have to walk to Morewood Gardens for all our meals, but soon learned to store food in our rooms for breakfast on cold, snowy mornings. For the next two years I lived in Morewood's B Tower. The summer before my senior year, I was asked to be a floor counselor and was given a single room in A Tower. Most of the girls on the floor were P and Ds—Painting and Design majors. They kept late hours and lived far different lives from the Maggie Murphs. I learned a lot.

I began at Margaret Morrison as a general studies major specializing in English. At the end of my sophomore year, I realized that I no longer wanted to become an English teacher, so I changed to Business Studies. Freshman English Composition class included students from all of Tech's colleges. The aim was to teach us to write clearly, concisely and effectively. One particular assignment stands out in my memory. We were told to describe in words —no drawings or diagrams—exactly how to build a paper airplane. Then we exchanged papers and were told to make a paper airplane by following the directions given to us. What a surprise! We soon discovered that what we thought were good instructions were not to someone else. It was a dramatic way to demonstrate the importance of clear, precise writing. I also remember fondly the Public Speaking course taught by Beekman Cottrell. It was perhaps the most difficult class I ever took. The first few assignments brought nothing but sheer panic and the desire to flee. But in time, with instruction and a kind audience, I began to enjoy the class and become a more confident public speaker.

Sorority life helped in that regard as well. I joined Delta Gamma and loved participating in Greek Sing and sorority skits. At that time sororities did not have houses, so each was assigned a closet in the lower level of Skibo for storing supplies and props. We reserved rooms there for meetings, parties and special events. For all of us young women, planning programs and holding offices in the sorority were most helpful in developing leadership skills.

All Tech grads remember certain special events and peculiar customs of their college years. Both students and faculty used to smoke in classes and extinguish their cigarettes on the wooden floors. No one complained. Housemothers routinely patrolled the many lounges of Morewood Gardens. It was their duty to ensure that female students kept both feet on the floor while visiting with their male friends. Climbing to the fourth floor of Margaret Morrison for a class was a strenuous workout, particularly when you were late. One of our married classmates became pregnant and was given a key to the elevator. We all crowded in as it groaned its way to the top of the building. I remember visiting Phipps Conservatory, triggering a lifelong love of gardening. Attending concerts and plays both on and off campus provided an important contribution to my cultural understanding. When my father visited campus, he took me to meet his close college friend and classmate, Professor David Moskovitz. Later, I became acquainted with David's daughter, Sema Faigen, when we attended Carnegie Clan meetings in the Boston area. Over the years, I learned to cherish Tech's traditions: Spring Carnival displays, buggy races, school songs, painting the Senior Fence. It was enjoyable to recall them with other Tech grads when we met at Boston Clan meetings while I was Clan secretary during the 1970s. Of course, I'll always remember being a finalist for queen of the Military Ball when I was a freshman and sweetheart of ATO a couple of years later. By then, I was a far different person from the shy freshman seeking to find her way on campus.

I met John Bertucci during my freshman year, but didn't begin dating him until I was a sophomore and he was a senior. He belonged to ATO and we spent a lot of our spare time at fraternity events. Occasionally, we went to Shadyside or Squirrel Hill or to New Castle to visit his family. John entered GSIA the September after graduation and studied there for two years to earn his master's degree. Back in the 1960s there was an often-quoted statement that 85 percent of college students met their future spouses while in school. John and I were part of that statistic.

In 1965, all within a single, hectic month, we graduated, married and moved to Texas, where John had a job with Texas Instruments. While we were in Texas, I worked for several years at Collins Radio in personnel and took courses in English and theology at the University of Dallas. In 1968 we decided to transfer to Massachusetts, where we stayed and raised our two daughters. John became vice president of MKS Instruments, Inc. and is currently president, CEO and chairman of the board.

Now that the children are grown, most of my time is spent playing with our grandchildren and doing volunteer work in Boston and our town of Lexington. I am actively involved in the local garden club and especially enjoy civic improvement projects and garden therapy work with the elderly.

Over the years, my family has remained close to Carnegie Mellon. My father passed away in 2000, but always loved reminiscing about his college years. He never failed to credit Tech for much of the success in his life. His story appeared in the Winter 2002 issue of the *Carnegie Mellon Magazine*. A graduate of the class of 1925, he invented the strain gauge, a sensor widely used in civil, mechanical and aeronautical engineering as well as in the automotive and construction industries. In 1959, he was presented an Alumni Association Merit Award. John and I have attended many of our reunions, are lifetime members of the Andrew Carnegie Society and recently established a Professorship in Electronic Materials. John is also a member of the Board of Trustees. We are, indeed, a Carnegie Mellon family.

Claire (Ruge) Bertucci
Business Studies '65

Left:
Claire with her future spouse, John, in June 1963

Right:
Delta Gamma and Alpha Tau Omega pins

The Way We Were:
From English Major to Business Executive

Marion J. Mulligan
Coshocton, Ohio

- *English '65*
- *Kappa Alpha Theta President*
- *Pi Delta Epsilon*
- *The Carnegie Technical*
- *Tartan*

Left bottom:
A sorority sister made this Kappa Alpha Theta doll for Marion.

Top right:
Marion Mulligan and her father Ed '37 at commencement in 1965

I have had an unusual series of jobs, most of which grew from my education in Tech's English Department. Maybe that's why I have such vivid memories of so many of my professors. Austin Wright, the department head, gave me an appreciation for Shakespeare, much as Fred Sochatoff opened my eyes to Greek and Latin writers—in translation, I admit. Ann Hayes taught Milton and was a superb model of an excellent teacher and a productive scholar. We all loved Beekman Cottrell, whose enthusiasm for the literature he assigned quickly infected everyone in the class. And Erwin Steinberg! I never had a class from him—he was dean during my years—but he used to appear now and then to talk about education and the importance of doing one's best. All the faculty had high standards; they worked us hard; we learned to love literature and to write well.

My father had graduated from Tech as a printing management major in 1937. We lived in Coshocton, Ohio, where he became an executive in the family's manufacturing business. I wanted a liberal arts education and Margaret Morrison's General Studies Department offered one. Having lived in a small town, I wanted to go to college in a city, and Tech was only a few hours away by train or bus. I visited campus and quickly fell in love with it, particularly with the beautiful fine arts building and the delightful array of people who studied and taught there. I saw drama students rehearsing in the halls while music from the practice rooms flooded the building. Who could resist?

So much about Tech appealed to me. My freshman year was tough; I wasn't as well prepared as I should have been, but the faculty was patient and I soon caught on. I took a fascinating course in calligraphy from Arnold Banks, another distinguished scholar/teacher. Morewood Gardens surrounded me with women from all Tech's departments preparing for careers in many walks of life. I attended plays in Kresge, the best theatre in town, and enjoyed taking the trolley downtown to shop or see the sights. I wrote stories for *The Tartan* and served briefly as an editor for *The Carnegie Technical*, Tech's journal featuring technical articles by faculty members and students. And who could forget the trolley parties? A fraternity would rent a trolley for an evening, fill it with guys and their dates, install a keg of beer, and tour the city. Can't do that anymore; like the old Skibo where I used to hang out, the trolleys are long gone.

I wasn't sure what I wanted to do when I graduated, so my father offered to pay for a year in Europe where I could study languages. He said that it was cheaper than graduate school. I had taken two years of Spanish and two of German, so I jumped at the chance, spending five months in Madrid and five in Vienna. Then I returned to Tech where I got a job as administrative assistant in food services and took some graduate work in English. When a job opened for a writer, I began working on proposals with the humanities and fine arts faculties. A Tech connection led to a similar job in planning with West Penn Hospital and then to two years of study for a master's degree in hospital administration—12 months in class at Pitt's Graduate School of Public Health and a 12-month internship in Lenox Hospital in New York City.

West Penn hired me back a few years later. I was in charge of day-to-day administration for a number of hospital departments for 10 years. Then when an organizational change took place at West Penn, I moved to Blue Cross for six years where I managed relationships with a number of hospitals. By this time, I had had on-the-job training both as a writer and as an administrator. Then in my middle forties, I married Tom Sutton, a 1956 Tech graduate in architecture, and we moved into an Ashland Park house where we still reside. For the past eight years, I've been involved actively in the Jones Metal Products Company. My father stepped down two years ago as head of the company, and I became chair. I've been devoting my energies and experience to re-invigorating the company with young, energetic people for both staff and board positions.

Throughout all these years, Carnegie Mellon has played an important role in my life. When I returned from New York, I served on the Alumni Association Advisory Committee and later for ten years on the Executive Committee of the Andrew Carnegie Society where I helped to get the society's newsletter started. Tom and I visit Carnegie Mellon fairly frequently. It's been wonderful to see it evolve into such a distinguished campus and university.

*Marion (Mulligan) Sutton
English '65*

Left:
The Suttons today

Below:
Two Andrew Carnegie
Society buttons

Tech Runs Nursery for All to Benefit

By Marion Mulligan

Carnegie Tech runs a nursery school, and students who don't believe it should visit the center, which is located in the basement of the new edition to Margaret Morrison College.

They will find a cheery and spacious room equipped to satisfy the activities of about twelve children aged 2-1/2 years to 3-1/2 years. They will also quite possibly meet Mrs. Marilyn Hammond, home economics teacher and supervisor of the nursery.

She explains that the school, which was started some twenty years ago, is run to provide an opportunity for Tech students, particularly those taking the child development course, to study the behavior of young children. In the laboratory these students, especially from the home economics and psychology departments, individually observe the children two hours weekly. They are required to watch the social, emotional, and mental development of the youngsters during one semester and to prepare a summary of their observations.

What they observe are the actions of normal youngsters playing in individual and group situations. The children have, at their disposal, toys and learning equipment from play telephones and dolls to picture books and blocks. No reading is taught to the youngsters. The department feels that at this age children need more experience in feeling textures and exploring their environment. With such a background it is hoped that the children will be prepared to tackle reading and other more advanced subjects in grade school.

"We are not a permissive school," says Mrs. Hammond, "We want the children to respect responsible authority."

The children enrolled in the nursery school are chosen from applications of parents within the Tech community and the immediate area. They are chosen by their age, sex, and readiness for nursery school, a factor which is determined by the instructor. The group is so small that the children may receive individual attention during their three-hour morning sessions five days a week.

The program benefits not only the children and Tech students, Mrs. Hammond was quick to note. Several of her colleagues are doing extensive research on child development and draw almost all of their data from experience in the nursery itself.

The Carnegie Tartan, Wednesday, February 27, 1963, p 8.

The Way We Were:
A Carnegie Mellon Trustee Remembers

Patricia Gail Askwith
Harrison, New York

- *French '66*
- *Alpha Epsilon Phi Rush Chairman, President*
- *Campus Chest*
- *Ski Club*

Right top:
Patti with daughter, Julie

Right center:
Patti with grandson, Canaan, three years old

Right bottom:
Patti with grandson, Wyatt, three months old

I have great memories of my four years at Margaret Morrison Carnegie College. Almost forty years later, I want to share my story with other women in the hope that they can get the most from their Carnegie Mellon experience.

I chose Margaret Morrison because Carnegie Tech offered a fine liberal arts education with the added attraction of renowned fine arts and drama departments. I was looking forward to living in a new city, Pittsburgh…not too close to my home in the suburbs of New York City, but not too far! I loved Pittsburgh but remember vividly the smokestacks and the strange smell in the air in the "City of Steel."

I majored in French and developed a great interest in French literature and culture. In the 1960s, Tech had no language labs, and I never learned to speak fluent, unaccented French. This was, perhaps, my motivation for my first named gift to Carnegie Mellon in 1990 to provide a language lab.

The hopes I had for being exposed to fine arts and drama were realized. I remember my Saturday morning calligraphy class with the wonderfully eccentric Arnold Banks…and still use my calligraphy on hundreds of occasions!

I lived in Morewood Gardens, where I met other young women from all different departments. I watched Iris Ratner and Caroline McWilliams cry and laugh for their drama homework assignments. Iris went on to write "Beaches" and is currently writing a Broadway show. Caroline performed "Love Letters" in New York City last year to benefit the drama department, and is a producer in Los Angeles. I did my French and Spanish homework every night with Joan Hoexter and Ellen Burstein, and we still talk almost daily.

The college experience was quite different from today's. Morewood was a "women only" residence, of course, where you "signed in" (and kissed your boyfriend goodnight in front of your housemother) before 12 midnight on Saturday night.

Several extracurricular activities added to my life. I was rush chair and later president of my sorority, Alpha Epsilon Phi, and enjoyed those responsibilities. Being a Campus Chest officer helped me to develop a sense of giving back to the community. And I learned to ski on trips to Seven Springs, a great diversion from academia.

The friendships I made have been lasting and very important to me. My college boyfriend, Tom Glassberg, a mechanical engineer who was president of the student body and of his fraternity Sigma Nu, and I have remained close friends. I loved my years at Margaret Morrison and left Tech determined to repay the school for all it had given me.

104

By the time I graduated in 1966, New York City needed teachers badly and offered a six-week training course. That fall, I became a third grade teacher in Harlem, where I had a wonderful experience. Then I went to Teachers College at Columbia University to earn a master's degree, and a year later returned to P.S. 76 and taught there for ten years.

In 1969, I married Jeffrey Kenner, an engineer who attended Lehigh University. We met after college on a ski trip to Vermont. Jeffrey began his career at Price Waterhouse and eventually left to start his own investment banking firm. Our daughter Julie, who was born in 1976, lives in Colorado with her husband John and our fabulous grandsons, Canaan and Wyatt.

After Julie was born, I decided to retire from teaching and join my family business. My father founded Campus Coach Lines in 1928 as a student at the University of Michigan, transporting students by bus from Ann Arbor to New York at a fraction of the cost of the railroad. Currently, I work with my Dad and we charter buses for private groups.

My outside interests include the Museum of Jewish Heritage – A Living Memorial to the Holocaust in New York City, as well as Democratic politics. I believe responsible citizens must participate in their governing bodies, and I have been privileged to become a supporter and friend of both my senators, Chuck Schumer and Hillary Rodham Clinton.

Photo by Zana Briski for TIME magazine

1   2   3   4

Over the years, I have been able to support Carnegie Mellon in ways that reflect what Margaret Morrison gave me. In addition to supporting the language lab, I have endowed a fund for international studies as well as French experiences in Pittsburgh, to enhance the college curriculum. I request that all students who receive a grant make an attempt to give back to the university in the future so other students will be able to have the same opportunity. I have chaired my class reunions in 1991, 1996 and 2001, and enjoy bringing our class together to reminisce and take pride in our alma mater. I am a member of the Andrew Carnegie Society and was a volunteer for the Centennial Campaign for Carnegie Mellon. I have been a member of the Board of Trustees since 1999, where I enjoy being part of the decision-making process for the great university Carnegie Mellon has become.

My college experience helped set a positive course for my life. I am hoping to be able to ensure that future generations of Carnegie Mellon women will be equally enriched.

Patti (Askwith) Kenner
French '66

For my 52nd birthday, I invited 60 of my female friends to dinner and the movies to see "The First Wives Club." The message we got from the movie was the depth of the friendships women share and the support women give each other. I asked each guest to make a gift in my name to any group that supports women. Time magazine did a cover story on the movie and sent a photographer to my party. They printed this photo (October 7, 1996 issue) of me and some of my guests, among them three Carnegie Tech friends.

Top:
MMCC friends,
1 Patti Askwith Kenner '66
2 Marge Levin Gerena '66
3 Marge Packard Thomas '66
4 Joan Hoexter Goldberg '66

Bottom:
Senator Hillary Rodham Clinton, Patti Askwith Kenner, and District Attorney Bob Morgenthau

The Way We Were:
From Student to Associate Dean

Betty Jane Lloyd
*Homestead Park,
Pennsylvania*

- *Secretarial Studies '44*
- *Carnegie Women's
Christian Association*
- *Citcom Clan*

Little did I realize on my first visit to campus—a warm September Registration Day in 1940—that I was destined to spend almost forty years of my life there. That is especially true when recalling that where I really wanted to be was at Penn State studying journalism. Parental pressure due to an unfortunate incident on that campus changed the plans.

The end of that first fall semester only reinforced my desire to be elsewhere. My only glimmer of hope was a statement by Dr. Charles Watkins, Dean of MMCC from 1929 to 1947: "Far be it from me to arouse sleeping dogs, but I don't know what you're doing here." He was referring to my lack of required math courses for acceptance. I'm sure he felt that I might do better elsewhere. Who could have guessed that eighteen years later I'd have an office adjacent to the one in which that very conference took place!

A series of fifty-cent-per-hour campus jobs, starting in the spring semester, changed my outlook considerably. The earnings helped to pay part of the $180 semester tuition. I worked for Dr. Lawrence Guild, secretary of a national honorary, Dr. John M. Daniels, Director of Admissions, and Edith Winchester Alexander, head of the Department of Secretarial Studies and later dean of MMCC (1947–56).

Expedited classes in the summer of 1943, fueled by World War II demands, required juniors in MMCC science and secretarial majors—as well as majors in all engineering departments—to complete the first semester of our senior year during that summer. Consequently, we finished our course work in December and graduated.

My final semester was cut short by a request to join the faculty of Munhall High School, from which I had graduated in 1940. My five-year association with them started on November 11, 1943. It was required, however, that I turn in all class assignments and attend class one day a week at MMCC for the duration of the semester.

Because I was commuting and working the maximum number of hours permitted under NYA (National Youth Administration) rules, I participated minimally in campus activities. One of my favorites was the commuter organization, Citcom Clan. It was there I met Ed Schatz, later a vice president at Carnegie Mellon, and Virginia Wright, his future wife.

In the spring of 1948 came an unexpected invitation to join the faculty of the Department of Secretarial Studies in MMCC. There was no hesitation in accepting the offer. For ten years, teaching departmental and elective courses, participation in some recruitment activities, and outside consulting provided full-time professional activity. I planned and presented secretarial improvement classes and seminars for employees at Carnegie Tech and a number of large companies. There were campus related activities, too, such as holding offices in the MMCC and General Faculty organizations.

Also in 1948, a Faculty Club came into existence. Housed in Forbes Hall (formerly a women's dormitory where Warner Hall now stands), it provided dining and recreational facilities along with lounges and meeting rooms. It provided its membership the opportunity on an informal basis for greater exposure to colleagues from all colleges within Carnegie Institute of Technology. In the annex were sleeping rooms for unmarried, male faculty members. One of the highlights of membership for me was being elected as the only woman president in its twelve years of existence.

Right:
Betty Jane Lloyd at her
typewriter

When Dean Alexander retired in 1956, Margaret F. LeClair (1956–60) was appointed to the office. It was she who lured me into the Dean's Office in 1958. My initial duties were to oversee the scheduling, orientation and counseling of all incoming freshmen and to assist in their transition to their departments of choice. At the other extreme was the responsibility for the College's diploma ceremony following the main commencement program.

Throughout that year and the ones to follow, duties escalated. In 1960 when Erwin Steinberg succeeded Dean LeClair, and during his term as Dean of the College of Humanities and Social Sciences (H&SS), I continued to be his associate. While in the Dean's Office, I served simultaneously for one year as acting head of the Department of Business Studies (formerly Secretarial Studies) and three years (1970–73) as head of the Department of Business and Resource Management, comprised of the final graduates in home economics and business majors.

These three years were beyond a doubt the unhappiest of my academic tenure. I was caught in a situation that required survival or resignation. Like many fellow alums, I was extremely bitter about the demise of my college. Yet I needed to maintain a loyalty to the university I served (concurrently, I was acting in behalf of the new college freshmen). At the 1973 commencement that marked the last MMCC graduation, I was honored to be the first woman to serve as faculty marshal.

Betty Jane Lloyd
Associate Dean
Director of Academic Advisory Center
College of Humanities and Social Sciences

CARNEGIE-MELLON UNIVERSITY
PITTSBURGH, PA. 15213

Betty Jane Lloyd as faculty marshall in 1973

Two major emphases of the 1960s were 'publish or perish' and 'the changing role of women.' My research on the way other women's and coordinate colleges were providing counseling and curricula related to the latter, provided substance for frequently published articles in national journals. Also helpful was knowledge from numerous convened conferences and seminars related to women's issues and held on our own campus.

Development of the Academic Advisory Center in H&SS in 1978 was a huge accomplishment for me. The Center, which was under my direction for the first year, provided central advising, especially for freshmen but also for all students requesting or requiring academic help or support. I'm happy to say that the Center is alive and well today.

Since my retirement in 1983, I have continued living in the house next door to the one in which I was born and from which I commuted for those almost forty years. I am still not a joiner but do some traveling and get great satisfaction from assisting friends and neighbors with tasks they can no longer perform for themselves.

Betty Jane Lloyd
Business Studies '44

GREGG PUBLISHING DIVISION
McGRAW-HILL BOOK COMPANY, INC.
330 WEST 42ND STREET
NEW YORK 36, N.Y.

January 29, 1958

ss Betty Jane Lloyd
garet Morrison College
negie Institute of Technology
Wood Street
sburgh, Pennsylvania

Miss Lloyd:

A very tardy "thank you" for your
pation in WQED's typing "spectacular"
is month. I thought you might like to
enclosed picture as a reminder of your
ervice."

From what Bill White tells me, you may
e seen yourself in the Kinescope,
ly "sharp" for a gal of 1892.

ain, many th...
sure

The Way We Were:
A Dean Reminisces

Erwin Steinberg
*Pittsburgh,
Pennsylvania*

• *Dean of MMCC*

I had earned my Master's degree in English at what is now the State University of New York at Albany, spent a little over three years in the Technical Training Command of the Army Air Force during World War II, and applied to Columbia University for further graduate study before I ever heard of Carnegie Tech. When Tech hired me in 1946 as an instructor in English, Columbia accepted me; and I was off to an unexpected academic career. Wartime service and the opportunity offered by the GI Bill encouraged a lot of us to rethink our futures.

A bachelor, I lived in Forbes Hall, once a women's dorm before Tech acquired Morewood Gardens, and then a faculty club. (Warner Hall sits on that site now.) Instructors in the English department taught English Composition, four sections of 25 students each. We received 100 essays each Friday and spent most of the rest of the weekend and the next week teaching and working over the papers—word by word, line by line. With a heavy teaching load, few of my colleagues of any rank did research, let alone published. Except for the grinding pressure of grading papers and wanting to perform well, I remember the department as collegial and low-stress.

Summers I devoted to graduate study: Columbia in 1946 and 1947, Oxford in 1948, and then New York University starting in 1949. Then I was awarded $500, promoted to assistant professor, and sent off on leave for 18 months to complete my coursework for the Ph.D. After half a dozen years of teaching, grading papers, and writing my dissertation, during which time I was married, in one week in June of 1956, I was awarded my Ph.D., was appointed head of the Department of General Studies in MMCC, and my wife and I had our first child. That put the cap on ten strenuous years.

The department headship was a strange job. Margaret LeClair, with whom I had previously shared an office in the English Department (in those days almost all faculty members shared offices), had been head before me. The General Studies Department had no faculty since all the people who taught general studies courses belonged to their own departments—English or history

or psychology, for example. I was only dimly aware of any problems that existed in Margaret Morrison because General Studies was expanding rapidly, and from that perspective, things were going well.

Looking for kinds of education to build onto a liberal arts program in a way that would provide career opportunities for women, I started a program in Technical Writing and Editing in 1958, which grew out of consulting work in writing I had been doing for Westinghouse and other Pittsburgh firms. The program grew slowly— we usually had eight or ten students a year— but it continues to this day as a B.S. in Technical Writing. Alongside of it grew today's Professional Writing major and M.A. program in Professional Writing. These programs are a legacy from Margaret Morrison to Carnegie Mellon.

I often taught Margaret Morrison girls, as we called female students in those politically incorrect days. All the classes were in the Margaret Morrison building. What a comfortable place to be! The halls were always spotless, and the janitorial staff washed the chalkboards between classes. The students were universally polite and well behaved—no running in the halls and no unusual dress. Most of them came from Pittsburgh and the surrounding counties, and many had been friends in high school. Largely commuters, they shared lockers and studied together on campus. It was like a small, safe, private world.

I got along well with the MMCC faculty, which used to put on a skit each year in the large hall on the fourth floor of the building. In one of these memorable productions, I walked across stage wearing a turned-up rain hat shaped like a fedora, manipulating a yo-yo as I went. I was the hit of the show; at least that's what my students told me just before grades were due.

In 1960 when Dean Margaret LeClair left, President Jake Warner appointed me to succeed her as dean of MMCC and told me that he would work as hard as he could to revive the college. He kept his word; he advocated new Bachelor and Master of Arts degrees, provided funds for a new wing on the building, and brought Dr. Jules LaBarthe over from Mellon Institute to try to promote research in clothing and textiles. Unfortunately, Jules' health was failing, and the numbers in that program and others continued to decline. Looking back now, I see that the demise of Margaret Morrison Carnegie College was inevitable.

For a few years, I was, at the same time, dean of both Margaret Morrison and the new College of Humanities and Social Sciences. Then I returned to the English Department, where I held the Baker Professorship from 1980 to 1992, continuing my scholarship in Modernist Literature, writing mainly about James Joyce, Franz Kafka, and Virginia Woolf.

Lots of funny incidents enlivened my day-to-day activities as dean. I returned to my office one day, for example, to find that all the furniture had been rearranged. We just put it back and made no fuss. I never learned who did it or why. Once I had a ticklish negotiation with someone in the dean of women's office. It turned out that a Maggie Murph was living with her boyfriend in an apartment off campus in violation of several of the school's cardinal rules. The dean wanted to expel her—right at the end of her senior year. When the young woman refused to return to the dorm, I found her a room in the YWCA and persuaded the person in the dean's office to let her stay there. A dozen years later, the young woman wrote me a note to thank me, saying that I had saved her life; she was now happily married and had two wonderful children. Deaning was like that some days.

I remember another day when all the books from the Margaret Morrison library had been moved into the new Hunt Library. As I stood looking at the dusty walls, two curious strangers asked politely what was going on. I explained and they thanked me pleasantly. Soon after, I learned that Alfred and Estelle Andrews, MM'26, had generously provided funds to renovate the rooms into a suite for the dean's offices. That office is now a conference room that is still the pride of the building. I kept looking for similar visitors during the rest of my tenure as dean, but no such luck.

During the height of the anti-Vietnam War unhappiness in the late 1960s, I heard a commotion outside and was told that the ROTC offices, several floors below my office, were being invaded. Fearing a fire, I snatched a completed book manuscript out of a cupboard and hurried outside to my car. There was no fire, and the book was published in 1973.

In 1991, President Robert Mehrabian asked me to take a new assignment as Vice Provost for Education, a position I held until 1996, when I returned full time to a far different English Department than the one I had joined exactly a half-century before. It features a scholarly, nationally known faculty, with excellent undergraduate programs in creative writing, literary and cultural studies, and rhetoric, as well as widely respected graduate programs in literary and cultural studies and rhetoric, all in a distinguished university.

As I look back over the past 57 years, I couldn't have planned a more interesting, satisfying career: a variety of challenges, good colleagues, bright students, and the opportunity to be part of an organization that grew from a good regional educational institution to a widely recognized university with an international reach and reputation—and with more women students and faculty than ever before.

Erwin Steinberg

The Way We Were:
Thirty Years of Devotion to Carnegie Mellon

Hilary Zubritzky
*McKees Rocks,
Pennsylvania*

- *Costume Economics '70*
- *Commuter Rep*
- *Home Ec Club*
- *Commuter Counselor*
- *Omicron Nu*

In 1972, I received my Master of Science in Home Economics Education. I watched in disappointment during my graduate years as the college in which I had earned two degrees during a six-year period was phased out. Yes, I was angry; but time healed my feelings. The positive experiences I had overshadowed any negative feelings. I was also very proud of having had the privilege of attending an institution of the caliber of Carnegie Mellon. My experiences were unique, formative, and hold a special feeling for me.

It is that special feeling that made me remain an active alum. I did not want to give up my connection to Carnegie Mellon and I was able to keep in touch via Clan meetings and alumni events. Louise (Wunderlich) Manka, MM'37, was president of the Pittsburgh Women's Clan when I graduated. The Clan sent invitations to all Pittsburgh grads to attend a Clan meeting, a scholarship luncheon at the College Club in Oakland, and I met Louise and perhaps 100 others, mostly MMCC graduates. I found beautiful tables set with thistles and Tartan plaids, and I had a delightful afternoon with graduates from a variety of eras, reminiscing about their days at Tech.

I joined the Women's Clan, eventually becoming its treasurer and then its president. Today, I work with the scholarship committee and am still a member of the board. Recently I joined the Pittsburgh Alumni Clan, where I am the secretary and serve on the board. You can usually find me at Clan events during homecoming celebrations, doing a variety of things all to benefit the Clan!

Working with alumni has been a delightful and refreshing experience. I have worked with the Carnegie Mellon Admissions Council to recruit students at college fairs in my area. I have also called prospective students to describe the university. I served two three-year terms on the Alumni Executive Board and chaired several class reunions. For this work, I received an Alumni Service Award in 1990. It was an honor to be recognized for something I truly enjoyed doing.

Why did I attend Margaret Morrison in the first place? My father was a physician and my mother a teacher. One of my mother's friends from eastern Pennsylvania had lavished praise on Tech; and although she attended Bucknell, she wanted her daughter to go to Tech. It was my choice because of MMCC's reputation for home economics education and because I wanted to remain in Pittsburgh. I went for an interview in my senior year, being quite frightened about whether I had the credentials to make it in. I remember the day my mother drove to school to pick me up when the acceptance letter came—I do not know who was prouder that day!

I commuted from home, an hour each way on buses or streetcars. I studied on the bus, my personal introduction to time management skills. However, after commuting five and a half years, I vowed I'd never take a bus again, and I haven't!

I joined the commuter's club, becoming one of its 100 or so members, and later served as commuter representative to the student government. I also joined the Home Economics Club. Most of its meetings were teas where we had a chance to talk informally with faculty members. And I was elected to Omicron Nu, the home economics honorary society. I attend its social events at conferences to this day.

My six weeks in the Home Management House gave me a stint as a real campus resident, and many memories. I remember trying to keep the off-white rugs clean during a particularly sloppy, wet January in 1970. What a year it was for Bissell Rug Cleaner!

Graduation,
May 1970

From right to left:
Dr. Gladys Spencer, dean of Home Economics, Sheri Sivitz, Hilary Zubritzky, Carol (Sutherland) Ellis, two unknown grads, Margaret Culgan.

I also had the privilege of serving President Guyford Stever veal parmigiana, broccoli, and strawberry parfait. I think anyone who spent time in the Home Management House, squeaky and drafty as it was, will always remember that house as it stood on Margaret Morrison Street, today a parking lot!

Even in the late 1960s and into the 1970s, it was a given that if you were attending a home economics class, you had better not wear slacks. Ms. Patricia Tengel, the Home Management House manager and an instructor of management and finance, was the youngest faculty member in the department and led the revolt for the women of MMCC when it came to introducing slacks. Ms. Tengel had the audacity to wear them!

Many other excellent faculty included F. Louise Bailey (clothing), Dr. Martha Eggers (microbiology and bacteriology), Dorothy Thomas Kolodner (nutrition), Doris Meyers (fashion design), and Dean Betty Jane Lloyd. Two faculty members who particularly helped to shape my life are Dr. Gladys Babcock Spencer and Dr. Ann Baldwin Taylor.

Dr. Spencer was head of Home Economics Education. She taught all of us the true meaning of professionalism. "Keep up to date," she advised. "Join professional organizations and attend professional meetings." I did. I became president of the Pennsylvania Home Economics Association, held offices in the American Home Economics Association, and attended national meetings year after year. Dr. Spencer was my faculty advisor and mentor, and we remain friends today. She always keeps abreast of my accomplishments!

Dr. Ann Baldwin Taylor, director of the Children's School, was my other favorite professor. Her love for children shaped my own teaching. When I took Child Development, she assigned each of us an individual child to observe for the semester. We watched their behavior through the one-way glass in the nursery school, spent time playing with our child, taught an occasional lesson, and even went to the child's home. I learned to pay close attention to children's behavior for clues to how to teach them.

I think there is a little of Dr. Taylor in me whenever I enter the classroom, and that is definitely a good thing. Dr. Taylor and I remain friends today as well. We often meet at Margaret Morrison events on campus.

After I graduated from college, I studied for my M.S. in Home Economics Education. Then I was employed by Montour School District in Coraopolis, a suburb of Pittsburgh. I am still teaching there thirty years later, and I love it. I teach Family and Consumer Sciences to both girls and boys in sixth, seventh and eighth grades. This is the new name—definitely 21st Century—for Home Economics.

I'm still applying what I learned at Margaret Morrison from classes, faculty involvement, and the hard work ethic. It shaped the way I teach, my professional philosophy and the way I approach anything. I guess the (paraphrased) words of Andrew Carnegie—"my heart is in my work"—really rang true for me. Yes, I still think outside the box when I approach a problem, and that can also be attributed to Carnegie Mellon. My years of association with Carnegie Mellon continue to be one of the proudest things in my life, and I will always remain a Loyal Scot.

Hilary Zubritzky
Costume Economics '70
M.S. Home Economics
Education '72

HOME MANAGEMENT AND HOME EQUIPMENT

NELL WHITE
MARY LOUISE FOSTER

Ours was the beginning of an era no longer tied to panty raids and sign-in sheets. The new generation of Sally Rides and Iris Ratners would shuck those white gloves and prim hats we wore to the Margaret Morrison teas and enter a world of new freedoms and expectations for women.
—Marilyn Bates

Chapter 6

1956–73
More Memories from Maggie Murphs

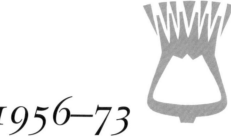

In the first class of Maggie Murphs to take a course in GSIA—Programming in Basic—we punched cards and processed them on a system not far removed from ENIAC. Ours was the beginning of an era no longer tied to panty raids and sign-in sheets. The new generation of Sally Rides and Iris Ratners would shuck those white gloves and prim hats we wore to the Margaret Morrison teas and enter a world of new freedoms and expectations for women. But something was lost of the old order that cared about our bodies in the milk bars of the 1920s and our reputations guarded by something that now seems antiquated—housemothers. Today when I see a young woman in a tank top with a pierced navel and a tattoo in the small of her back, I hark back to those who lived in the gentility of Whitfield House in the early '40s.
Marilyn "Bobbie" Bates
Business Studies '61

I didn't have to think very long to figure out the most important benefit from my years at Carnegie Tech as an MMCC student. That's the ability to solve problems. Most of the courses that I took as a history major, as well as the electives, emphasized going through steps to arrive at a solution. I'll never forget a blue book that I wrote for a history exam, in which I confused the causes of one war with those of another. Although I did not receive a high mark for that particular question, I received a compliment from Professor Roy Curry, praising the logic and methodology I had used.
Gladys (Stalinsky) Maharam
History '64

At Margaret Morrison, women students had the best of both worlds: the leadership training that comes with single-gender education and the social life of a lopsidedly male university. When we ventured out to take classes in other colleges, we were often the only, or the first, girls in the class. A management class in GSIA was a hoot. The male professor didn't know what to make of us. We knew what to make of him. We all got As.
Regina (Uliss) Frank
Clothing and Textiles '64

The goal of the Catalyst on Campus Conference in 1964 was to formulate a program based on the joint efforts of fifty colleges and Catalyst (a non-profit agency) to meet more effectively the motivational, educational, counseling and placement needs of educated women.

During the last semester before graduation, senior biology majors participated in a course entitled Senior Seminar. I chose as my project a genetic study of a specific trait transmitted through several generations of fruit flies. I remember carrying vials of fruit flies to all my classes in order to count the emerging flies, identify which ones had the desired trait, and choose the flies needed to start the next generation.
Nancy (Grasmick) Barnard
Biological Sciences '58

Only 12 women enrolled in the 1962 class of the Department of Biological Sciences. Being so few, we had virtually all of our academic science courses together over a four-year period, and we became a closely-knit group. Most of us loved to play basketball, but most women joined their sorority teams. Our small group had representatives from most of the sororities plus independents, so it seemed natural for us to form our own intramural team. We kept on winning. As the season progressed, our professors started coming to the games to cheer us on. Of course, we won the championship.
Patricia (Michael) Gottemoeller
Biological Sciences '62

The best part of the MMCC experience was being in a place that felt right, a place where you could be serious about your studies and not feel like an outsider for doing so. I had come from an undergraduate school—the University of Texas— where football was king and academics were tolerated. Of course, the administration there would deny that, but at least among the students back in the late 1960s, that was a given. Few of us played football, but partying for football was the rule. MMCC meant that it was OK to be serious about Shakespeare.
Michael Clark
English M '68

What I remember most is how one professor changed my life and launched me into the career I love. Dr. Eugene Caliendo, Professor of Italian and Spanish, was an extraordinary man, a mentor of the finest caliber. For four years, he took me under his wing and showed me the way. Today I am the president and founder of the Mentor Consulting Group. I would not be where I am today if it were not for Carnegie Tech and Professor Caliendo. I still stay in touch with his wife every Christmas.
Susan (Gordon) Weinberger
Modern Languages '62

I was in the first class of technical writers and have a newspaper clipping with a photo and story about the program. The photo shows five of us freshmen along with Dr. Erwin Steinberg, the founder of the program. The headline says something about girls preparing to write about outer space or something silly like that. I doubt if any of us ended up writing about outer space. However, the subjects that I've written about over the years are amazingly diverse.
Janis (Geisler) Ramey
Technical Writing and Editing '62
English M '67

My favorite professor and my mentor was Ms. Martha Peadon Eggers. She was compassionate and had an abiding interest in her students. In my sophomore year, I spoke to her about changing my major from biology to French. She encouraged me to stay in biology, with a strong conviction that she knew I would improve when I took advanced courses. Well, I did, and in 1970–73, I taught biology in the Biology Department at Carnegie Tech. For two of those years, I served as assistant department chair. Presently I teach biology, microbiology, or anatomy/physiology in a local community college. I fondly remember Maggie Murph.
Donna (Dalton) Opoku-Agyeman
Biology '65

After I graduated from Pitt, I came to Margaret Morrison for my master's in English. It was a wonderful experience. I remember the community of fellowship students in the program I was in. I never had this community experience at Pitt. We all got to know each other. I spent time in the dorms, which I never did at Pitt. It was so nice to be in small classes and discussion groups. It was a warm and wonderful experience. Michael Clark was one of the people in my fellowship group. I loved reading his memories of Margaret Morrison that were in the last alumni newsletter. He was delightful.
Anita Mallinger
English M '68, D H&SS '73

I was assigned to Tech's Military Science Department in 1964 and obtained an M.A. in history from Margaret Morrison in night school while I was there. The knowledge gained at MMCC was most beneficial in my assignments in Korea, the Pentagon, the U.S. Army Center for Military History at the Pentagon, the Research Center at the Army War College, and at NATO. I am still using the knowledge I gained in Professor Mandelbaum's course on the growth of cities as I work with candidates running for public office in Peachtree City and Fayette County, Georgia.
James Steinbach
History M '68

History and philosophy professor Robert Schwartz told our philosophy class how he personally arrived at some philosophical opinions. One of his conclusions was that if it makes you feel better to believe in God, then believe in God. That conclusion is important to me.
Renee (Marks) Cohen
History '63

Memories:
Home Economics

*I*n the 60s, as a married woman and the mother of three, I was stimulated by Carnegie Tech's interest in having women complete their college credits. My undergraduate credits from other schools, interrupted by war and marriage, were evaluated, and I was encouraged to complete my work, earn a degree, and launch a teaching career. Two graduations occurred in 1965: our daughter graduated from high school as I received my bachelor's degree from Carnegie Institute of Technology. That was the key to my entry into the work force, which also enabled our three children to further their education. Thanks for the open door.
Carol (Stiefel) Swift
Home Economics Education '65, M '71

My memories include being in a lab and having the professor come up behind me and ask why I had done a procedure in a certain way. It wasn't enough to be able to repeat the facts; we were constantly challenged to think and question. It was just as fearful, however, to be seen above the first floor of Margaret Morrison in slacks or jeans. Home Ec majors knew that once we left the safety of the first floor lounge, we had better be dressed professionally before we went up the staircase. It took many years for me to be comfortable in pants suits! Both are examples of the way MM left an indelible but positive mark on my standards and expectations.
Judith (Lomakin) Dodd
Foods and Nutrition '62

In retrospect, some of the skills we learned in the Home Management House were too restrictive. We were not permitted to repeat a meal preparation that someone had used. We could not watch television. We had to purchase the food left in the kitchen by the preceding cook. We used supermarket coupons to stretch our budgets. After last week's terrorist attack (September 11, 2001), however, I think back to those gentler times. Maybe they weren't so terrible.
Nancy (Tapper) Smith
Home Economics Education '69

When I studied textiles, manmade fibers were becoming a major industry. A wonderful professor who raised my interest in this field was Dr. Jules Labarthe. He was a chemist at Mellon Institute, who came to MMCC to teach our organic chemistry classes. I wrote my thesis on protective clothing in the atomic industry and hoped to become a scientist. But, I discovered that our program only qualified us to become buyers or designers. So I decided to go to Carnegie Library School for an M.L.S., emphasizing science, and became a science librarian.
Verna (Robinson) Brem
Clothing and Textiles '60
M.L.S., Carnegie Library School '62

Eurythemics in the Child Development Laboratory

I was one of about seven non-traditional students on campus in 1958. I had been out of school for about 15 years, was married, and had a 12-year old son and a nine-year old daughter. Miss Crow, the head of the department, admitted me on probation since I did not meet all of the entrance requirements. I was admitted as a regular student at the end of the first semester after the faculty evaluated my work. I commuted 20 miles each way to school, and carried a diminished schedule because of my family responsibilities. From Monday through Friday, I didn't get much sleep, but I loved it and am very proud of my degree. Margaret Morrison enriched my life and my relationship with my husband and children as well.
Arla (Mitchell) Gwynn
Home Economics Education '64

Even though my husband, who is an engineering alum, and I come back for reunions, having my department close and then my school close somehow made me feel that I don't have a little place there anymore. Certainly the days I spent at Carnegie were wonderful, and the MMCC history should be interesting. My husband tells this story about a dinner I prepared at the Home Management House. We weren't going together at the time, but he was my friend so I invited him to share the dinner I was planning. Everything went pretty well. However, the dessert I chose to make was cream puffs—I've never made them since—and I served them on paper doilies. At the end, we were going around critiquing the meal, and everyone sort of had this clump of soggy doily on their plate. It obviously was not a good idea...something you learn.
Susan (Seibert) Pontano
Home Economics Education '65

Memories:
Pot Pourri

Memories. Tina Crawford's presence on campus (a real celeb). Walking across the Cut through the seasons—good exercise. Meals at the dorm. Observing the dramats' unique dress and behavior. Curfew, 1:00 a.m. Saturday night. Housemothers. Wall pay telephones in constant use. Buggy races. Skibo bridge games. Always having a deadline to meet. Attending the Pittsburgh Symphony on Friday evenings. Having Korean War vets on campus. Constant contact with individuals of amazing foresight and intelligence. Carnegie Tech was an extraordinary place to be and an experience that I have always held dear.
Barbara (Jones) Horton
Secretarial Education '59

I was a transfer student so I had only two years at Tech. They turned out to be the best years of my life. So many wonderful memories. Studying late into the night. Sorority sisters. Meeting my future husband and his friend at his brand new fraternity house and an invitation from him to all the '57 Homecoming activities. My '59 graduating class was the first in many years not to wade in the pool in front of Morewood Gardens, thanks to the girls in the preceding year's graduating class, who were too noisy, plus "other things" that brought an end to this annual event.
Dorothy (Acklin) Leete
General Studies '59

Chi Omega played a large part in my life, and I have fond memories of Spring Carnival, Greek Sing practices and performances (remember Toga parties?) and most of all, the good friendships and bonds that have continued. As sorority president, I learned leadership skills that I have been able to use throughout my life, even in my own business.
Mary (Cruikshank) Hymes
Home Economics Education '68

Pittsburgh

You city of my growing up,
I hardly know you.
Downtown, in memory
baroque, haphazard, horizontal
has become metallic, prestine,
                              vertical

And the soot that indiscriminately blackened
white collars, cuffs, new-fallen snow,
lungs, lace curtains, attitudes
has been transformed into a
white-washed legend.

Gone, too, the clanging streetcars,
so much a part of you and your scene
that the streets seem ghost-like
in their rubber-tired quietness.

But your trinity of rivers yet remain
to form the triangle forever guarded
by the brooding hills,
and the friendly people living, loving
in the close-built, dark-bricked houses
still welcome me
                              and call me home.

M. Kathryn "Tassie" (Truxell) MacDonald
Business Studies '45

*Written in 1970 after returning for
her 25th Homecoming*

My fondest memory is of the nighttime view down Forbes Avenue from my seventh floor dorm room in Morewood Gardens. I liked being up high and seeing the lights. Seventh floor girls were always interesting. My second fondest memory is of the lilacs on the lawn of Morewood Gardens. Each spring they were, although briefly, so lush, so lovely, and so fragrant. It was wonderful to be able to see serious drama on campus. Having fine arts students in some of my classes made them more interesting because of the expansion of points of view. There are other memories popping up now, of 2:00 a.m. walks up Fifth Avenue from that bar (the Greeks) on Forbes, the free meals at the Unitarian church, walking in the middle of the street the day of the blizzard, and doing homework in Skibo to have company nearby.
Gail Whitacre
English/Psychology '67

As a recycled student 20 years after getting my B.S. in chemistry, I wanted to learn what was new in biology and chemistry, so I earned an M.A. in Natural Sciences. I often brought my fellow students home with me. One of them from India became my husband's co-leader of a Boy Scout camp. He got lost in the Pennsylvania woods. I remember my canoeing trip on the west branch of the Susquehanna River on an Easter vacation with the CMU Explorer's Club. We experienced three seasons in a few days, slept in pup tents, and ate meals using rocks as tables. Dr. Hugh Young was our leader. All of us had a great wilderness experience.
Ruth (Knight) Ernsberger
Natural Sciences M '65

One evening after our Thanksgiving break, I, like half the resident campus, was stuck in slow-moving traffic and was hours late getting back to the dorm. With only 15 "late minutes" allowed before we were "campused" for the following weekend—no exceptions—you can imagine the rowdy crowd confined to the dorm from Friday evening to Monday morning.
Pauline "Polly" (Speiglman) Ginsberg
English '63

Our biology professor in 1962 was a new teacher with a heavy Greek accent, Dr. Ethymio, I recall. About halfway through the semester, we were required to dissect live frogs. The lab's teaching assistant was a young man whom we all considered adorable. How we used to torment him! (I think he enjoyed it.) However, none of us was willing to anesthetize the frog without his help. Picture this, a lab full of young women, squealing at the sight of live frogs ready to be sacrificed in the name of science! In the spirit of the Sixties, we all released the frogs at once; they were jumping all over the old wooden tables and onto the floor when the door opened and in walked Dr. Ethymio.
Susan (Hartmann) Kantrowitz
Social Studies '66

Memories: ridiculous dormitory rules, Edwin Fenton, Pete Granville Jones, Scotch 'n Soda, mingling with students from the various departments by living in the dorm and being in Scotch 'n' Soda, enjoying the film festival, having the chance to see great theater on campus, and feeling pride when I see various CIT individuals who have made it big in the movie and theater world.
Martha (Cohen) Pheneger
General Studies, '64

I never did understand why all the windows that faced the Cut had to have the blinds at the same height. My teachers were adamant about that. Seemed not a big deal to me.
Marjorie (Steiner) Hylen
Home Economics Education '57

I was a commuting student who lived within walking distance of the school. On the day of a final exam, however, I awoke too late and drove to school. Since I had no time to look for a legal parking space, I parked right in front of the Margaret Morrison building, clearly in a NO PARKING zone. Much to my chagrin, as I was walking out of the building after the exam, I saw my car being lifted from its perch by a tow truck. I ran over to the tow person and tried to convince him to leave my poor car alone. Despite crying, cajoling, and other types of feminine persuasion, I watched in dismay as my vehicle vanished down the street. A cab ride to the "pound" and $50 (a lot of money in those days) got my car back. It was almost worth it. I got an A on the exam.
Dorothy (Steerman) Samitz
Clothing and Textiles '61

It started on a hot, Spring Sunday, and everyone was washing cars. Well, it got a little out of hand, and pretty soon water balloons were falling out of windows. A bucket of water fell on some poor, unsuspecting parent. Students coming back from the library were soaked by hoses, balloons, and buckets of water. Someone hosed down oncoming cars, and one poor convertible owner got so wet that he called the police. Well, as the guys were loaded into police cars, they ran out the other side and escaped. It was like a Laurel and Hardy show right before our eyes.
Barrie (Dinkins) Simpson
Costume Economics '68

Scotch 'n' Soda's 1963 "Miss Stars and Stripes"

I remember a concert in 1958 or 1959 that I thoroughly enjoyed. The Kingston Trio came to CMU and entertained. In 2000, I had an opportunity to see them again and remembered the experience.
Sylvia (Braunstein) Belle
Home/Costume Economics '62

When I graduated with my MMCC psychology degree, I approached WQED TV in search of a job and met Fred Rogers—"Mister Rogers"! He advised me to study child development at the University of Pittsburgh, so I followed his advice and earned my master's in 1967. By that time, I had been working for one year with "Mister Rogers' Neighborhood" and I have stayed there ever since, drafting responses to viewer mail, and speaking and presenting workshops nationwide. I have also worked closely with Fred Rogers on his books for children and adults.
Hedda (Bluestone) Sharapan
Psychology '65

Memories:
Career Preparation

As an education major, I was not required to take the pattern-drafting class. I elected to do so, however, and worked with all the clothing majors. Little did I ever dream that one course would help me with my future business. I taught for three years, and once I was married and the children came along, I opened my own home-based business: Jean's Fashions. I not only sewed custom-made clothing but did hundreds of alterations, some of which people never dreamed could be done. Because I had taken the pattern-drafting course, I was able to correct patterns and make garments to fit each individual person. I could also look at a ready-made garment and make a copy from scratch for a client.
Jean (Stana) Lotz
Home Economics Education '62

Aside from the knowledge that prepared me for a career in home economics, the most important aspect of my education at Margaret Morrison was learning how to approach projects or tasks with an organized plan. Organization and its concomitant prioritization, inherent requirements for every class at Margaret Morrison, have helped me succeed in every facet of my life. After being out of college for 19 years, I went to law school. I had a husband, two teen-age children, a spacious home, and a dog to take care of, along with a full load of classes and a job at the district attorney's office. If it were not for the training in organizational management I received at Margaret Morrison, I never would have graduated from law school.
Rhoda (Shear) Neft
Home Economics '61

We roommates at Tech get together every year, and we reminisce about our days at Margaret Morrison. We recall the high standards that were set for all of us in the Home Management House regardless of our duties as cook, hostess, laundress, or cleaning staff. Those standards have rarely been met in our real lives, but the importance of having standards, setting goals, and planning how to achieve them has stayed with us.
Judith (Rau) Dunlop
Costume Economics '61
Minerva (Hawkins) Nelson
Costume Economics '61

I found that the preparation given the graduates of the business studies program was very thorough, very comprehensive. I had a large number of job offers, and I literally had my pick because of my background.
Lana (Kubasak) Andrews
Business Studies '62

Attending Carnegie Mellon changed my life. My husband (Bob, E'70) and I often say, "We learned how to think, we learned how to problem solve, and not be afraid to try things. And that's what the school did for us." In our families, we were the only ones to go to college. Now Bob and I both have advanced degrees, our daughter has advanced degrees, and our son has just graduated from Carnegie Mellon. Mrs. Kolodner, who taught nutrition, was a very confident woman, who was very much in charge and yet very kind in helping us to be our best. Helene Bourke, who taught child development, is the reason I went into child development.
Toni (Sapet) Ungaretti
Home Economics Education '70

Memories of MMCC include moving into Morewood Gardens and being surprised at the building. There were some nifty fireplaces, bay windows, lofts, and unique shapes. At classes we were taught to be ladies. It seems funny now, but we were to dress and act as ladies at all times, and most of our Maggie Murph teachers worked on this. When I graduated and moved to New York City in 1964, I was the only woman from Pittsburgh leaving my roots and going off by myself to the big city. Though many of my friends didn't understand, I was excited and felt well prepared. It turned out I was right. Any job I had was never as difficult as school had been, and so that whether I was an interviewer at Lord and Taylors, a legal secretary, or an executive assistant at an advertising agency, I was never intimidated.
Janet (Harton) Von Twistern
Business Studies '64

As I calculate my household monthly food cost and reach for my updated home management file, I am reminded of the standards that were instilled in us as students at the Home Management House so many years ago. Aside from the academics, the values that were taught at Margaret Morrison remained with us for a lifetime. We all seemed to do pretty well while contributing something to society and at the same time always learning something new. Many thanks to CMU and its dedicated teaching staff that put up with us, and for the opportunities and the memories.
Dorothea (Manners) Goedel
Home Economics '57

IN COSTUME ECONOMICS (1945)

The class of 1945 was the last to receive Costume Economics degrees. We had heard rumors that the department was about to be folded into the Home Economics Department. So some of us decided to take action. Margie (Volk)Troy and I took the matter to the top. We made an appointment to meet with President Doherty and told him that most of us were interested in careers in clothing, not cooking and household management. We persisted until President Doherty became utterly exasperated and ushered us to the door. He handed us our diplomas a few weeks later with a hint of a smile, perhaps in forgiveness for wasting his time.
Mary (Forman) Rice
Costume Economics '45

IN NURSING EDUCATION (1949)

Thanks so much. I think this is a great idea—the memoirs of Margaret Morrison alumnae—a little ointment for the wounds many of us felt when our departments were discontinued. After many years working in a variety of situations and working with nurses from other educational disciplines, I continue to evaluate our program as excellent.
Helen Louise (Biesecker) Moe
Nursing Education '47

IN SOCIAL WORK (1953)

When the graduate social work program was phased out, I did 101 flips. I'm still angry, still resentful. I don't believe I will ever resolve my conflicts with the change. Even with the proliferation of schools of social work, the quality of education at Margaret Morrison School of Social Work is not duplicated anywhere.
James Pantalos
Social Work M '51

IN BUSINESS STUDIES (1969)

I think I had one of the worst educations possible to prepare me for the technology that was to come; and it was senseless to have a school just for women at that time. However, it was the name of the school (CIT) that opened doors for me. My four years at Tech were gruesome, grade-wise, but I learned to think, handle challenges and solve problems.
Carol (Karnell) Lampe
Business Studies '67

IN HOME EC EDUCATION (1969)

I was graduating the year before Margaret Morrison was closed, so our statistics class decided to do an analysis of why there should be a Home Economics Department offering a master's program in this part of the country. Geographically, there was no other school offering a home economics education master's. Our analysis didn't carry any weight whatsoever, but it was very interesting to those of us who did it. Shortly after Carnegie Mellon started closing its department, other departments started closing across the country. I think it was felt that they weren't cost effective and that the market had changed to mass-produced clothing, which was less expensive than handwork and tailoring. Also, there was the impact of the availability of mass-produced, prepared foods.
Carol (Birth) Burrows
Home Economics Education M '71

A 1973 GRADUATE

As a member of Margaret Morrison's last graduating class, I was very upset that they closed MMCC. Once we heard what was happening, we went to President Stever's office. He had just come on board, and supposedly the decision was made before he got here. We pointed out that women's issues—nutrition, health, and childcare—were finally getting attention in a whole new way. More women were returning to work than in the past. We were thought of as just little home ec teachers, and we were trying to make changes in that image. We soon discovered, however, that we were beating our heads against a wall. The decision to close had been made, and it didn't matter what we said or did. But at MMCC, we learned how to think and how to problem solve. I think that this is true of the entire university. We were taught to think instead of just being fed miscellaneous information. We really received a great education.
Suzan (Bowden) Krauland
Home Economics Education '73

A DIFFERENT VIEWPOINT

I never resented the closing of Margaret Morrison. It no longer fulfilled the expectations of women in a new era. It had not met the promise of Ellen Swallow Richards, the founder of home economics. Only the large state schools, manned by specialists in food science, nutrition, textile technology, business and management, marriage counseling, and child development survive. Perhaps they understand more than the old-time home economists that the world's business, not just the home, is the rightful territory of those important subects.
Mildred (Cook) Luckhardt
Home Economics '41, M '66

I find the idea that the University,
almost from its inception,
had a college for women—
a college for the daughters of
steelworkers as well as the sons—
to be a very exciting concept,
historically ahead of its time and
part of a rich tradition.
—*Season Dietrich, H&SS '01, Heinz M '02*

Chapter 7

1973–and Beyond

The Legacy of Margaret Morrison

*T*hirty years have passed since the last Margaret Morrison graduate received her diploma from Dean Steinberg at the 1973 commencement ceremony held on the lawn before the fine arts building. During these thirty years, Carnegie Mellon University has continued to rise steadily in quality and prestige and has taken its place among the nation's most distinguished universities. Margaret Morrison Carnegie College has played a significant role in the new university that Carnegie Mellon has become.

The Margaret Morrison Carnegie School opened its doors in 1906 to enroll the first women students in the Carnegie Technical Schools. For decades, they were somewhat isolated from the academic programs in engineering and science, whose departments refused to take women students until World War II. Margaret Morrison students, however, pounded on these closed doors and gradually won their ways through them, proving by their achievements in classes that they could hold their own academically with men. Today women make up 32 percent of the university's total student enrollment and study in every one of its 50 departments. The proportion of women in computer science, a field notori-ous for its overwhelmingly male population, leads the nation. The chart on this page gives the numbers. Margaret Morrison students blazed the way to a university that enrolls women throughout its entire student body.

Current Programs with MMCC Origins

A number of contemporary Carnegie Mellon programs had their origins in Margaret Morrison. The ancestor of today's distinguished Biological Sciences Depart-ment was the Biological Sciences program at Margaret Morrison that was transferred to

HEADCOUNT ENROLLMENT BY GENDER
FALL SEMESTER 2002

	MALE	FEMALE	TOTAL
College of Fine Arts	553	667	1,220
Carnegie Institute of Technology	1,742	491	2,233
Graduate School of Industrial Administration	1,111	385	1,496
Heinz School of Public Policy & Management	269	249	518
Humanities & Social Sciences	700	611	1,311
Interdisciplinary	416	272	688
Mellon College of Science	501	302	803
School of Computer Science	805	299	1,104
TOTALS	**6,172**	**3,329**	**9,501**

—Carnegie Mellon Factbook 2003, v. 17, p. 27

Winners of Alumni Merit Awards

Rachel E. Beatty '18

Helen (Jaffurs) Cacheris '46

Lucille (Wissolik) Campbell
  Thane '42

Margaret A. Carver '43

Marie A. Davis '41, L'45

Hannah K. Eastman '28

Josephine (Gibson) Eckert '24

Marcella (Cohen) Goldberg '31

Alma E. Hiller '14

Elaine (Lobl) Konigsburg '52

Stephanie L. Kwolek '46

Erma (Teitelbaum) Meyerson '39

Doris E. Myers '24

Henrietta (Accipiter) Parker '29

Marlene (Peternel) Parrish '57

Mary Louise (Milligan)
  Rasmuson '32

Helen A. Reitz '21

Grace M. Rupert '18

Alma (McCloud) Salter '57

Mary E. Schlayer '38

Margaret Stroud '39

Sara C. Tesh '21

Veronica Volpe '34

Marlene Parrish, 2002 Alumni Merit Award winner, speaking at the Margaret Morrison Tea, Homecoming, October 2002

Mellon College of Science. Similarly, various majors in the humanities and social sciences originated in the General Studies Department at Margaret Morrison. Margaret Morrison granted the first Bachelor of Arts and Master of Arts degrees in the humanities, which were transferred to the new College of Humanities and Social Sciences in 1968. The Early Childhood Education Program of the Department of Psychology originated in the nursery school of MMCC's Home Economics Department. The Technical Writing and Editing program continues as a Technical Writing bachelor's degree; alongside of that program grew today's Professional Writing major and Master of Arts program in Professional Writing.

Faculty and Alumnae Honors

Alumni records list 6,300 Margaret Morrison graduates, including both undergraduate and graduate students and about 90 master's degree men. About 3,000 of these alumni are living today, continuing in vital roles in professions and families and communities. Five members of the Margaret Morrison faculty are listed among Carnegie Mellon's current emeriti faculty: F. Louise Bailey, Associate Professor of Textiles and Clothing; Lois Fowler, Professor of English; Betty Jane Lloyd, Associate Dean and Associate Professor of Humanities and Social Sciences; Gladys B. Spencer, Associate Professor of Home Economics Education; and Ann Baldwin Taylor, Director of the Children's School.

Many Margaret Morrison alumnae have had their distinguished careers recognized by the university. Three women, Elaine (Lobl) Konigsburg '52, Stephanie Kwolek '46 and Mary (Berg) Wells Lawrence '51, have been awarded the Distinguished Achievement Award, given annually for "distinguished service and accomplishment in any field of human endeavor that brings honor to the recipient and the university." Dr. Kwolek and Mrs. Lawrence also received honorary doctoral degrees, from Mellon College of Science in 2001 and the College of Fine Arts in 1974 respectively; joining them is Mary Louise (Milligan) Rasmuson '32, who received her honorary doctorate from the College of Fine Arts in 1959. Twenty-three Margaret Morrison alumnae have won Merit Awards for "exceptional accomplishment in the nominee's chosen occupation." And 47 hold the Service Award granted for "especially active participation in alumni or university affairs."

The Margaret Morrison Building

The Margaret Morrison name figures prominently on campus, prompting incoming students to ask what (or who) it (or she) was. The Margaret Morrison building served for many years after Margaret Morrison was phased out as the first home of the School of Urban and Public Affairs (SUPA). When SUPA moved to Hamburg Hall and became the H. John Heinz III School of Public Policy and Management, the Margaret Morrison building became the second home of the College of Fine Arts. CFA now has all or parts of three of its schools in the building: Design, Architecture and Music. Atop the west wing of the building, the School of Architecture has built a laboratory, the Center for Building Performance and Diagnostics (also called "The Intelligent Workplace"), that has, in its short life, made significant contributions to improved building practices both in the United States and abroad. Plans are under discussion for a possible new east wing on the Margaret Morrison building.

One of the intriguing ideas that has emerged from conversations between Mary Phillips and Margaret Morrison alumnae is

the creation of an alumnae space where their contributions and achievements could be recognized for posterity. The administration applauds this idea and will incorporate it into future discussions of facility planning.

Alumnae Support of the University

Another legacy of Margaret Morrison alumnae is their generous support of university fund drives. Although MMCC has the smallest number of alumni of all of the colleges, the Maggie Murphs had the highest percentage of donors to the Centennial Campaign in 1995–2000—almost 50 percent. Currently, 86 MMCC alumnae belong to the Andrew Carnegie Society, the university's philanthropic organization. The Pittsburgh Women's Clan, the lineal descendant of the Margaret Morrison Alumnae Association that held its first meeting in 1909, today numbers 38 Margaret Morrison graduates among its 82 active members. The names of Margaret Morrison alumnae also appear on donor wall plaques in the University Center, the Purnell Center for the Arts, and buildings in four of Carnegie Mellon's seven colleges. Signs outside of classrooms, offices, and laboratories in these buildings acknowledge gifts to their construction by individual Margaret Morrison alumnae. In 1989, Steven Fienberg, Dean of H&SS, began a fund drive to build a lecture hall connected to a new media center to be named the Margaret Morrison Media Wing. Although plans for the lecture hall failed to reach maturity, the media wing was built in two classrooms in Porter Hall. Led by the chair of the fund drive, Joan (Casey) Leisure, MM'49, 1,303 Margaret Morrison alumnae

gave gifts totaling $225,000. The media wing's two classrooms are the Patricia Askwith Kenner, MM '66, Language Learning Resource Center and the Joan Casey Leisure Multi-Media Classroom.

In 1999, the university established the Margaret Morrison Carnegie College scholarship program to support undergraduate women and commemorate the history of the college. To date (May 2003) alumni and friends of the college have contributed close to a million dollars toward the scholarship program. The program includes individually endowed scholarships, charitable gift annuity scholarship funds, and a pooled scholarship fund. Fifteen donors have endowed and named individual scholarships for a total of $625,000. Over $300,000 from more than 2,500 annual gifts have been committed to the MMCC pooled scholarship fund, which has awarded 12 scholarships to undergraduate women in the past three years.

The MMCC Lecture Series debuted in April 2000 and has welcomed hundreds of alumnae and their spouses back to campus to reminisce with old classmates and experience the innovation and creativity that is the hallmark of Carnegie Mellon. Through these quarterly lectures, alumnae have heard leading faculty present on current research, enjoyed outstanding student performances, and toured campus locations such as the National Robotics Engineering Consortium, Mellon Institute, and the Intelligent Workplace atop the Margaret Morrison Carnegie Hall.

Major Contributors to the MMC Media Center

Sylvia Ann Martin Arthur '48
Adah Borgerding Brownlee '24
Virginia Campbell '51
Margaret A. Carver '43
Gloria Cofsky Casey '60
Thelma Laylander Chandler '32
Norene G. DiBucci Christiano '64, '71
Dorothy L. Stauff Corey '45
Thelma E. Adams Covalt '22
Anne J. Exline '49
Sema D. Moskovitz Faigen '49
Velma F. Fritsch Ferrari '57
Geraldine Hill Fox '64
Janet E. McVicar Fugassi '33
Helen McCrea Greiner '37
Nina L. Gearhart Haro '58
Carol Knestrick Henderson '61
Lois Jacobs '33
Patricia Askwith Kenner '66
David Klahr GSIA '15, '68
Ethel Cooper Kurtz '57
Ruth Lieberman Levaur '31
Joan Casey Leisure '49
Janet Zehfuss Le Hane '51
Silvia J. Levie '29
Marion J. Mulligan '65
Nancy McKenna Murrin '39
Ann Parker Peterson '53
Mary Louise Milligan Rasmuson '32
Mary Foreman Rice '45
Lenore R. Engelmann Riegel '68
Martha Robinson Ritter '34
Mary Lou Lerch Rosencranz '46
Lila Oyen Schadel '46
Laura Bugher Sillers '22
Phyllis Grant Silverman '48
Jeanne E. Hecht Steele '47
Katherine E. Kutscher Tibbetts '40
Adelaide McCloskey Van Norman '32
Florence Bechtel Whitwell '18
Elsie J. Terry Zug '31

Top left:
The Intelligent Workplace sits atop Margaret Morrison Carnegie Hall.

Bottom right:
In 2003, craftsmen began restoring the Margaret Morrison Carnegie Hall Portico, modeling brick and granite work after Henry Hornbostel's College of Fine Arts Terrace.

The Margaret Morrison Tea at Homecoming is another popular event. In the early nineties, Susan Henry, Dean of Mellon College of Science, invited Margaret Morrison science graduates to a tea at Mellon Institute. A few years later, the deans of the College of Humanities and Social Sciences and the Graduate School of Industrial Administration joined Dean Henry in hosting all returning Margaret Morrison alums at an MMCC Tea at the Hunt Institute for Botanical Documentation, located on the top floor of the Hunt Library building. Over the years, the location for the tea has varied, but it has become a traditional event for Maggie Murphs on the Friday afternoon of Homecoming each fall. In 2003, the program for the MMCC Tea will be the first presentation of this book.

As mentioned at the beginning of Chapter 4, we are so appreciative of the more than 200 graduates who generously shared reminiscences of their days as students at Margaret Morrison Carnegie College for this history. The memories and knowledge they provided helped us to shape the entire volume. And readers will be captivated and delighted by their many stories of MMCC college life.

Margaret Morrison Tea, Homecoming, October 2000

MMCC's Legacy into the 21st Century

Margaret Morrison Carnegie College's legacy is many faceted. Its greatest legacy, however, lies neither in buildings nor academic programs but in the contributions its graduates have made to American society. Many Maggie Murphs have been wives and mothers, imparting to husbands and children the high standards and loving personal relationships that marked their collegiate education. Almost a third became faculty members in elementary schools, secondary schools, and colleges, where they were able to influence the lives of thousands of students. Others embraced occupations such as health care providers, executives in many fields, entrepreneurs and dozens of additional pursuits. The interviews in this volume speak eloquently to the talent and achievements of Margaret Morrison graduates. The Maggie Murphs have bequeathed a rich legacy to Carnegie Mellon.

When the shovels split the earth on that summer day in 1906 for the Margaret Morrison Carnegie College building, the groundbreakers envisioned the rise of a splendid edifice. What they could not have envisioned was the impact and legacy left on the city, and indeed the nation, by the thousands of young women who would be educated in the very classrooms whose foundations were begun that day. The lofty columns and rotunda endure, standing silent witness in a new century to the pioneering women of years past, whose lives and labors opened the doors of opportunity to a new generation of young women who sit beneath the same columns today.

In 2006, the university will commemorate the 100th anniversary of the founding of Margaret Morrison Carnegie College. We are looking forward to sharing this festive occasion with you. It will be a wonderful opportunity to celebrate the triumphant, pioneering spirit of seven decades of Margaret Morrison graduates.

The Margaret Morrison Legacy Continues

Contributors of Reminiscences

These wonderfully generous contributors of reminiscences, photographs and memorabilia have our enduring gratitude. Each contributor played an important role in shaping this book.

Please note that only Carnegie Mellon degrees are included. Most degrees refer to MMCC bachelor's degrees, except for the following codes:

CFA   College of Fine Arts
D   Doctoral degree
H   Honorary Doctoral degree
H&SS   College of Humanities and Social Sciences
L   Carnegie Library School master's degree
M   Master's degree
MCS   Mellon College of Science

(Acklin), Dorothy Leete, '59
(Alessio), Evelyn Murrin, '57
Andrews, Lana (Kubasak), '62
Anguish, Virginia (Rowley), '49
(Aronson), Marjorie Ravick, '49
(Aschmann), Adelaide Brady, '38
(Askwith), Patricia Kenner, '66
Austen, Anne (Martin), '51
(Baldwin), Ann Taylor
Barnard, Nancy (Grasmick), '58
Barr, Barbara (Bulger), '55
Bates, Marilyn "Bobbie", '61
(Bechtel), Florence Whitwell, '18
Behrend, Celeste (Silberstein), '49
Belle, Sylvia (Braunstein), '62
Benson, Mary (Crago), '30
Bertucci, Claire (Ruge), '65
Bice, Eleanor (Bright), '39
(Biesecker), Helen Moe, '47
(Birth), Carol Burrows, M '71
(Bluestone), Hedda Sharapan, '65
Blumberg, Ruth (Steinman), '43
(Bowden), Suzan Krauland, '73
(Brackemeyer), Helen McCulloch, '43
Brady, Adelaide (Aschmann), '38
(Braunstein), Sylvia Belle, '62
Brem, Verna (Robinson), '60, L'62
(Bright), Eleanor Bice, '39
(Brown), Frances Newhams, '33
(Bruce), Virginia Walker, '44
Budd, Elaine (Levin), '44
(Bulger), Barbara Barr, '55
Burrows, Carol (Birth), M '71
Busler, Frances (Timms), '33
(Campbell), Mary Lou Clarkson, '40
Campbell, Agnes (Cancelliere), '35
(Campsey), Lois Stauffer, '54
(Cancelliere), Agnes Campbell, '35
Carhart, Jean (Jacobs), '64
(Carlson), Mildred Eilertson, M '67
Carver, Margaret, '43
Caughill, Rita (Schmidt), '40
(Cerutti), Eileen McConomy, '56
(Chersky), Martha Orringer, '41
(Chetlin), Janet Rosecrans, '44
Christiano, Norene (DiBucci), '64, M '71
Clark, Michael, M '68
Clarkson, Mary Lou (Campbell), '40

(Clyde), Pauline Gaffney, '50
Cody, Jayne (McCann), '49
(Cohen), Martha Pheneger, '64
Cohen, Renee (Marks), '63
Condio, Mary (Roe), '53
(Connor), Jane Wiseman, '51, M '53
(Cook), Mildred Luckhardt, '41, M '66
Cooney, Carol (Ford), '45
Cost, Ruth (Lauffer), '39
(Crago), Mary Benson, '30
Craig, Barbara (Woods), '48
Crooks, Lucille (Orr), '43
(Cruikshank), Mary Hymes, '68
(Dalton), Donna Opoku-Agyeman, '65
Dana, Mary Frances (Nichol), '35
Darby, Helen (Sacco), '45
Davis, Mary (Sperring), '54
(Denslow), Janet Landerl, '44
Devoy, Patricia (Mitchell), '57
(DiBucci), Norene Christiano, '64, M '71
(Dinkins), Barrie Simpson, '68
(Ditty), Kathryn Updike, '52
Dodd, Judith (Lomakin), '62
Doerfler, Theresa (Pepine), '55
Drischell, Patricia (Snedden), '51
(Duffy), Eleanor Kasehagen, '33
Dunlop, Judith (Rau), '61
Easley, Ruth (Siegle), '38
Eilertson, Mildred (Carlson), M '67
Ekiss, Barbara (Kinner), '58
Elias, Rea (Simon), '45
(Ellison), Joanne Nydegger, '57
(Emert), Anna Mae Statti, '50
Ernsberger, Ruth (Knight), M '65
Faigen, Sema (Moskovitz), '49
Farrahy, June (Haskell), '48
Fedor, Shirley (Gill), '51
Flegal, Jean, '43
Florida, Mary (Waite), '51
(Ford), Carol Cooney, '45
(Forman), Mary Rice, '45
Fowler, Lois (Shoop), '47
Frame, Louise (Rickard), '60
Francis, Jean (Guthridge), '46
Frank, Regina (Uliss), '64
Friedheim, Charlotte (Savage), '38
(Friedman), Lorine Hertz, '18
(Friel), Nancy Huey, '61
Fullerton, Dolores (Walker), '52
Gaffney, Pauline (Clyde), '50
Gardner, Mary (Rial), '45
(Geisler), Janis Ramey, '62, M '67
Gephardt, Helene (Holzworth), '51
(Gerlach), Dorothy Nemy, '54
Gibbon, Suzanne (Rau), '62
Gibson, Mary (Yorke), '38
(Gill), Shirley Fedor, '51
Ginsberg, Pauline "Polly" (Speiglman), '63
Glosser, Ruth (Taubman), '44
Goedel, Dorothea (Manners), '57
(Goldsmith), Gretchen Lankford, '43, M HNZ '90
(Gordon), Susan Weinberger, '62
Gottemoeller, Patricia (Michael), '62
(Grant), Phyllis Silverman, '48
(Grasmick), Nancy Barnard, '58
Gruver, Lois (Speed), '38
Gumell, Doris (Otto), '42
(Gustafson), Ruth Johnson, '35

(Guthridge), Jean Francis, '46
Gwynn, Arla (Mitchell), '64
(Hammers), Sandra Samuelson, '57
Harris, Jean (Metzger), '45
(Hartmann), Susan Kantrowitz, '66
Hartmann, Helen (McAleese), '63
Hartner, Elizabeth (Pearsall), '31, M MCS '37
(Harton), Janet Von Twistern, '64
(Haskell), June Farrahy, '48
Hasley, Anne (Sweeney), '46
(Hawkins), Minerva Nelson, '61
(Hecht), Jeanne Steele, '47
Henneberger, Mary (Keefer), '47
(Herman), Shirley Townsend, '51
Herron, Clara, '47
(Hertz), Nancy Muskin, '45
Hertz, Lorine (Friedman), '18
(Hill), Mary Ina Jones, '53
(Holzworth), Helene Gephardt, '51
Horton, Barbara (Jones), '59
(Houston), Mary Shaffer, '55
Huey, Nancy (Friel), '61
Hussey, Rhoda (Mears), '46
Hutchins, Lucile (Meyer), '36
Hylen, Marjorie (Steiner), '57
Hymes, Mary (Cruikshank), '68
(Jacobs), Jean Carhart, '64
Johnson, Ruth (Gustafson), '35
(Johnston), Helen Martin, '44
(Johnston), Margaret Thomas, '42
(Jones), Barbara Horton, '59
Jones, Martha (Wainwright), '44
Jones, Mary Ina (Hill), '53
Jones, Ruth (Templeton), '44
Kantrowitz, Susan (Hartmann), '66
(Karnell), Carol Lampe, '67
Kasehagen, Eleanor (Duffy), '33
Keaton, Sally (Ray), '43
(Keefer), Mary Henneberger, '47
Kehew, Betty (Ogilvie), '40
Kemper, Gertrude (Novak), '32
Kenner, Patricia (Askwith), '66
(Kinley), Catherine Sillins, '44, M '47
(Kinner), Barbara Ekiss, '58
(Klein), Phyllis Levy, '40
(Knight), Ruth Ernsberger, M '65
Kostyo, Elsie (Pestner), '51
Krasik, Natalie (Nathan), '45
Krauland, Suzan (Bowden), '73
(Kubasak), Lana Andrews, '62
(Kutchukian), Diana Thomasian, '49
Kwolek, Stephanie, '46, H MCS '01
(Lacey), Joanne Ritchie, '58
Lackner, Margaret "Judy" (Skeehan), '44
Lampe, Carol (Karnell), '67
Landerl, Janet (Denslow), '44
(Lang), Jeanne Schlicht, '49
(Lang), Margaretha Neu, '36
Langkamp, Ruth (Young), '43
Lankford, Gretchen (Goldsmith), '43, M HNZ '90
Laub, Louise (McCullough), '41
(Lauffer), Ruth Cost, '39
Leeper-St. Clair, Dorothy (Magnuson), '38
Leete, Dorothy (Acklin), '59
Leighton, Carolyn (Smith), '43
(Levin), Elaine Budd, '44
Levy, Phyllis (Klein), '40

Lewis, Hilda (Rugh), '38
(Linder), Sylvia Mason, '43
(Lipman), Reva Swartz, '38
Liversidge, Helen (Zimmerman), '42
Lloyd, Betty Jane, '44
(Lomakin), Judith Dodd, '62
Lotz, Jean (Stana), '62
Luckhardt, Mildred (Cook), '41, M '66
Luther, Joanne (Tishlarich), '42
MacDonald, Kathryn "Tassie" (Truxell), '45
(Magnuson), Dorothy Leeper-St. Clair, '38
Maharam, Gladys (Stalinsky), '64
Mallinger, Anita, M '68, D H&SS '73
Manka, Louise (Wunderlich), '37
(Manners), Dorothea Goedel, '57
(Marks), Renee Cohen, '63
(Martin), Anne Austen, '51
Martin, Helen (Johnston), '44
Mason, Jane (Merrill), '38
Mason, Sylvia (Linder), '43
(Maurhoff), Norma Pickard, '48
(McAleese), Helen Hartmann, '63
(McCann), Jayne Cody, '49
(McCaslin), Mary Margaret Robinson, '39
McConomy, Eileen (Cerutti), '56
McCulloch, Helen (Brackemeyer), '43
(McCullough), Louise Laub, '41
(McKenna), Nancy Murrin, '39
(Mears), Rhoda Hussey, '46
(Merrill), Jane Mason, '38
Mervis, Rosalyn, '50
(Metzger), Jean Harris, '45
(Meyer), Lucile Hutchins, '36
(Michael), Patricia Gottemoeller, '62
(Miller), Barbara Trellis, '51
(Miller), Patricia Uhl, '53
(Milligan), Mary Louise Rasmuson, '32,
    H CFA'59
(Mitchell), Arla Gwynn, '64
(Mitchell), Patricia Devoy, '57
Moe, Helen (Biesecker), '47
(Moore), Barbara Ramsey, '56
(Morgan), Virginia Obrig, '30
(Moskovitz), Sema Faigen, '49
(Mulligan), Marion Sutton, '65
Murrin, Evelyn (Alessio), '57
Murrin, Nancy (McKenna), '39
Muskin, Nancy (Hertz), '45
Muzzey, Betty (Yagle), '41
(Myers), Barbara Nightingale, '53
(Napoli), Grace Ruscitti, '49
(Nathan), Natalie Krasik, '45
Neft, Rhoda (Shear), '61
(Neiman), Ruth Winer, '43
Nelson, Minerva (Hawkins), '61
Nemy, Dorothy (Gerlach), '54
Neu, Margaretha (Lang), '36
Newhams, Frances (Brown), '33
(Nichol), Mary Frances Dana, '35
Nightingale, Barbara (Myers), '53
(Novak), Gertrude Kemper, '32
Nydegger, Joanne (Ellison), '57
Obrig, Virginia (Morgan), '30
(Ogilvie), Betty Kehew, '40
Opoku-Agyeman, Donna (Dalton), '65
(Orr), Lucille Crooks, '43
Orringer, Martha (Chersky), '41
(Osborne), Ruth Rouleau, '52, L'53
(Otto), Doris Gumell, '42

Pantalos, James, M '51
Parker, Nancy (Sitler), '52
(Pearsall), Elizabeth Hartner, '31,
    M MCS '37
(Pepine), Theresa Doerfler, '55
(Pestner), Elsie Kostyo, '51
Pheneger, Martha (Cohen), '64
Pickard, Norma (Maurhoff), '48
Pollis, Angela, '50
Pollis, Helen, '45
Pontano, Susan (Seibert), '65
(Raab), Patricia Schuetz, '68
Ramey, Janis (Geisler), '62, M '67
Ramsey, Barbara (Moore), '56
Rasmuson, Mary Louise (Milligan), '32,
    H CFA'59
(Rau), Judith Dunlop, '61
(Rau), Suzanne Gibbon, '62
Ravick, Marjorie (Aronson), '49
(Ray), Sally Keaton, '43
(Reiber), Lydia Strehl, '54
(Rial), Mary Gardner, '45
Rice, Mary (Forman), '45
(Rickard), Louise Frame, '60
Ritchie, Joanne (Lacey), '58
(Robinson), Verna Brem, '60, L'62
Robinson, Mary Margaret (McCaslin), '39
(Roe), Mary Condio, '53
Rosecrans, Janet (Chetlin), '44
(Rosendahl), Alberta "Bertie" Walker, '45
Rosenthal, Louisa (Saul), '44
Rouleau, Ruth (Osborne), '52, L'53
(Rowley), Virginia Anguish, '49
(Ruge), Claire Bertucci, '65
(Rugh), Hilda Lewis, '38
Ruscitti, Grace (Napoli), '49
(Sacco), Helen Darby, '45
Saibel, Janice (Yent), '55
Samitz, Dorothy (Steerman), '61
Samuelson, Sandra (Hammers), '57
(Sapet), Toni Ungaretti, '70
(Saul), Louisa Rosenthal, '44
(Savage), Charlotte Friedheim, '38
Schalles, Virginia (Wade), '41
Scheafnocker, William, M '53
Schlicht, Jeanne (Lang), '49
(Schmidt), Rita Caughill, '40
Schuetz, Patricia (Raab), '68
(Schultz), Margaret Tsiang, '53
(Seibert), Susan Pontano, '65
(Sekey), Martha Wayman, '43
Shaffer, Mary (Houston), '55
Sharapan, Hedda (Bluestone), '65
(Shear), Rhoda Neft, '61
(Shermer), Maxine Slesinger, '38
(Shoop), Lois Fowler, '47
(Siegle), Ruth Easley, '38
(Silberstein), Celeste Behrend, '49
Sillins, Catherine (Kinley), '44, M '47
Silverman, Phyllis (Grant), '48
(Simon), Rea Elias, '45
Simpson, Barrie (Dinkins), '68
(Sitler), Nancy Parker, '52
(Skeehan), Margaret "Judy" Lackner, '44
Slesinger, Maxine (Shermer), '38
(Smith), Carolyn Leighton, '43
Smith, Nancy (Tapper), '69
(Snedden), Patricia Drischell, '51
(Speed), Lois Gruver, '38

(Speiglman), Pauline "Polly" Ginsberg, '63
(Sperring), Mary Davis, '54
(Stalinsky), Gladys Maharam, '64
(Stana), Jean Lotz, '62
Statti, Anna Mae (Emert), '50
Stauffer, Lois (Campsey), '54
Steele, Jeanne (Hecht), '47
(Steerman), Dorothy Samitz, '61
Steinbach, James, M '68
Steinberg, Erwin
(Steiner), Marjorie Hylen, '57
(Steinman), Ruth Blumberg, '43
(Stiefel), Carol Swift, '65, M '71
Strehl, Lydia (Reiber), '54
Sutton, Marion (Mulligan), '65
Swan, Joy, '44
(Swartz), Edith Zober, '38, M '45
Swartz, Reva (Lipman), '38
(Sweeney), Anne Hasley, '46
Swift, Carol (Stiefel), '65, M '71
(Tapper), Nancy Smith, '69
(Taubman), Ruth Glosser, '44
Taylor, Ann (Baldwin)
(Templeton), Ruth Jones, '44
Thomas, F. Irene, '37
Thomas, Margaret (Johnston), '42
Thomasian, Diana (Kutchukian), '49
(Thompson), Alice Volkwein, '35
Thurston, Eve, '50, L '51
(Timms), Frances Busler, '33
(Tishlarich), Joanne Luther, '42
Townsend, Shirley (Herman), '51
Trellis, Barbara (Miller), '51
(Truxell), Kathryn "Tassie" MacDonald, '45
Tsiang, Margaret (Schultz), '53
(Udman), Lillian Weitzenkorn, '43
Uhl, Patricia (Miller), '53
(Uliss), Regina Frank, '64
Ungaretti, Toni (Sapet), '70
Updike, Kathryn (Ditty), '52
Vincent, Mary, '46
Volkwein, Alice (Thompson), '35
Von Twistern, Janet (Harton), '64
(Wade), Virginia Schalles, '41
(Wainwright), Martha Jones, '44
(Waite), Mary Florida, '51
(Walker), Dolores Fullerton, '52
Walker, Alberta "Bertie" (Rosendahl), '45
Walker, Virginia (Bruce), '44
Wayman, Martha (Sekey), '43
Weinberger, Susan (Gordon), '62
Weitzenkorn, Lillian (Udman), '43
Whitacre, Gail, '67
Whitwell, Florence (Bechtel), '18
Winer, Ruth (Neiman), '43
Wiseman, Jane (Connor), '51, M '53
(Woods), Barbara Craig, '48
(Wunderlich), Louise Manka, '37
(Yagle), Betty Muzzey, '41
(Yent), Janice Saibel, '55
(Yorke), Mary Gibson, '38
(Young), Ruth Langkamp, '43
(Zimmerman), Helen Liversidge, '42
Zober, Edith (Swartz), '38, M '45
Zubritzky, Hilary, '70, M '72

Photography & Illustration Sources

Unless otherwise noted, photos may be found in the Carnegie Mellon Univeristy Archives.

Cover
Illust: Thistle, *Thistle,* 1915
Photos: Far left, Stephanie L. Kwolek from Lemelson/MIT Found., Boston, MA; Far right, Mary (Houston) Shaffer, Below Mary, Dean Breed; All others unidentified.

Inside Front and Back Covers
Illust: MMC Hall, Charles H. Overly
© Overly Publishing, Worcester, MA

Page 8
Photo: MMCC students attend class, 1906
Poem: The Woman's Song, *Thistle,* 1908

Page 9
Illust: Thistle, *Thistle,* 1909
Photo: Andrew Carnegie reads letter *Pittsburgh Dispatch,* Nov. 15, 1900

Page 10
Photo: "My Heart is in the Work," Baker Hall stairwell, Carnegie Mellon
Photo: Mrs. Hammerschlag digs the first shovelful, 1906
Photo: original campus, April 1906

Page 11
Paint: Margaret Morrison Carnegie, First Floor, Margaret Morrison Carnegie Hall, Carnegie Mellon, 1925
Illust: Woman in Stripes, *Thistle,* 1908
Illust: Why He Flunked, *Thistle,* 1912

Page 12
Photo: Charter Class, Story of *Carnegie Tech,* 1937
Photo: Margaret Morrison Carnegie Hall, 1907

Page 13
Illust: Women of MMCS, 1909
Photos: Classrooms, *Carnegie Technical Schools,* circa 1910

Page 14
Photo: MMCC lunchroom, circa 1915
Map: Redrawn from original map, circa 1906

Page 15
Photo: MMCC Basketball *Thistle,* 1909
Illust: MMCC Spirit, *Thistle,* 1909

Page 16
Photo: Dean Smith, *Thistle,* 1908
Photo: MMCC Faculty, *Thistle,* 1909

Page 17
Photo: Drawing Class, *Carnegie Technical Schools,* circa 1910
Illust: MMCC Graduate, *Thistle,* 1906

Page 18
Photo: Clara Herron, *Thistle,* 1947
Photo: Catherine C. Ihmsen, *Thistle,* 1909
Invitation: Fourth Annual Banquet, 1909

Page 19
Photo: Pi Delta Epsilon, *Thistle,* 1946
Photo: Mortar Board Certificate, Herron Collection, 1947,

Page 20
Photo: Costume Design, circa 1920

Page 21
Illust: Thistle, *Thistle,* 1924
Illust: Women with Yarn, *Thistle,* 1918

Page 22
Illust: Woman with Fan, *Thistle,* 1916

Page 23
Illust: New MMCC Wing, Tenth Annual Report of the Director of CIT, 1913
Illust: Woman Blown by Wind, *Thistle,* 1917
Photo: New Forbes St. Entrance, circa 1925

Page 24
Illust: Girls' Dorms, Thistle, 1919
Photo: MMs dine in Home Management House, n.d.
Photo: Forbes Hall, circa 1935
Photo: Mellon Hall, circa 1923

Page 25
Map, *C.I.T. Alumnus,* August 1921
Photo: Mellon Hall Residents, *Thistle,* 1928
Map: *C.I.T. Alumnus,* August 1921

Page 26
Photo: Dean Breed, *The Story of Carnegie Tech,* 1937

Page 27
Photo: MM Social Work Club, *Thistle,* 1921

Page 28
Illust: I Loved Her Knot, *Thistle,* 1914
Illust: MMCC Glee Club, *Thistle,* 1913

Page 29
Photo: Maypole Dance, *Thistle,* 1919
Illust: Girl, *The Carnegie Tech Puppet,* 1928

Page 30
Photo: Campus Week Program, 1928
Photo: Attendants of the Campus Week Queen, circa 1924
Photo: Geisha Girls, Campus Week, 1923
Photo: Women's Sweepstakes, Campus Week, 1924
Dance Card: Cora Elizabeth Wright Scrapbook, 1917–22

Page 31
Photo: Plebes Bury Regulations, Campus Week, circa 1920
Illust: MMCS Plebes, *Thistle,* 1917

Page 32
Photo: Sema(Moskovitz) Faigen, *Thistle,* 1949
Photo: David Moskovitz, *Thistle,* 1925
Photo: WCIT Staff, *Thistle,* 1949

Page 33
Poem: Late Afternoon, *Cano,* 1948
Photo: The Lady's at Work, *Thistle,* 1947

Page 34
Photo: Elizabeth Pearsall, *Thistle,* 1931

Page 36
Photo: Mary Louise Milligan, *Thistle,* 1932
Photo: Mary Louise and Family, Rasmuson Collection, 1922

Page 37
Photo: WAC Director, 1946, Rasmuson Collection
Photo: Elmer and Louise Rasmuson, Rasmuson Collection, June 2000

Page 38
Photo: Morewood Gardens, circa 1940s

Page 39
Illust: Thistle, *Thistle,* 1937

Page 40
Photo: Skibo sign, circa 1947

Page 41
Photo: Thistle Hall, *Carnegie Alumnus,* April 1932
Illust: Playing Cards, *Thistle,* 1946

Page 42
Illust: Girl Tiptoeing Up Stairs, *Thistle,* 1949
Photo: Carnegie Union exterior, circa 1943
Photo: Carnegie Union interior, 1939
Illust: Addition to Morewood Gardens, Alfred D. Reid Architects, circa 1950

Page 43
Photo: CIT Nursery School Pamphlet, n.d.
Photo: MM with Fade-Ometer, *Carnegie Alumnus,* 1943

Page 44
Illust: Mannequin, *Thistle,* 1949
Photo: MM with mimeograph, *Thistle,* 1940
Photo: Secretarial Studies Class, circa 1947
Photo: Nurse with child, circa 1938

Page 45
Photo: Library Work, *Campus Views,* circa 1930
Photo: Dean Watkins, *Thistle,* 1939
Illust: Science Equipment, *Thistle,* 1951

Page 46
Photo: Dean Green, *Thistle,* 1935
Photo: Home Economics Faculty, *Thistle,* 1946

Page 47
Photo: Dean Edith Winchester, *Thistle,* 1944
Photo: MMCC Senate Party, Grant Collection, 1947
Artifact: Western Union Telegram, Grant Collection, May 1947

Page 48
Photo: Calendar Girl, *The Scot,* July 1954
Photo: One in a Million, Scotch 'n' Soda, *Thistle,* 1954
Illust: The Girls' Roller Derby, *The Scottie,* May 1949
Photo: Homecoming Queen candidates, *Thistle,* 1954

Page 49
Photo: Women's Clan officers, *Carnegie Alumnus,* Sept. 1943
Illust: Fancy Kiss, *The Scot,* May 1951

Page 50
Photo: Hilda Rugh, *Thistle,* 1938
Photo: 1933 Nursing Class, Lewis Collection

Page 51
Photo: Hilda and Lib, Lewis Collection, 2000
Photo: Hilda as Nurse, Lewis Collection, circa 1938
Photo: Lib as Football Player, *Thistle,* 1934
Photo: Irish Stew, *Thistle,* 1934

Page 52
Photo: Betty Yagle, *Thistle,* 1941
Photo: Intersorority Council, 1941

Page 53
Photo: Betty in Government Service, Muzzey Collection, 1945–46
Photo: 1941 Graduates, Muzzey Collection

Page 54:
Photo: Margaret Carver, *Thistle,* 1943
Photo: *Dorm Bagpiper,* Oct. 1948

Page 55
Photo: Women's Glee Club, *Thistle,* 1943

Page 56
Photo: Gretchen Goldsmith, *Thistle,* 1943
Photo: Carnegie Inn, 1928
Photo: Skibo Interior, circa 1950

Page 57
Illust: *The Scottie,* Jan. 1941

Index

Please see also *Contributors of Reminiscences* listed on pages 126 and 127.

Please see also *Contributors of Reminiscences* listed on pages 126 and 127.

Please see also *Contributors of Reminiscences* listed on pages 126 and 127.

Please see also *Contributors of Reminiscences* listed on pages 126 and 127.

Please see also *Contributors of Reminiscences* listed on pages 126 and 127.

Please see also *Contributors of Reminiscences* listed on pages 126 and 127.

In appreciation to the hundreds of Maggie Murphs and friends
for their generosity to the Margaret Morrison Carnegie College Scholarship program.

Endowed Scholarships

Evelyn Alessio Murrin, MM'57: *The Dean Margaret F. LeClair Scholarship*

Dr. Joy Swan, MM'44: *The Joy Swan Scholarship for Women in Science*

Patricia Kenner, MM'66: *The Patricia Askwith Kenner Scholarship*

Pittsburgh Women's Clan: *The Pittsburgh Women's Clan Scholarship*

Maureen & Jared Cohon: *The Maureen B. Cohon Scholarship*

Mary Ann, MM'66, & Charles Cardani: *The Mary Ann Petras Cardani Scholarship for Women in Science*

Sema & Ivan Faigen: *The Sema, MM'49 & Ivan Faigen, E'48, Scholarship for Women in Modern Languages*

Sema & Ivan Faigen: *The Sema & Ivan Faigen Scholarship for Women in Science*

Florence Minifee, MM'43: *The Florence Minifee Scholarship*

John Lehoczky: *The John & Mary Lou Lehoczky Scholarship for Women in Humanities & Social Sciences*

Louisa Rosenthal, MM'44: *The Louisa Saul Rosenthal Scholarship for Women in Creative Writing*

Selma P. Ryave, MM'69 & Rosalyn C. Richman, MM'68: *The Selma Podolsky Ryave Scholarship*

Selma P. Ryave, MM'69: *The Rosalyn C. Richman Scholarship*

Dwight Schultheis: *The Emmy & Richard Schultheis, Sr. Scholarship*

Sharon, MM'64 & David Robinson, E'65: *The David & Sharon Robinson Scholarship*

Charitable Gift Annuities

Betty Jane Lloyd, MM'44

Joanne Lacey Ritchie, MM'58 & M. Delmar Ritchie, Jr., IM'57

MMCC Pooled Scholarship Fund

...And the hundreds of alumni who designate their annual gifts to this fund.

Thank you.